Islam, Education, and Freedom

Educational Leadership: Innovative, Critical and Interdisciplinary Perspectives

Series Editors: Jeffrey S. Brooks, Alan J. Daly, Yi-Hwa Liou, Chen Schechter and Victoria Showunmi

The Educational Leadership series provides a forum for books that push the conceptual boundaries of educational leadership and that introduce novel perspectives with the promise of improving, challenging and reconceptualising the field of study and informing practice. Books in the series take a global, interdisciplinary focus and cover educational phases ranging from early years to higher education. They aspire to be field-leading innovations that advance new theories, topics and methodologies. The series will be of interest to those working across disciplines such as educational leadership, school leadership, teacher education, sociology, anthropology, economics, psychology, political science, philosophy and public policy.

Also available in the series:

Educational Leadership and Critical Theory, edited by Charles L. Lowery, Chetanath Gautam, Robert White and Michael E. Hess

The Relational Leader, edited by Yi-Hwa Liou and Alan J. Daly

Women Navigating Educational Research, Jana L. Carlisle

Forthcoming in the series:

Leadership for Society, Rima'a Da'as and Chen Schechter
Gender and Educational Leadership in Greece, Emmy Papanastasiou
Equity and Influence in the Funding of Schools, Matthew P. Sinclair
Socialisation of School Leaders in Sub-Saharan Africa, Pontso Moorosi and Callie Grant

Islam, Education, and Freedom

An Uncommon Perspective on Leadership

Melanie C. Brooks and Miriam D. Ezzani

BLOOMSBURY ACADEMIC
LONDON • NEW YORK • OXFORD • NEW DELHI • SYDNEY

BLOOMSBURY ACADEMIC
Bloomsbury Publishing Plc, 50 Bedford Square, London, WC1B 3DP, UK
Bloomsbury Publishing Inc, 1359 Broadway, New York, NY 10018, USA
Bloomsbury Publishing Ireland, 29 Earlsfort Terrace, Dublin 2, D02 AY28, Ireland

BLOOMSBURY, BLOOMSBURY ACADEMIC and the Diana logo are trademarks of Bloomsbury Publishing Plc

First published in Great Britain 2024
This paperback edition published in 2026

Copyright © Melanie C. Brooks and Miriam D. Ezzani, 2024

Melanie C. Brooks and Miriam D. Ezzani have asserted their right under the Copyright, Designs and Patents Act, 1988, to be identified as Authors of this work.

For legal, purposes the Acknowledgments on p. xviii constitute an extension of this copyright page.

Series design by Tjaša Krivec
Cover image © shock / Getty Images

All rights reserved. No part of this publication may be: i) reproduced or transmitted in any form, electronic or mechanical, including photocopying, recording or by means of any information storage or retrieval system without prior permission in writing from the publishers; or ii) used or reproduced in any way for the training, development or operation of artificial intelligence (AI) technologies, including generative AI technologies. The rights holders expressly reserve this publication from the text and data mining exception as per Article 4(3) of the Digital Single Market Directive (EU) 2019/790.

Bloomsbury Publishing Plc does not have any control over, or responsibility for, any third-party websites referred to or in this book. All internet addresses given in this book were correct at the time of going to press. The author and publisher regret any inconvenience caused if addresses have changed or sites have ceased to exist, but can accept no responsibility for any such changes.

A catalogue record for this book is available from the British Library.

Library of Congress Cataloging-in-Publication Data

Names: Brooks, Melanie C., 1972- author. | Ezzani, Miriam D., author.
Title: Islam, education, and freedom: an uncommon perspective on leadership / Melanie C. Brooks and Miriam D. Ezzani.
Other titles: Educational leadership: innovative, critical and interdisciplinary perspectives
Description: London; New York: Bloomsbury Academic, 2024. | Series: Educational leadership: innovative, critical and interdisciplinary perspectives | Includes bibliographical references and index. | Summary: "Islam, Education and Freedom explores six key areas of freedom: identity, acceptance, pedagogy, conflict, trust, and love. Based on a qualitative case study of a progressive Islamic school in Southern California, North Star Academy, the book illustrates through the voices of the participants how each particular freedom was applied in the school. The authors show how the six freedoms were understood, taught, and practiced with the aim of developing courageous and confident American Muslims. It explores the ways the school leaders facilitate and impart each freedom and the influence this has on the development of American Muslim students' identity. The book includes a Foreword written by Khaula Murtadha, Associate Vice Chancellor for the Office of Community Engagement, Indiana University-Purdue University Indianapolis, USA"– Provided by publisher.
Identifiers: LCCN 2023051058 (print) | LCCN 2023051059 (ebook) | ISBN 9781350231184 (hardback) | ISBN 9781350231221 (paperback) | ISBN 9781350231191 (epub) | ISBN 9781350231207 (ebook)
Subjects: LCSH: North Star Academy (Springwater, Calif.) | Islamic education–California–Case studies. | Muslim students–Ethnic identity.
Classification: LCC LC1099.515.C85 B76 2024 (print) | LCC LC1099.515.C85 (ebook) | DDC 371.828297–dc3/eng/20231116
LC record available at https://lccn.loc.gov/2023051058
LC ebook record available at https://lccn.loc.gov/2023051059

ISBN: HB: 978-1-3502-3118-4
PB: 978-1-3502-3122-1
ePDF: 978-1-3502-3120-7
eBook: 978-1-3502-3119-1

Series: Educational Leadership: Innovative, Critical and Interdisciplinary Perspectives

Typeset by Deanta Global Publishing Services, Chennai, India

For product safety related questions contact productsafety@bloomsbury.com.

To find out more about our authors and books visit www.bloomsbury.com
and sign up for our newsletters.

For Holland, Bronwyn, Clodagh, and Jürgen—
Keep learning, for in education you will find freedom.

For Ahbab Ummah Amariyah, Aydin, and Reya—
Seek life's purpose through
faith, knowledge, and courage
imbued with freedom.

Contents

List of Figure	viii
List of Table	ix
Series Editors' Foreword	x
Foreword *Khaula Murtadha*	xiii
Acknowledgments	xviii
Introduction: Intersections of Islam, Education, and Freedom	1
1 North Star Academy: A Progressive Islamic School	13
2 Freedom of Identity	31
3 Freedom of Acceptance	49
4 Freedom of Pedagogy	63
5 Freedom for Conflict	83
6 Freedom to Trust	101
7 Freedom to Love	115
8 Five Years Later	133
9 North Star Academy: A Model for Freedom	155
Methodological Appendix	177
Glossary	180
Note	182
References	183
Index	193

Figure

1 A model for freedom in progressive Islamic schooling   156

Table

1 Tripartite Framework 72

Series Editors' Foreword

Jeffrey S. Brooks, Curtin University School of Education, Australia
Chen Schechter, Bar-Ilan University, Israel
Alan J. Daly, UC-San Diego, USA
Victoria Showunmi, UCL Institute of Education, England
Yi-Hwa Liou, National Taipei University of Education, Taiwan

The history of thought and practice in educational leadership can be conceived as a punctuated equilibrium (English, 2008). The arc of the field's history is a steady evolution of traditional ideas centered around management, administration, efficiency, rational decision-making, authority and power (Beck & Murphy, 1993). Heavily influenced by business administration and management literature, the field is also shaped by sociology, anthropology, economics, psychology, political science, philosophy and public policy. As an applied field, scholarship in educational leadership shapes—and is shaped by—developments in schools, universities, policy making processes, and in other formal and informal education settings (Brooks & Miles, 2006). This has meant that there is space in the field for both highly theoretical work and for research grounded in a specific context. Of course, quite a lot of scholarship in the field seeks these aims at the same time as a way of generating relevant knowledge *in situ* while also advancing thought and practice throughout the world (Gunter, 2016).

Occasionally, ideas are introduced that compel scholars and practitioners to reconsider the foundations of "what they know" and adopt new ways of thinking about and practicing their work. Among intellectual movements that upset educational leadership's orthodoxy were postmodernism, critical theory, feminist theories, social justice, culturally relevant school leadership, distributed leadership and more purposeful studies of the relationship between leadership and learning (Brooks & Normore, 2017). Each of these domains of inquiry produced novel perspectives on educational leadership (to be sure there are others—we do not pretend this is an exhaustive list) that inform contemporary conceptual and empirical research. Additionally, each of these intellectual movements initiated a paradigmatic shift in the way people engage in the practice of educational leadership, think about their work, and conduct themselves as leaders and followers in formal and informal education settings.

For all this innovation, the arc toward improvement has been slow, and often the emphasis on the traditional has subdued the exploration of the radical. This book series seeks to establish a space for research that (a) explores promising concepts at the edges of the field, (b) encourages the publication of new ideas, and (c) critiques contemporary assumptions about educational leadership. Our hope is that the series may play some role in prompting future conceptual and empirical revolutions that will move the field forward via emergent scientific and artistic revolutions.

New perspectives are emerging from across the field and other disciplines that have great potential to influence (and be influenced by) educational leadership scholarship and practice. Among these are exciting developments related to sustainability and climate change, social networking, religion and spirituality, immigration and globalization, student-centered leadership, and innovative contributions to traditional topics such as community-school relations, gender, race, ethnicity, sexuality, diversity, intercultural/cross-cultural studies, globalization, early childhood and adult education, student voice, and activism. To be sure, there are others. While it is easy to point to individual articles or small groups of scholars working in these areas, there is no clear publication outlet for deeper, focused and nuanced works that explore and challenge such ideas in the detail afforded by a full-length book or highly-focused edited volume. Reaching out beyond the field of educational leadership, there are developments in sociology, anthropology, political science, policy studies, psychology, curriculum studies, brain-based research, environmental science, creativity studies, medicine, law, and other fields that have yet to be deeply explored or understood in terms of their possible applicability to educational leadership. We see the series as a place where such disciplines, ideas and lines of inquiry can come into dialogue and create innovation. We see this book series as a forum for interdisciplinary, innovative, creative, and indeed controversial work.

In addition to providing a forum for such exciting ideas, we aim for this series to also include a diversity of authors and contexts under-represented in many extant book series. This means diversity of author, geographical context and perspective. As this is a series of research books, we anticipate the primary audience being academics, but we also anticipate that the topics will be of interest to practicing school leaders, teachers, policy makers, and scholars working across disciplines such as educational leadership, school leadership, teacher education, sociology, anthropology, economics, psychology, political science, philosophy and public policy. We invite you to join us in the conversation—

to share your work and your insights as we explore and extend the field of educational leadership.

References

Beck, L. G., & Murphy, J. (1993). *Understanding the principalship: Metaphorical themes, 1920s–1990s.* Teachers College Press.

Brooks, J. S., & Miles, M. T. (2006). From scientific management to social justice...and back again? Pedagogical shifts in educational leadership. *International Electronic Journal for Leadership in Learning,* 4(1): 2–15.

Brooks, J. S., & Normore, A. H. (2017). *Foundations of educational leadership: Developing excellent and equitable schools.* Routledge.

English, F. W. (2008). *Anatomy of professional practice: Promising research perspectives on educational leadership.* Rowman & Littlefield Education.

Gunter, H. (2016). *An intellectual history of school leadership practice and research.* London: Bloomsbury.

Foreword

One of the essential skills an ethical leader must cultivate is the building and rebuilding of a principled community. From the very beginning of this text, authors Melanie C. Brooks and Miriam D. Ezzani ask that we reflect on the ethic of freedom and the effects of "unfreedoms" on community. They expose the reader and urge awareness of the overt surveillance and targeting of Muslim communities in the aftermath of the September 11, 2001 attacks on the World Trade Center and the Pentagon. The authors set a backdrop against the presidency of Donald Trump, whose anti-Muslim racism coded in public speeches, executive orders, and proclamations vilified Muslims. The growth of underground social media platforms spewing hatred is referenced, as are the consequences of religious discrimination and unrelenting investigations. The federal government, via the FBI and the Justice Department, has maintained its censorious lens on Islamic movements and perpetuated, in some, the ideas that Islam poses a significant threat to American society. Concomitant immigration laws have been enacted to reify issues of racial alignment.

What then does it mean to be a leader in a school that has named its mission as progressive and its purpose to develop an American Muslim identity so that students are "well-prepared to succeed, lead, and serve?" For the authors, the September 11 attack, subsequent acts in the United States, and the heightened US awareness of global violence linked to Islam have generated an increasing distrust and fear of Muslims. And this fear, as well as apprehension of what Islam represents, is enacted in schools across the country. The Othering of Muslims, microaggressions, and even physical violence have become commonplace. These are just reasons for this important book about educational leadership, faith, and the development of a community (*ummah* in Arabic) nurturing self-realization, principled interactions among its staff and student body, and the profundity of love.

Brooks and Ezzani recount the historical presence of Muslims, connecting the current era to the past horrors of slavery and its vestiges. This text presents an opportunity to further understand Islam amid historical circumstances and the education of Muslim children while examining the challenges of a widening US sociopolitical and religious divide. The authors remind us that absent from most high school history texts are the records of Islamic narratives and practices or the Muslim faith with West African origins. This book, *Islam, Education, and Freedom: An Uncommon Perspective on Leadership*, provides the reader a glimpse into that record and an emergent understanding of how Islam became a movement *within* a migration movement of Black people from the south to northern cities. The loss of the confederacy, Jim Crow laws, lynchings, and black codes forced newly freed people to leave the Southern lands they knew to seek a way of life in northern cities and, for many, the passionate hope for identities distinct from enslavement. Many African Americans on that northern journey gained support from religious groups and the means for some notion of racial unity. During those years, roughly from 1910 until the 1960s, different Muslim organizations offered the new arrivals a rethinking of religiosity, cultural roots, and connections to the African continent, and an axiological divergence from US mythologies of white supremacy and subjugation of Black life worth. The book is not about that aspect of history; the chapters veer into a direction that allows the reader to examine how leadership for freedom is taken up as discourse and discursive practice in an Islamic school in this troubling US context.

The authors' first research site is an office park set in Southern California. The ethnographic, rich descriptive methods of observations, interviews, and focus groups yield an understanding of how schools can be places where families, students, and educators with different religious beliefs can break through the bonds of homogeneity. The imagery was of a carefully trimmed landscape, offices, and an apartment complex—a flagpole with red, white, and blue waves. After the greetings and safe entry, the qualitative research ensues as Ezzani and Brooks describe a twenty-year timeline for the development of the North Star Academy, a school developing American Muslim identity in a progressive environment.

Freedom to educate, freedom to teach the young the fundamentals of Islam, and freedom to pursue knowledge (*ilm* in Arabic) present a critical juncture in this book. The authors assert that leaders can create an expansive space for differences, where trusting relationships are developed, difficult questions can be asked, and the questioner feels regarded. It is the reasoning behind the launching of the Nation of Islam schools and the schools where thousands of "non-Black immigrant families" enroll their children in sites reflective of their sociocultural and ethnic practices of Islam. Issues of educator preparedness and the failure of teacher and principal preparation programs to include topics of religious diversity in their programs of study are noted in this book, as well as the perpetuation of Muslim stereotypes and inaccurate information. Without educator knowledge or epistemological discernment, differences between Muslims with African, Arab, or Middle Eastern origins and African American Muslims fail to become a strand of a culturally engaging, multicultural curriculum. Therefore, many educators lack the ability to dispel misinformation about Islam and Muslims.

Muslim parents, adult caregivers, and extended families often seek a safe and healthy climate for their children to develop academically and become skilled in reading and writing in Arabic while also having access to religious experiences aligned with their Islamic beliefs and practices. These different schools appear to be unified on Islam's tenets of the oneness of God, on the Qur'an and *hadith*, and the duty of Muslims to seek knowledge. However, as recounted in the text, they are at variance in their schooling of the political, social, and cultural milieu and are often quite different in teaching Islamic values. Some are very conservative and attached to a mosque with specific understandings of Islamic doctrine. One of the challenges to Islamic school leaders is to address religious and human complexity, such as national and global immigration, religious refugees' life chances, racial and ethnic biases, or ways to examine, with their students, the international consequences of war. The challenge is to foster critical thinking and analysis, the values of kindness, sympathy, and far more, through the teachings of the Islamic faith.

Social learning theory suggests that moral formation consists or develops in the acquisition of behavioral norms that are imbued from one's external environment. Interviews with administrators of the school's lower and upper divisions speak about students' moral development through daily practice not only of religious rituals but shared values. One leader's comment suggested the need to create a "curriculum of resistance," thus creating environments where there is a need to be proactive when injustices are exhibited within and outside the school.

Read and reflect on the interviews of North Star alumni, now high school students. They reminisce about shared fun times but also what it meant to be elementary school-aged children having experienced the building of a foundation where their confidence is nurtured so they subsequently could speak up for themselves in spaces where beliefs were contradictory to theirs. They remembered their "lower school" educators who maintained high expectations while having faith in them as capable students. The alumni share how valuable it was to have someone who genuinely cared for their personal well-being. There is value in having what one alum called the cultivation of a "strong moral compass." They told of instances in their high schools when they had to be respectful but correct teachers who were citing information from erroneous text. It is a lesson for educators that even young students can be provided with the ability to question what others may contend.

Attending to, while respecting, differences is another theme woven throughout this book. Students are encouraged to be okay with differences, including diversity of thought. The parents of students discuss its importance as related to the teaching staff, different ethnicities, and different faith groups. The leaders discuss how their immigrant parents navigated Christmas traditions and offer insight into cultural understandings of being raised in a country where the Muslim worldview is dominant contrasted with that of a Christian country. The board leadership references diversity in families' ability to afford tuition. Knowing the "other" also meant acknowledging that the notion of community does not equate to cohesion and commonality. When the students spoke of what foods to eat and what was *zabiha* or how *wudu* (see the text explanations for these Arabic terms) was performed, they understood the differences and were taught to regard those differences as part of being human. How did these North Star leaders create schools where students can talk about their differences, their feelings—where their social emotional well-being is as important and linked to their academic growth? Where can a middle school student confide it is okay to cry in this place? Herein is another lesson shared for compassionate leaders who wish to foster a caring school climate.

North Star Academy educators embraced a curriculum of inquiry and critical questioning about the injustices evident all around them, amid the social construction of race and other inequities. They used curriculum and co-curricular activities emphasizing character development and values of respect, honesty, self-restraint and control, justice, kindness, and care. While adopting community service-learning projects with their students and programs like the Leader in Me or Zones of Regulation, the leaders grounded these values in light of Quranic teachings. As critical social justice scholars, the authors reviewed the school's curriculum documents and noted that there exist challenges to historical heteronormativity and attempts to promote gender equality and progressive Islam through paternalistic interpretations. Yet, a curriculum of resistance, media literacy, and discussions of current events are referenced as a powerful means to foster students' consciousness, as well as their ability to question gendered power relationships. Six specific freedoms (identity, acceptance, pedagogy, conflict, trust, and love) are developed in the school as students' American Muslim identities, as was their critical consciousness of community and the importance of treating others humanely.

US education systems appear to be in constant flux, subject to many different notions of school reform and attempts at improvement. Viewed through a power analysis and critical lens, these reforms are partial and fragmented attempts at curriculum/standards-based reform, teacher education reform, principal and site-based management enactments, and charter school or market-based voucher-driven school reform measures. Nevertheless, each of these approaches includes references directly or indirectly to leadership changes.

At this time when there are mounting cries for a national reckoning and critical examination of racial, gendered, and classist inequities, school leadership must evolve toward a more culturally engaging, social justice-focused, participative form of leadership. Readers of this book may learn about creating a vision for broad school-community engagement, where school students see themselves in civic roles beyond the schoolhouse walls. One of the senior leaders articulated a vision of relational leadership that was not merely about interaction but of connection and commitment, a vision where students "look outside themselves and identify ways to contribute to their community, society, and the wider world."

Pedagogical journeying of students, teachers, and parent leaders is a valuable concept raised throughout *Islam, Education, and Freedom: An Uncommon Perspective on Leadership*. New teachers and veteran educators share their explorations with ideas, their joys with student brilliance, and difficulties with progressive concepts. Take the journey with the researchers, the students, the parents, and educators of North Star Academy. The authors take time to explain the ideas behind learning to be moral: to ground educational practices in democratic voice, collective understanding, faith, and freedom. You will gain insight into Islam and a deeper understanding of a spectrum of faith-laden practices with expansive interpretations. There is much to learn about leadership and teaching/learning for freedom and justice.

Khaula Murtadha
Professor and Associate Vice Chancellor for Community Engagement
Indiana University-Purdue University Indianapolis
USA

Acknowledgments

We express our profound gratitude to D. E., head of school, who understood and appreciated the purpose and potential of our project and the importance of capturing it for the benefit of Muslim communities. You are a precious gem! We sincerely appreciate the Islamic Center and O. R., who served as Chair of the Board of Directors at the time of the study. This book would not have materialized without the School and Center's consent and participation. We extend our heartfelt thanks to the leaders, teachers, parents, and community members who generously gave their time to share their experiences and perspectives. Thank you for the confidence you placed in us.

Thank you to Bloomsbury for accepting this as a worthwhile project. We offer our heartfelt appreciation to Jeffrey S. Brooks for believing in this project and being a sounding board and staunch supporter of our research for nearly a decade. We pay our deepest respects to the students and alumni of the school. Their self-awareness, courage, and commitment to the principles of progressive Islam exemplify the tremendous value that arises through an education centered on freedom. Thank you for teaching us this.

I am deeply indebted to my mom and dad for their love and support. Your belief in me has been a constant source of inspiration. I also extend my love to the Ezzani family, who always welcomed me with open arms, laughter, and delicious food. To my sister and friend Miriam, your kindness, compassion, and determination inspire me to push myself and believe in my own abilities. To my husband, who always says, "Yes, and . . .." you are my better half and I adore you. M. C. B.

To my parents, Dabia and Mohamed, for their love and faith in me. To my children by birth and through love, Jamila, Miles, Zahir, Vani, Avanti, Hiwot, and Natasha, who are always attentive and whose eyes light up when I share a bit of myself with them. To my sister, Huda, Khalid, Heba, Sophia, and Yousef, thank you for your love and care. To Melanie, I have learned so much from our raw and humbling discussions for over a decade. I am grateful for how they shaped our partnership, sisterhood, and friendship. To my partner and soulmate,

Mahebub, who checked in, cooked meals, brought chai, and offered unwavering love, support, and counsel. Your.love.is.liberating. M. D. E.

Lastly, we extend our gratitude to our extended family, friends, and colleagues who demonstrate genuine interest in our work as scholars and uplift us with their encouraging inquiries and words of support.

Introduction

Intersections of Islam, Education, and Freedom

When you think of freedom in the United States of America,[1] what comes to mind? Do you think about the founding documents, such as the Declaration of Independence, the US Constitution, or the Bill of Rights? Do you think about the civil liberties enshrined in these documents, such as the freedoms of conscience, speech, press, expression, assembly, or religion? Do you regard freedom in the United States as ensuring the right to equal treatment under the law, due process, and fair trials? Do you equate freedom in the United States with the right to privacy, security, and liberty? Is freedom held in the symbols of the US Flag, the Bald Eagle, the Statue of Liberty, or the celebrations of the 4th of July, Memorial Day, and Juneteenth? Or does a particular song, film, or television show remind you of freedom in the United States (Cantor, 2012; Dooley, 2017; Romanowski, 2012)? For many Americans, freedom is loosely associated with one or more of these concepts. For others, freedom is inseparable from American identity and the mainstay of the country's greatness.

Throughout the United States, freedom is taught through formal schooling (Pavlick, 2019) and realized through societal norms and mores that maintain its salience. For example, politicians repeatedly promise to protect or increase individual freedoms (Mearsheimer, 2021). Many schoolchildren begin their day reciting The Pledge of Allegiance. Scholars defend academic freedom as one of the great intellectual traditions of the United States (Reichman, 2019). Capitalistic narratives link the United States' economic prosperity to freedom (Friedman & Friedman, 1982). Those who fight and die for freedom's cause are revered as heroes and martyrs (Railton, 2021). Americans are proud to claim freedom as one of their most cherished values and uphold it as an indisputable marker of superiority (Plunkett & Kimble, 2018). Indeed, the United States' exceptionalism as an "empire of liberty" (Reynolds, 2010, p. xiii) is a familiar paean passed from generation to generation.

Yet, freedom for all remains an incomplete project. For Americans who identify as Black, Indigenous, and people of color, freedom is a "hollow mockery"

(Douglass, 1852, p. 20). US history is replete with unfreedoms: slavery (DuBois, 2015); Jim Crow laws (Gates, 2019); genocide and the forced removal of Native Americans (Saunt, 2020); the internment of Japanese Americans during the Second World War (1942–5) (Reeves, 2015); surveillance on Muslim American citizens after September 11, 2001 (Herman, 2011); and the ongoing detainment of enemy combatants without charge in Guantanamo Bay, Cuba (Roth, 2005)— among numerous other violations to individual freedoms (Chabon, 2020; Hing, 2018; Jeffries, 2004; Snowden, 2019). These inhumanities have shaped the United States where freedom is easily afforded to some and elusive and nonexistent for others (Douglass, 2009/1846).

The September 11, 2001, attacks on the World Trade Center and the Pentagon irrevocably altered the idea of freedom in the United States (Nguyen & Danticat, 2005). Seven weeks after the attacks, reminiscent of Orwellian Newspeak, the *Uniting and Strengthening America by Providing Appropriate Tools Required to Intercept and Obstruct Terrorism Act of 2001* (USA Patriot Act) passed Congress with little dissent. This Act allowed the US government to expand surveillance and law enforcement powers to investigate individuals suspected of terrorism (Etzioni, 2005). With a public overwhelmed with fear, grief, and anger, little was done to stop the United States government's prioritization of national security at the expense of individual freedoms. Given that the attacks were made in the name of Islam, American Muslims and those who appeared to be Muslim were targeted and surveilled.

The increased powers to mark Muslim communities effectively moved Islam from a peripheral and nonthreatening faith to that of a despised religion and suspect enemy group (Aizpurua et al., 2017; Cainkar, 2011; Powell, 2018). Subsequent attacks, such as the 2013 Boston Marathon bombing, the 2015 San Bernardino mass shooting, and the 2016 Orlando Nightclub shooting, increased affective distrust and hostility toward Muslims (Green, 2019). During this time, extreme right anti-Muslim hate groups gained traction through smaller, underground social media platforms, such as Discord, 4Chan, Gab, Rumble, MeWe, Telegram, and others. With little to no restrictions to regulate these online platforms, an increasing number of anti-Muslim groups began to spread disinformation to discredit and malign Islam and Muslims. In addition, the religious right used conservative mainstream media outlets to promote conspiracy theories, one of which warned viewers of an eminent civilization *jihad* (spiritual struggle) whereby the Muslim Brotherhood would unseat the government to establish a new Islamic caliphate on US soil (Sutliff, 2016).

This upswell of anti-Muslim racism and rhetoric successfully persuaded a majority of American citizens to see Islam as a political ideology to be feared rather than a world religion (Warner, 2020). Anti-Muslim narratives have become normalized in politics (Bell, 2014; Council on American-Islamic Relations, 2019), and continue to shape perceptions that Muslims either choose not to or are simply unable to integrate into US society. Consequently, Muslims experience bias, religious discrimination, defamation, harassment, and assaults in workplaces, public venues, and schools (Acquisti & Fong, 2012). However, this is not a new phenomenon. Rather, one could argue that its origins reside with the arrival of enslaved West African Muslims to the shores of the British colony of Virginia over 400 years ago (Jones, 2021; Williams, 2010).

America's Greatest Shame: Slavery and the Duplicity of Freedom

Estimates indicate that 12 million Africans were forcibly transported to the Americas between the seventeenth and nineteenth centuries. Of the 305,326 West Africans involuntarily brought to North America, only 252,652 survived the voyage (Eltis, 2018). Of those who survived, upward of 20 percent were West African Muslims originating from pre-colonial Islamic kingdoms (Curiel, 2015; Esposito, 2011). Before their enslavement, many West Africans received an Islamic education, and a significant number were *hafiz*, a title of respect bestowed upon those who memorized the entire Qur'an. Many could read and write in Arabic and use unstandardized systems of writing in local languages (Curtis, 2009; Diallo, 2012; Einboden, 2020; Esposito, 2011). Yet, there is no indication of a link in the transmission of Islam from enslaved West African Muslims to the Islam African American Muslims practice today (Diouf, 1998).

The absence of enslaved Muslims in American history is partially due to a collective absence in scholarly research (Diouf, 2021). Albeit some scholars have documented the barriers West African Muslims faced in practicing their faith amid the violence and dehumanization inherent in chattel slavery (Diouf, 1998; Halverson, 2016). Despite horrific challenges, some Muslims continued practicing their faith (Gomez, 1994), which set them apart from other enslaved individuals through practices of prayer, dietary observances, fasting, modesty, and charity (Diouf, 2021). These acts of resistance included keeping their names or giving their children names that reflected their Islamic heritage, such as Bilal, Fatima, or Salih (Diouf, 2021). Although deprived of sacred texts and communal gatherings, they wrote or recited verses from the Qur'an in Arabic. Some of these writings have been preserved as historical documents, such as the autobiography of Omar ibn Said. Teaching new generations to read and write was another barrier. Enslaved African Muslims performed Islamic rituals in secret, such as prayers, fasting, and charity (Diouf, 2021; Gomez, 1994). They clandestinely formed networks with other Muslim slaves who shared their culture and faith. They wore turbans, caps, beads, and other items that were of religious significance as a form of protection and as symbols of resistance against slavery and oppression. Primary sources curated by the National Museum of African American History and Culture reveal that enslaved Muslims utilized bilingualism and their faith to "build community, resist slavery and pursue freedom" (Smithsonian, 2019).

Slaveholders found various methods to force conversion to Christianity. These included but were not limited to physical violence, psychological pressure, and manipulation to the offering of rewards and privileges to those who converted (Grant, 2015). They stole identities through Christian renaming (Curtis, 2009) and distributing Bibles translated into Arabic to coerce conversions (Grant, 2015). Thousands of enslaved West African Muslims converted to Christianity. Others converted because of the perceived benefits of conformism. Chattel slavery existed in the United States for 246 years, which effectively stripped enslaved Muslims of their humanity and their faith.

Despite the founding fathers' awareness of Islam's presence in the young nation, their focus remained on whether Protestantism should be the nation's civic religion (Spellberg, 2013). Thomas Jefferson advocated for a clear separation of church and state, citing reason, scientific knowledge, and liberty as the tools to propel humanity forward (Ragosta, 2013). Jefferson's vision did not entail a ban on religion; rather, he supported religious liberty for "the Jew and the Gentile, the Christian and Mahometan, the Hindoo, and infidel of every denomination" (Jefferson & Washington, 1853, p. 45). In a fledgling nation, religious freedom was codified through the First Amendment to the United States Constitution in 1791, though this freedom was granted to some while denied to others (Winters, 1978). Thomas Jefferson never extricated himself from the "deplorable entanglement" of slavery (Araujo, 2020, p. 154). He enslaved 600 individuals at Monticello (Jefferson, 1824; Wiencek, 2012). Alongside other founding fathers, Jefferson failed to acknowledge or rectify the duplicity of freedom, a hypocrisy upheld until emancipation in 1863.

Although Jefferson identified as a Christian deist, he owned George Sale's 1734 English translation of the Qur'an. He used this translation as a legal reference

(Hayes, 2002). Yet, over time, Jefferson came to see Islam as a more enlightened and rational religion than Judaism and Christianity (Hammer & Safi, 2013). This perspective did not alter Jefferson's stance on religion, however. As with Judaism and Christianity, Jefferson denounced Islam and remained critical of religion in toto until his death. Antithetical to his personal views, Jefferson did not see a reason to bar Muslims, or individuals of any religion, from holding office in the young nation. Remarkably, it was not until 242 years later, in 2007, that the first Muslim was elected to serve in the United States Congress. Representative Keith Ellison poignantly took his oath of office by laying his hand on Thomas Jefferson's 1734 Sale translation of the Qur'an. This defining moment announced to Americans, many for the first time, that Islam is deeply rooted in the "American experiment" (Dionne & Dilulio, 2000, p. 1).

Liminal Space: Life between Freedom and Subjugation

The confederacy's defeat in the Civil War (1861–5) compelled White landowners to establish segregationist laws to maintain political power and racial supremacy. Violence, intimidation, and lynching of African Americans, sanctioned by Jim Crow laws and Black Codes, continued subjugating formerly enslaved African Americans and limited their freedom (Boustan, 2017; Wallenstein, 2004). Beginning in 1916 and continuing through the 1970s, an estimated six million African Americans participated in the Great Migration north to escape Southern racism. Most migrants settled in Detroit, Chicago, Pittsburgh, New York, and Washington, DC. They secured work in factories, mills, railroads, and other industrial and labor-intensive jobs with low status and low remuneration (Boustan, 2017). New arrivals turned to religious groups for networking, spiritual uplifting, and racial unity (Jackson, 2005). Among the varied religious groups were burgeoning "proto-Islamic Black American" organizations led by charismatic African American leaders (Jackson, 2005, p. 46). These groups brought thousands of African Americans into the fold of Islam, providing members with needed camaraderie among pervasive oppressions (Bowen, 2011; Hammer & Safi, 2013).

The earliest African American Islamic organizations began in the first decades of the twentieth century, most notably the Ahmadiyya Muslim Community, the Moorish Science Temple of America, and the Nation of Islam. Each organization linked Islam's "figures, place names, texts, events, and themes" to the "historical destiny of black [sic] people" (Chande, 2008; Curtis, 2005, p. 559;

Weisenfeld, 2016). The Ahmadiyya organization emphasized African heritage and contributions to Islam (Bayoumi, 2001). The Moorish Science Temple of America centered its teachings on the belief that the Moabites of Northwest Africa were the ancestors of African Americans (Chande, 2008). Similarly, the Nation of Islam preached that the Tribe of Shabazz, located in Egypt's Nile Valley, was the origin of African American lineage. African American Islamic organizations skillfully blended elements of traditional Islam with Black pan-nationalism. In doing so, they offered converts a rich history rooted in the lived experiences of Africans and African Americans (Jackson, 2005). Yet, arguably, it was Islam's narratives of resistance, struggle, and hope that drew African Americans to Islam.

The rapid expansion of African American Islamic organizations did not go unnoticed by the US government (Chande, 2008). From the 1930s onward, the Federal Bureau of Investigation and the Justice Department viewed the growing Islamic movement as a significant threat to American society. Driving these suspicions were concerns that African American Islamic organizations were involved in activities threatening the United States (Curtis, 2013). These included, but were not limited to, conspiring with the Japanese during the Second World War, collaborating with the Communist Party, inciting Black empowerment, cultivating radicalization, inflaming violence, and provoking racial insurgency (Curtis, 2013; Evanzz, 2017; Johnson, 2017). In response, the federal government separated organizations from their religious missions, purposefully recasting them as dangerous political cults. In this way, the federal government circumvented First Amendment protections and used covert and illegal operations to "expose, disrupt, misdirect, or otherwise neutralize" African American Muslim leaders from their organizations (Curtis, 2013; Deflam, 2008, p. 182). In addition, the US intelligence operatives employed a variety of clandestine operations to "frustrate any efforts of the groups to consolidate their forces or to recruit new or youthful adherents" (Kamali, 2017, p. 70). Undercover informants, infiltration of meetings, warrantless surveillance, the spread of disinformation via media outlets, and the incitement of intragroup divisiveness were common tactics used to suppress the perceived threat African American Muslims posed to society (Curtis, 2013). Despite these surreptitious efforts, African American Muslims continued to fortify the links between African American Islam and liberation (Howell, 2013).

In 1965, the passage of the Hart-Celler Act opened the United States to immigrants from Muslim-majority countries. This legislation abolished the *National Origins Formula* (1921–65), which restricted immigration to percentages that mirrored America's population. With restrictions lifted, a critical mass of Muslims immigrated to the United States from around the world, many in search of America's promise of freedom. They settled in ethnic enclaves divided along geopolitical, racial, ethnic, and intrafaith lines, which helped them preserve their cultural identities (Abdullah, 2013). The US government classified Muslim immigrants from the Middle East as Caucasian/White (Maghbouleh, 2017). This categorization afforded new arrivals the ability to retain aspects of their heritage culture and selectively assimilate dominant White cultural norms and mores into their day-to-day lives (Ajrouch & Jamal, 2007). This racial liminality allowed Middle Eastern/Arab Muslims to deftly shift between racial and ethnic identities. Some could "open or close the door to whiteness [sic] as necessary"—a freedom not afforded African American Muslims (Guhin, 2018; Maghnouleh, 2017, p. 5). Muslim immigration changed the religious, racial, ethnic, and linguistic landscape of the United States, in large part due to the rich cultural diversity of the *ummah* (Muslim global community). However, race and racism fundamentally shaped—and continue to shape—the lived experiences of American Muslims, creating an American *ummah* historically, racially, ethnically, socially, and religiously complex (Guhin, 2018; Maghnouleh, 2017).

On February 26, 1993, a truck bombing organized and detonated by Al-Qaeda operatives killed six and injured over 1,000 people in New York City's World Trade Center. This bombing not only heightened Americans' awareness of global violence done in the name of Islam but also served as a precursor to the September 11, 2001, attack, which killed 2,977 individuals. With subsequent attacks in the United States after 2001, American Muslims have become increasingly distrusted and feared (Abu El-Haj, 2006; Bleich et al., 2015b; Karim, 2006; Said, 1996; Sirin & Fine, 2008). This trepidation toward Muslims extended into the schooling sector, where leeriness has fostered microaggressions, bigotry, and, in some cases, physical violence against Muslim and Muslim-appearing students and their families. Being othered was commonplace and expected for most Muslim students attending public schools (Saada, 2017).

Marginalizing Muslims: Still Schooling the 'Other'

Muslims experience public schools like other minoritized groups, enduring derogatory slurs, racist policies, discriminatory curriculum, and inequitable practices (Bonet, 2011; Douglass, 2009; Kendi, 2019; Zine, 2004). In effect, schooling positions Muslims as immutable subalterns. Most teachers are underprepared to recognize and push back against organizational norms and educational practices that continue to subjugate those of the Muslim faith (Apple & Buras, 2006; Hall, 2001; Said, 1978). For non-Muslims, intrafaith differences are often not readily apparent. Consequently, non-Muslim teachers and students perceive Muslims through their Eurocentric and hegemonic Western gaze, whereby they stereotype male Muslims as misogynistic and threatening and female Muslims as dependent and oppressed (Burney, 2012, p. 26; Said, 1978; Van Es, 2016). Further to this, many non-Muslim teachers do not understand the differences between Arab, Middle Eastern, and Muslim and have difficulty developing culturally responsive and inclusive pedagogy (Gay, 2018). Arab culture is rarely included in the multicultural paradigm of schooling (Abu El-Haj, 2006), and when it is included, it often contains inaccurate and/or erroneous information (Wingfield, 2006). These misconceptions contribute to Muslim students feeling alienated and marginalized in public schools (Abu El-Haj, 2006; Brooks et al., 2021; Suleiman, 2004).

Compounding the problem is the failure of teacher and principal preparation programs to include the topics of religion, religious diversity, and religious bias in their coursework (Poole, 2015). This begs the question as to whether schoolteachers and school leaders are cognizant of or have the requisite knowledge to identify religious bias, dispel misinformation, or teach religious literacy skills (Brooks et al., 2021; Ezzani & Brooks, 2015; Greenawalt, 2007; Heinrich, 2013; Khuwaja & Ezzani, 2022; Wuthnow, 2011). Schools have the power and potential to be religiously responsive and religiously inclusive. Nevertheless, unlearning racist beliefs and practices requires educators to move from unlearning, unseeing, and undiscerning to critical learning, critical awareness, and critical discernment. The ongoing failure to decolonize White, Christian, Western curricula reinforces the privileging of canonical knowledge, languages, and spiritualities over non-Western ways of knowing and being. Essentially, hegemonic curricula delegitimize freedom of thought outside the colonial project, proffering othered students a maleducation (Said, 1978; Zeus, 2018).

Even in 1932, the Nation of Islam was acutely aware that their children were being taught a colonized curriculum in Detroit public schools. Not willing to subject their children to a dehumanizing and unaffirming educational system, the Nation of Islam established the first private Islamic school in the United States, naming it The University of Islam. The name reflected the universal nature of the school's teachings and the advanced Blackcentric K–12 curricula that focused on students being able to "know self," "love self," and "do for self" (Rashid &

Muhammad, 1992, p. 179). Wanting to free themselves from the psychological and physiological impacts of racism, the University of Islam taught a curriculum that was timely and impactful. For example, music and athletics were not included in the curriculum to deliberately remove the stereotype of African Americans as entertainers and athletes (Shalaby, 1967). Students learned about White hegemonic and racist culture to engage in a "process of cultural renewal" that developed pride in their Black identity, African heritage, and Islamic faith (Shalaby, 1967, p. xi). In 1975, the Nation of Islam divided into two distinct groups after the death of Elijah Muhammad. The branch following Warith D. Muhammad (Elijah Muhammad's son) aligned itself with orthodox Sunni Islam. The University of Islam schools revised their curricula to include traditional Sunni Islamic beliefs and changed their name to Sister Clara Muhammad schools in honor of Elijah Muhammad's wife (Rashid & Muhammad, 1992). The other branch followed Louis Farrakhan, an outspoken and controversial leader who continues to shape the Nation of Islam's Black nationalist and separatist discourses.

It is important to note that non-Black immigrant families did not enroll their children in Sister Clara Muhammad schools, attended by the children of the African American Muslim community. They also did not attend Black mosques. Rather, immigrant families preferred their children to attend schools and mosques reflective of their ethnic, linguistic, and sociocultural understandings and practices of Islam. These preferences in schooling were grounded in pervasive anti-Black racism. Immigrant families saw value in being viewed as White and were content to receive its privileges. As a result, immigrant families enrolled their children in schools that mirrored their racial, ethnic, sociocultural, historical, and economic characteristics. These deep divisions persist today.

The most recent report by the Islamic Schools League of America identified over 300 immigrant community-based schools and Sister Clara Muhammad schools in operation (Keyworth, 2015). Collectively considered, Islamic schools in the United States educate upwards of 32,000 students annually (Keyworth, 2015). Yet, contrary to public perceptions, Islamic schools vary in regard to denominational divisions (i.e., Sunni, Shi'a, Ismaili, Ahmadiyya), schools of jurisprudence (i.e., Hanafi, Maliki, Shafi'i, Hanbali), socioreligious movements (i.e., Progressive/Liberal, African American, Ibadi, Salafi, Wahhabi), and for reasons related to educational philosophies, geopolitics, race, ethnicity, and language, among other differences. Despite these many differences, Islamic schools share three important key concepts: (1) *tawheed*, the oneness of God, the creator, and sustainer of the universe; (2) *ta'lim*, imparting the teachings of the Qur'an and *hadith* (the collections of traditions containing sayings of Prophet Muhammad); and (3) *'ilm*, the duty of Muslims to seek knowledge. Most Islamic schools teach state curricula (with variations in offering music and art) and add lessons in Arabic, Qur'an, and Islamic studies to the curriculum (Haddad & Smith, 2009). Islamic schools also include prayer during the day, require modesty in dress, and provide food that is *halal* (permissible) and meat that is *zabiha* (slaughtered in a permissible way). Parents who enroll their children in Islamic schools do so for myriad reasons. Common reasons include learning about Islam, developing Arabic language skills, having a safe and secure environment, providing academic excellence, and integrating religious experiences that are aligned with their Islamic beliefs and practices (Brooks, 2019; Grewal & Coolidge, 2013; Meer, 2007; Merry, 2018).

Yet, the diversity of the Muslim *ummah* brings complexities to the schoolhouse, raising questions as to whether certain types of diversity are a threat to freedom. Some parents and school stakeholders carry with them "their own colonial ideals about skin color and ethnic differences" along with personal experiences that shape the way they engage with difficult topics (Abdullah, 2013, p. 72). Racial and ethnic conflicts, civil and national warfare, international military interventions, politics, and contested histories and geographies bring varied opinions and perspectives to the fore (Selod & Embrick, 2013). Whether or not Islamic school leaders and teachers engage with controversy to foster productive discussion and debate, promote complex reasoning and integrated thinking skills, or develop in students a critical consciousness rooted in the Islamic faith, entirely depends on how freedom is understood, taught, and used in Islamic schooling.

We began this research during the second half of the Trump presidency in January 2019. By this time, Trump's anti-Muslim racism was well-established through a series of executive orders and proclamations (Patel & Levison-Waldman, 2017). For half of the population, Trump's bigotry fed into social, economic, and racial antagonisms that reinforced White middle and working-class resentments toward Black, Asian, Latinx, and others perceived as making notable gains at their expense. The rationalized ignorance of his followers in choosing to remain uninformed and loyal despite his espoused racism was perplexing and confounding. We were bewildered at the ease by which Trump's hate speech was cheered and extolled by many, even people we called family and dear friends. Be that as it may, Trump's public statements and vilification of Muslims as anti-American and liberticidal compelled us to explore Islamic schools in the United States and the concept of freedom.

Before we begin deconstructing how freedom is understood, taught, and used in an American Islamic school, we must concede the political nature of education and the inherent biases embedded in research (Wolcott, 2002). Education research is never value-free nor neutral, especially on topics of faith, race, gender, and ideology (Griffiths, 1998). We acknowledge the impossibility of conducting research on these issues without our biases, which have developed through our personal histories and decade-long research partnership. As scholars working in the critical tradition, we support racial, gender, social, and economic justice. We align ourselves with a progressive understanding of Islam, one that advocates for human rights, inclusion, dignity, compassion, and justice (Safi, 2003b). To mitigate against our biases, we present the narrative as we experienced it, alongside the firsthand accounts of the participants in their own words.

We recognize the inevitability of political and ideological reactions to this research. We welcome passionate responses, critical conversations, and follow-up investigations that seek to better understand the myriad problems, issues, and perplexities raised through this qualitative case study on American Islamic schooling, leadership, and freedom. It is only through this collective action that new knowledge is generated and uncommon understandings acquired. It is our aim that this collective energy will help bridge the widening socioreligious divide in the United States and beyond.

1

North Star Academy

A Progressive Islamic School

At first glance, North Star Academy looked like any other private elementary school in Southern California. Its facade was of the modern Spanish Mission Revival style common to the area. Its red clay tile roof met a cream-colored stucco exterior. Rounded arches lined the length of the main school building, which was flanked by neatly trimmed and mature landscaping. Located in an older office park, its neighbors included a Chinese school and cultural center, two music academies, an attorney's office, three tutoring centers, and a large apartment complex. Near the main entrance, a sign displayed the school's name next to a National Blue-Ribbon School banner. In the center of the lawn was a tall flagpole on which a US flag fluttered in the breeze. There was also a mosque in the office park, although it was not affiliated with the school. Even with these accouterments, most people driving past the building would not recognize it as a school, much less an Islamic school.

We arrived at North Star Academy a little after 9:00 on a Monday morning in January 2019. It was easy to find parking, as the school day had already started. We were ready for a full day of data collection. We gathered our bags from the trunk of the rental car and walked across the parking lot to the main entrance to the school. The front door was located in a large vestibule, which we found dark, cool, and a welcome respite from the sun. At the far end of the vestibule was a locked rod-iron gate that separated us from the school's main hallway. We heard the bustle of a busy school morning and were excited to go inside. We rang the doorbell. Wendy, one of the school's two administrative assistants, stood, smiled, and slid open the window. She said, "Hi, are you here for the research project?" "Yes," we both replied. Wendy nodded and handed us a clipboard to record our visit. Miriam wrote our names, affiliations, and the current time and passed the clipboard back through the window. Wendy pushed the buzzer to unlock the door, and we walked in. She pointed to a row of chairs, "I'll call Ms. Fatemi and let her know you are here. Please take a seat." We sat down and placed our bags on the floor.

A portable bookcase separated the office space from the waiting area, which was more of a hallway than a welcoming place to sit. The front office was small. Stacks of books and papers lined the far wall. Two administrative assistants' desks were crowded with books, papers, and computer equipment. Three closed-circuit televisions hung just above Wendy's computer monitors. These added to the feeling of clutter and confinement, yet also offered a sense of safety. As we waited for Ms. Layla Fatemi, we noticed a historical timeline on a nearby wall. "Miriam let's take a look," whispered Melanie.

The timeline on the wall began in 1998. In that year, members of the Islamic Center of San Rico, a leading Islamic Center known for its work in social justice, community building, and interfaith outreach, gathered to discuss the possibility of establishing a new Islamic school in Field County. Earlier that year, a market analysis conducted by the Islamic Center indicated significant interest in supporting an Islamic school south of the city. The school would be a sub-entity of the Islamic Center of San Rico, which retained complete control over the land purchase, building design, and approvals. In 1999, a Founding Committee formed and identified a tract of land for the school in the city of Hermantown, twenty-eight miles south of the City of San Rico. When the Hermantown residents learned that the tract of land was for a new Islamic school, they mobilized quickly and stood against the purchase. They argued that the town could not accommodate the increased traffic that would result from a new school. Yet, the underlying motivations for the staunch resistance were evident in the racist and anonymous hate-filled messages left on the Islamic Center of San Rico's phone messaging system. Facing this intense opposition, the Founding Committee decided to revoke its purchase of land in Hermantown and begin searching for suitable land in a city further south. Finally, in 2000, both the Islamic Center of San Rico and the City of Springwater approved a new site for the school. The groundbreaking was a ceremonial event. Two pictures were captured that day. The first showed smiling adults in hard hats posing with decorated new shovels. A second picture displayed the community standing in prayer on a tarp, seeking Allah's (God's) assistance and blessings for this new school.

A year later, on September 10, 2001, North Star Academy welcomed eighty-five students in preschool to grade five. The following day, on September 11, 2001, the cover of the Springwater Daily News featured the opening of the city's new Islamic school. The article included a color photograph of young boys and girls at *dhuhr* (midday) prayer and a short interview with the head of school, Dr. Muna Ramsey. On that same day, 2,996 individuals lost their lives in a suicide terrorist attack on the World Trade Center, the Pentagon, and in a field near Shanksville, Pennsylvania. In our first interview with Dr. Ramsey, she reflected on the terrorist attack and how it occurred on the second day of the school's inaugural year. She said, "It was just news, 'New Islamic school opens in the heart of the City of Springwater.' Of course, there was no imagining what would happen that day on the East coast. Yet, the attack framed our purpose and what we needed to do, not only for our kids and our families but also for the community in recognizing who we are and what we do."

Despite this challenging start, the school flourished. The following year, fifty-four new students enrolled. In 2006, the school had a waiting list for entry and received accreditation from the California Association of Independent Schools (CAIS) and the Western Association of Schools and Colleges (WASC). Several years later, the school was named a National Blue Ribbon of Excellence school by the U.S. Department of Education and became one of 300 FranklinCovey Leader in Me Lighthouse Schools. By 2018, the school had outgrown its physical space. The Islamic Center decided to add an upper school campus for grades six through eight.

The school advocated for years to have its own 501(c)(3) status, as it was classified as a sub-entity of the Islamic Center of San Rico. In other words, the Islamic Center's Board of Trustees insisted on maintaining control over the school to ensure that the center's ideology was not lost or modified. This arrangement required North Star Academy to obtain center support and approval for its annual budget and strategic plan. Just two weeks before we arrived, the school acquired 501(c)(3) status to align with the opening of the upper school campus. As we finished reading the 2019 panel of the timeline, Ms. Layla Fatemi entered the hallway and greeted us with a firm handshake and a warm hello.

Ms. Layla Fatemi—Lower School Director

"Let's go to the conference room to talk," Ms. Fatemi said. We turned and picked up our belongings and followed her down the hallway. We sat at a rectangular table that filled the entire room. We pulled out our voice recorders, pens, and notebooks, reviewed the informed consent with Ms. Fatemi, and pressed record. Miriam started the interview, "Please tell us about yourself and your role in the school." After thinking for a few seconds, Ms. Fatemi said enthusiastically, "I'll tell you. Let me begin with the school first, and then I'll talk about my personal journey that led me to the role of lower school director." She shifted her weight in the seat. "The school opened in 2001. I wasn't here, but I think our beginning was poignant. On September 11th, we were featured in the Springwater Daily News." We nodded as Ms. Fatemi spoke, remembering the timeline and the newspaper article we had read moments earlier.

Ms. Fatemi continued, "Looking back, September 11th was such a significant marker for us. I was teaching at a conservative Islamic school when 9/11 occurred. The tragedy impacted me in a very personal way. I felt threatened. When I reflect on that time, I can see how the aftermath fueled Islamophobia in a new way, a way that Muslims had never felt before 9/11. I experienced it head-on, and it was terrifying. I wore a scarf back then too, so I had to make a conscious decision to continue covering. I was working at a very conservative Islamic school that required all females to wear a *hijab* (head covering), whether Muslim or not. I was frightened because I had just started wearing a *hijab* the year before."

Miriam commented, "Yes, I remember the media reports of Muslims—and anyone looking Muslim—being attacked verbally and physically. It was a scary time." Ms. Fatemi leaned forward, adding emphasis to her reply, and said, "After 9/11, the realization of being Muslim in America and having a Muslim identity hit us all at once. Prior to 9/11, we saw ourselves as part of the melting pot of America, part of the larger society. I moved from Pakistan to California when I was nine years old. I never thought of myself as anything but an American Muslim. I guess I never realized until now, in my forties, that the things I did in my life were for a reason; although, at that young age, when you're making those choices, it's not so evident."

Ms. Fatemi cleared some papers in front of her as she took a deep breath. She continued to reflect on her past.

"It's interesting to think about my own life choices. First, I went into journalism with the intent to work at a big city magazine. I didn't like the work. I didn't find it fulfilling. Near the end of my bachelor's degree, I took some classes in education. I had enough credits to qualify as a substitute teacher. I decided to return to school to obtain my teaching credential. All teachers go into teaching to make a difference. I remember a pivotal moment where I thought, 'I don't know what I'm doing.' It was literally a divine moment. I believed in my faith, but I wasn't like, 'I'm going to work in an Islamic school.' That wasn't my intention. When I returned to university, my only experience in education was working as a Sunday school teacher at our local mosque, similar to the

Islamic Center of San Rico. I knew the value of a young person teaching the next generation of Muslims about their faith. I thought, 'This is fun and interesting, but I only have them for two hours. Wouldn't it be cool if I opened a school?' I was ambitious. It's like what I was trying to do initially with journalism. I wanted to create a magazine with my friends that merged the two worlds. Growing up Pakistani, I only had access to shoddy fashion magazines that were just horrible; the grammar was all wrong, and the pictures were lame. I wanted to do *Vogue*. My ambition was to show Muslim identity and hold on to tradition."

Ms. Fatemi took a deep breath and looked for our approval to continue, which Miriam gave by way of a slight nod. "Long story short, that was my concept for an Islamic school. I didn't want a mosque-oriented school. I wanted something that blended both worlds. So, when I interviewed for a position at North Star Academy, I didn't know much about the school; however, I knew that the school was progressive. I didn't understand what that meant though. It was a label, and I knew it reflected a division in our community."

Ms. Fatemi stopped for a moment to collect her thoughts. She said, "I last worked at a charter school. That school terminated my employment. I needed a job. Along with interviewing at North Star Academy, I interviewed at many public schools. Islamic schools turned me off because of the bureaucracy, the politics, and the instability. I wasn't feeling confident at that time. My husband encouraged me to apply to North Star. Then I met Muna. This school felt unlike any other Islamic school. The school was an actual building, and the office was professional. North Star was different. I thought, 'Oh my gosh, my dream of an Islamic school already exists!' My journey makes sense to me now because I haven't left. It's my fifteenth year. I've been a teacher, curriculum director, and now the director of the lower school."

"How does your faith influence your professional life?" asked Melanie. Ms. Fatemi replied after thinking for a moment, "Muslim identity is part and parcel of who I am. I've seen the benefits of this in my own kids who went here. I want to instill this identity in the next generation." Ms. Fatemi looked at her watch. "I am so sorry, but I have a meeting with the Parent Association. Feel free to stay as long as you would like." Miriam pressed stop on the two audio recorders. Ms. Fatemi gathered a few items from her desk and left the room.

Miriam reflected, "It's too bad we had to stop. It was interesting when she spoke about her experiences after 9/11. She felt targeted, and she had just begun wearing the *hijab*."

"I remember that time. It was scary. American flags were everywhere—on every mailbox and lining all of the streets. I became much more aware of my identity as an American, so I understand where she is coming from. I think the mission statement says something about identity. Can you pull it up on the website?" Melanie asked.

Miriam opened her laptop and went to North Star Academy's homepage. Under the tab 'About us' was the mission statement. Melanie read it aloud.

> North Star Academy offers outstanding academics in a progressive Islamic environment, developing in each child an American Muslim identity, so that they are well-prepared to succeed, lead, and serve.

"That captures the school well. Let's make a note to follow up with Layla."

"Sure thing," said Miriam. "Oh, look at the clock. We need to get to the upper school to meet Dr. Ramsey. Let's get going."

Dr. Muna Ramsey—Head of School

North Star Academy's upper campus was in an office park eight miles from the lower school campus. The newly constructed school was situated between manufacturers, wholesale supply distributors, furniture stores, and, at the far end, a Coptic Orthodox Church. As we approached North Star Academy's upper campus, we were surprised to see only two parked cars in its large parking lot. The empty parking lot seemed strangely quiet for the middle of a school day. We grabbed our bags and headed to the front door. As we walked, it was obvious that the building was new. Landscaping had yet to be planted. The school's name was embossed on a stand near the main entrance. The building's design was of a modern Islamic style, with echoes of traditional Islamic architecture, including a *minaret* (a slender tower connected to mosques used to project the call to prayer), geometric and pointed arch windows, stonework, and stucco. We reached the glass entryway and pulled on the door. It was locked.

The receptionist saw us approach and unlocked the glass front door. "Welcome to North Star Academy's upper school! We were expecting you. Please follow me to a room where you can wait." We noticed that there were no pictures on the walls. No plants. We did not see any students. The building was quiet. We later learned that the school was still under construction. Only half of the school was being utilized. The walk to the room was not far and took us through a large staff kitchen and past a row of offices. The office doors were open, and a few staff members were working at their desks. The receptionist ushered us into a workroom with a circular table and four chairs. We started to unpack our bags, taking out our recorders, pens, informed consent paperwork, and notebooks. As we were unpacking, Dr. Ramsey appeared in the doorway. "Hello!" exclaimed Miriam in a high-pitched and excited tone, holding her arms out for a hug. "Hi!" replied Dr. Ramsey, accepting Miriam's hug. In their embrace, they rocked side to side for a few seconds saying how nice it was to see each other. They were excited to reconnect. When they both let go, Miriam turned and introduced Melanie to Dr. Ramsey. "Why don't you both come to my office," Dr. Ramsey said.

We picked up our equipment and bags. Our arms were full as we walked around the corner to Dr. Ramsey's office. Her office was a comfortable size with a desk, chairs, and sofa. Artwork hung on the walls, and family pictures were interspersed along her bookshelves. Coffee, tea, and pastries sat on top of a sideboard near the entrance of her office. She invited us to help ourselves to refreshments.

"Thank you for the warm welcome, Muna, and for finding time to talk with us today. To begin, could you please tell us about your childhood?" asked Melanie.

Dr. Ramsey leaned back in her executive chair and said, "I identify as an American Muslim with Egyptian heritage. Both of my parents were raised in Egypt. I was born in the 1960s and grew up in the early 1970s in a relatively privileged area. My early school experience was more about color than my religion. My religion, too, but they're intertwined. There were very few—let me be blunt with you—Brown kids in my school. Because I'm from Egypt, North Africa, I'm darker with curly hair. I was called out as Brown. I became aware of this when I was seven years old. My hair didn't do the same things as other kids. When an African American boy enrolled in our school, I got teased that he was my boyfriend. I thought, 'Oh, okay. They think I'm like him or look like him in their eyes.' That was an 'aha' moment for me. Although I knew I was a smart kid, I remember having to fight my way through school and advocate for myself. I think my motivation was just to be with my friends. I don't think it was a political thing, but I had to be my own advocate. I remember all the other kids got into schools through teacher recommendations, but I had to take a test to prove I could keep up in advanced academics. My parents didn't know how to advocate for me because they were immigrants."

Miriam commented, "I get it. My parents were immigrants too. They valued education but didn't understand the importance of engaging in the school experience with me. Part of it was that they did not have a formal education."

"How was public school for you overall?" Melanie asked.

Dr. Ramsey nodded and said, "Well, I attended only Southern Californian public schools. A lot of what was going on when I was growing up was centered on politics. In junior high school, it was the Kurds and Druze struggling against oppression. When I was in high school, it was the Iranian hostage crisis that dominated US media. My social studies teachers were interested in politics and what was going on in the world. When they discovered I was Egyptian, they asked me questions as if I had insight into that world. The peace talks at Camp David with Menachem Begin and Anwar Sadat were also a big deal. The media always framed these events around politics. It was never about Islam. Anwar Sadat was a hero in the eyes of Americans. I felt a sense of pride without really understanding the context. I think I was too young to understand.

"There were a lot of things I didn't understand. There was an assumption that everyone celebrated Christmas. In first or second grade, when I returned from winter break, my class had to write to the prompt, 'What did you receive for Christmas?' In fact, I had to write about that every year. My family didn't celebrate Christmas. I came home from school in second grade and asked my mom, 'Why do I not have Christmas presents? Why don't we celebrate Christmas?' In response, my parents put up a tree and lights for a couple of years to make me feel that we weren't different from my friends' families. They explained to me that we were Muslim.

"I think when you're raised in a country where the norm is Muslim, you really don't ask questions. The same is true if you live in a predominantly Christian country; you don't ask why. For example, my parents, raised in Egypt, never asked why they fast or pray five times a day. They never had to ask. It was just something everybody did. My parents didn't have answers to my questions. On the other hand, Christians living here in America probably could not answer similar questions, such as 'Why Christmas trees? Why lights?' Most of them wouldn't know how to respond. It's just a part of their childhood. They didn't need to ask why because everyone else was doing it. So, I was caught between the two. I didn't understand why there were Christmas trees and lights or why people exchanged gifts. My parents really didn't have the language to explain it to me."

Miriam nodded in agreement. "My parents did the same thing. I remember the whole family piling into the VW van and driving to Sears. Baba bought us a silver tinsel Christmas tree with all the decorations."

Dr. Ramsey laughed and continued, "Well, here are my thoughts. I believe religion for my family was cultural more than anything else. I wouldn't say they were devout because it wasn't like they held onto the faith because they understood and loved it. I think it was just something they grew up with. I think their devotion came later because of things that happened to me and because I did ask questions. I spent a lot of time pushing back and questioning.

I would often say, 'Well, why?' or 'It doesn't make sense,' or 'Why should I do it?' My family became involved with the Islamic Center of San Rico in my preteens. It was the only mosque in the region, and I remember some of my friends traveled 40 miles to attend. I joined the youth group when I was 11 or 12 years old. That's when we started going to the mosque, and I started understanding more about our faith. I joined the youth group, and for the first time, I was with people who were like me. By the time I was a senior in high school, I had finally found a group of people who shared my values, my family's values, and many of our daily practices. I clung to that. I decided to wear the *hijab* when I graduated from high school. Honestly, no women were wearing *hijab* in California; at least, it felt that way. I wore it for a year. I think it was a phase, but an important phase. When I was covering, people treated me like a foreigner. People would talk to me in very slow and short sentences. They spoke as if I was a second language learner. At university, people tolerated me rather than fully accepting me. No one approached me after class and asked me to hang out. In retrospect, the *hijab* served a purpose. In one way, I was able to talk about it openly when people asked me questions. In another way, it challenged me to be an activist. Wearing the *hijab* said to others, 'This is who I am.'"

"Muna, what do you see to be the big issues Muslim students face in the public school system now?" asked Miriam.

"9/11 was pivotal to the experiences of Muslim students. 9/11 happened, and suddenly Muslims became center stage. For me, growing up Muslim was a hidden component of my identity that no one really knew about. Then, all of a sudden, the whole country was focused on Muslims, and they had gross misunderstandings about who Muslims are and what we believe. I think Muslims growing up post-9/11 have to navigate a very different reality. They experience name-calling. In my youth, name-calling was Egyptian-related—'Where's your mummy and daddy?' instead of 'mommy and daddy.' There would be silly jokes, not necessarily mean-spirited, but used as a way for them to acknowledge that I was different. Some of our students will hear words like 'terrorist' or phrases such as, 'Oh, don't get him mad, he'll strap a bomb on himself' when they are in high school. They get a very different, uglier type of name-calling that's filled with bias and prejudice. Childhood teasing distinguished me as different. It wasn't as hurtful as some of the names kids are being called now."

"Do you think the current focus on multiculturalism in schooling is beneficial to Muslim students?" asked Melanie.

"I think the whole multiculturalism in education push has helped at least open the eyes of teachers. Some teachers still do not understand or practice multiculturalism in a very sensitive or deep way. I think the White middle-class teacher teaching children of color does not understand multiculturalism beyond focusing on food or clothing. They do not even try to understand the dynamics, such as 'What are the family's intentions regarding education?' Most teachers do not look deeply to recognize culture as a unique part of a child's home life. Even if you had a class of all White children, each home is a culture in and of itself. Teachers do not try to comprehend this and certainly do not connect with kids in that way.

"As you know, my environment is unique. We are an Islamic school with 99% Muslim students. We're trying to develop in each student a strong American Muslim identity. Most schools are conforming institutions designed to normalize. In our school, I have to prepare students who will be a religious minority and potentially a heritage minority. They need the skills to live in a world beyond our school. I don't want to create conformists because that would work against our mission. Instead, we aim for them to assert an identity that is authentically theirs in a society where the norm is not who they are. To do this, I needed to create a curriculum of resistance."

She smiled warmly and looked at her watch. "I have a meeting with the board president in about thirty minutes, and I need a few minutes to prepare. Let me end, though, by saying that I want educational leaders to create school environments of acceptance. I want them to react strongly if there are injustices within the school and to listen when a student or their family says a teacher has a certain point of view. We've had alumni come back to North Star Academy complaining about their social studies teacher making disparaging comments about Muslims in the classroom. Some alumni say they know that if they contradict the teacher, they'll be in trouble. Other alumni have told me that when they speak to their school's administration, they are disappointed when they are not as responsive as they would have hoped. Those are the things that need to be addressed. To be fair, however, we have heard other stories about administrators who bend over backward to provide their Muslim students with a private and safe place to pray. I want North Star Academy students to not be afraid to advocate for themselves. I want them to know their value."

Ms. Farah Rafiq—Upper School Islamic Studies Director

An hour later, we met with the upper school Islamic studies director, Ms. Farah Rafiq. She was young and in her mid-twenties and wore a flowing dress tied tight around her waist with a belt. "I'm sorry, but I'm on a tight schedule today," said

Ms. Rafiq. "Why don't we begin with you telling us about your upbringing," said Miriam.

"Sure. My family had progressive viewpoints, but up until third grade, I went to an Islamic school that was very conservative. Even the Saturday school that we went to was very restrictive, very black and white, very prohibitive. There was no in-between. There were no gray areas where you could question or wonder. My parents were not social activists but always gave in one way or another. Time. Energy. They gave from the heart. Giving doesn't always need to be tangible. My college experience shaped me. I learned about social justice. I also joined the Muslim Student Association, but I was uncomfortable with their approach to certain issues. It didn't feel right. I never veered too far to the right because my family kept me grounded.

"In 2010, my sister married Ziyad. Ziyad was a product of the Islamic Center of San Rico. He was Dr. Ahmed Salah's (one of the founders of the Islamic Center of San Rico) student from the age of fifteen. Although, if you ask him, he would say, 'Dr. Salah is my brother. He was my friend.' Their relationship was so special and unique. Ever since my sister married Ziyad, he and I have been in constant conversation. I learned a lot. It's not so much what I learned but how I learned to think. I developed a critical consciousness. The lens I look through now is a humanistic one. For example, some groups are still uncomfortable with homosexuality. I want to be held to a standard that shows mercy. The question I ask myself is, 'Am I being merciful to everyone?' That is what we are taught to do in Islam."

The receptionist entered the room after knocking quietly. "You have a parent to see you, Ms. Fariq."

That afternoon we drove to the Islamic Center of San Rico. Melanie said, "I could sense Dr. Ramsey's confidence. Her energy took up the whole room." Miriam replied, "Agreed. When we were young, our families were members of the Islamic Center of San Rico. Even though she was younger than me, and we were in different youth groups, we had an emotional bond because we were both products of the Islamic Center. You know, I can't help but think that the progressive ideology that she is advancing at North Star Academy might be more humanistic than that of the center."

Forty-five minutes later, we walked up the stairs to the entrance of the Islamic Center of San Rico. Miriam reflected, "Wow. It's been a long time since I stepped foot in the center. I wonder who's still working here? I wonder if I'll see familiar faces. You know, the Islamic Center Chair of the Board of Directors, Daod, is about my age. Now that he's the board chair, he may have a more conservative view to better cater to the congregation. Anyhow, we'll see."

We walked in, and the first person we saw was the director of the Islamic Center. Everyone called him by his last name—Patel. "*Assalamu alaykum,* Miriam!" "*Wa-alaykum assalam,*" said Miriam with a wide smile. Patel smiled and said to Miriam, "It has been a while! After thirty-five years of working at the center, I am going to retire. My mentee of five years, Beret, is going to take over as the new director."

"That is wonderful. I wish him much success. Congratulations on your retirement!" replied Miriam. He ushered us into the director's office. There was a large mahogany desk in the center of the room. Two Victorian tufted back chairs were placed in front of the desk. Persian carpets were on the floor, and mahogany bookshelves lined the walls. We set down our bags, pulled out an informed consent, and set up our recorders so as not to waste any time. Unlike Patel, Mr. Daod Bianchi and the board of trustees were volunteers who had full-time jobs outside of the center, and we had to be mindful of the time.

Mr. Daod Bianchi—Chair of the Board of Directors, Islamic Center of San Rico

Miriam greeted Mr. Bianchi with a hug. There was familiarity between Mr. Bianchi and Miriam. Hugs were not a customary greeting between women and men at the center; however, Miriam acted spontaneously. It had been about a decade since they last met. "Daod, this is my colleague, Melanie." Mr. Bianchi reached out his hand, which Melanie shook. Miriam interjected, "We want to be respectful of your time. We're all set up to start. Is that okay?" Melanie and Miriam took a seat.

Melanie started, "Let's begin with your current role and the roles you've played at the center, just to get some background."

Mr. Bianchi leaned forward and made direct eye contact with Melanie. "I'm currently the chair of the Board of Directors of the Islamic Center of San Rico. I've been in that role since 2015. I've been a part of the center for a better part of forty-two or forty-three years. So, I've been here since I was young. I've played various roles throughout my time here. In addition to being the chair, I'm also the spokesperson since the center engages in local, regional, state, national, and even international issues. That makes the center distinct from other centers or mosques.

"We recently reviewed our ideology and defined American Muslim identity. We had a group composed of board members and stakeholders who recently participated in a review of this statement, and while there were some minor tweaks to the language, we found that our statement fundamentally works. Like all documents that set the groundwork for an organization, it needs to stand the test of time. So far, our ideology has generally held up. The group wasn't composed of just old-guard people who say, 'Let's not change.' We also included people who are part of the up-and-coming generation of young Muslims. It was a thoughtful review. The changes in language were broader in scope, creating a more inclusive definition. Here is our new ideology statement."

Mr. Bianchi pushed a piece of paper to our side of the desk. It read:

> The Muslim community in the United States is a tapestry of races, ethnicities, cultures, and schools of thought. Respecting this diversity, we affirm our identity as Americans. We believe that the values and principles found in the U.S. Constitution align with the eternal message of the Holy Qur'an, promoting mercy (21:107), justice (4:135), peace (8:61), human dignity (17:70), freedom (2:256), and equality for all (49:13). We view the United States as our home. We believe in a representative democracy, as defined in The U.S. Constitution, and its congruence with the Islamic concept of *shura*, a collective and consultative form of decision-making. We embrace the pluralism of our country and are committed to constructively engaging in its betterment. We enjoy aspects of our nation's culture that do not conflict with Islamic values and avoid aspects that do. We believe that men and women should be equal participants in all activities and efforts.

Melanie's question broke the silence. "That is a nice statement. Do you see this statement as progressive?"

Mr. Bianchi leaned back in his chair.

"I think progressive is a relative term based on what's happening in the Islamic or Muslim world today. I'd like to think that we have an enlightened approach to practicing our faith, not just here in the United States but in general. Progressive relative to, for example, what you find in the Middle East? Progressive relative to what you find in mosques and Islamic institutions in the United States? I think a progressive ideology, or a progressive approach, means that we've gotten back to our roots. In the Muslim world, there is a lot of this false transitive thinking, meaning that the Prophet said A, therefore, if you do B, you are committing an act of *haram* (forbidden or unlawful). Putting things in a binary state of either *halal* or *haram* is very damaging. It drives a lot of people away. We're not in the business of preaching *haram*. Obviously, there are things that are *haram*, no question about it. We are in the business of trying to build community. We have a welcoming approach, not fire and brimstone."

"So, are you saying that Islam is essentially progressive?"

"Yeah, from my perspective, Islam fulfills the heart, the spirit, and the soul. It keeps you on a balanced path. Is that what you're asking?"

Miriam chimed in, "Perhaps the next question will help tease this out a bit. What is the role of social justice in Islam? And do you see the Islamic Center as a leader in social justice?"

"Yes, I see the center as a leader in social justice. For instance, the homeless situation in our city is out of control. The center has always taken a strong position of advocacy in working and engaging with the homeless. Because of gentrification, you have people who you wouldn't think are homeless or poor now coming to our food pantry every Saturday morning. One of the things we do is a collaborative food pantry. We are actively engaged with law enforcement, explaining who Muslims are and what Islam is. Beyond explaining, we propose, engage, and talk about the relationship between law enforcement and the Muslim community. The Muslim community, as you know, spans a wide variety of cultures, ethnicities, races, and economic strata. So, in that regard, we are very much engaged, and we see that as our primary purpose because that is what our faith teaches us.

"Beyond the belief in one God and that Prophet Muhammad is his final Messenger, social justice is one of the major themes in the Qur'an. For example, Moses and the Israelites. He brought them out of the Pharaoh's oppression, preaching a better life for people rather than engaging in a certain amount of sin that leads to the degradation of society and the degradation of an individual's heart. This is an essential tenet of the faith. Then you have to take, in my opinion, what you read in the Qur'an and figure out how to apply it to the modern day and the place in which you live. Helping the poor and engaging with those who are less fortunate are obligations of the faith.

"We also have to contend with the current political environment, especially with Donald Trump as president. Even if he wasn't targeting Muslims, it would be incumbent upon us to get out there and say something against injustice. For example, the way he talks about the Latino community, the disrespect towards handicapped people as he did in his campaign, the outlandish comments, the way he treats women, and all the scandals . . . these are things that shouldn't represent our nation. I think there's a definite role for us as a Muslim community. Then, beyond that is the targeting of Muslims. Out of this test, we have a great opportunity to really tell the story of what Islam is. There's a verse in the Qur'an, 'With every difficulty comes ease, with every difficulty comes ease.' That's the only verse in the Qur'an that repeats back-to-back. I see the difficulty as an opportunity to explain our faith, our culture, and our thinking as a way of easing Islam into the United States.

"I'm a reserve City of San Rico police officer. I do it because I love police work. I think it's a lot of fun, and I genuinely get satisfaction from helping people in a certain degree of distress. As a representative of the center, we work with law enforcement leaders at the city and county levels. They have the ability to influence national thinking. So, when we worked with the current chief, we said, 'Hey, here's the community. Here's where we stand on certain issues.' In 2004 and 2005, the city police department wanted to map where Muslims lived. It was put forward by a deputy chief who probably had some well-intentioned ideas but really had the blinders on in terms of what the impact would be. Blinders or not, it was not an acceptable thing to do. That provided an opportunity for us to engage with law enforcement. Our community was upset. It became a media story, and through that, they got to know who we are as Muslims. They had no idea about the diversity of the community. They didn't know Islam.

"I volunteered in the central division, and there was an officer who I used to work with. My last name is Bianchi, so it's not evident I'm Muslim. In conversation, he would say things about Islam and Muslims: 'You guys watch out for ISIS' or something like that. Then finally, one day, I said, 'Look, I'm Muslim.' It was like a rod went up his back because he said, 'Whoa, what's going on here?' It just completely threw him for a loop. I said, 'You're certainly entitled to your opinion,' but when you say, 'Muslims are trying to take over the United States and stuff like that . . . come on, give me a break.' Having those human interactions is just so important. Once you know the other, it allays and mitigates all these ignorant-based fears. When we're on patrol for twelve hours in a car, you talk about family, kids, and other things. Then I say, 'I'm Muslim,' and they're like, 'Oh . . . you're a Muslim?' These men are Iraq war veterans and Afghan war veterans and didn't know the culture of those countries. It's an opportunity."

"I'd like to circle back to social justice. Can you talk more about the center's stance on the LGBTQ community?" asked Miriam.

"Gay behavior, from our standpoint, and not at all from a perspective of hate, is the story of Sodom and Gomorrah. The Qur'an is very clear, but this remains a challenge. There's an identifiable gay Muslim community in the city. Do we say because you're gay, you cannot come to the Islamic Center? Of course not! You're welcome here. But we have to also strike a balance and say we're not going to adjust the tenets of the faith. That's not something we can do. If you wish to worship here, if you wish to pray here, by all means. We have a transgender person who comes to the center, a man who is becoming a woman. She goes by the name Susan. I think she's homeless. She comes because I guess she finds some spirituality here.

Forgive me for not using the right term . . . I'm not sure . . . she's still very clearly a man but dresses in women's clothing. She uses the women's bathroom . . . and that's where it gets real. We've had to say to her, 'We have another bathroom above on our mezzanine level that nobody goes to. You can use that one.'"

Miriam asked, "How did she receive that?"

"I think she was fine with it. I wasn't the person talking with her. Actually, I've never met her. The perspective of the Center is that we come from a place of love and respect. These people, for whatever reason, feel the way they feel. They are a miracle of God's creation. It's important that we demonstrate respect for all of God's creation. Do we agree with what's happening? Probably not. Gender equality is part of our ideology statement. Both men and women should be equal participants in the work, 100 percent. Our board chair last year was a woman and acted as such for a period of two years. She was the first woman chair. It's part of the fabric of this institution. The majority of people who work here are women, our employees, and our board members. We had a women's association here at the Islamic Center in the 70s and 80s that was disbanded because people asked, 'Why do you have a separate association for women when they're just as much a part of this mosque as anybody else?'

"I think it's okay to have a men's or a women's group because we're different. God created us differently. For example, the first all-female mosque was created because women do not have clear places in other Islamic Centers and Islamic institutions in the United States. When I was the chairperson of the Board, I insisted that for *Eid* (holiday) prayers, women would pray side-by-side with men. I want to do that here as well, but the logistics of the space will not work. We have to break down walls to make that happen or push out into the bathroom area. The idea of men and women praying side-by-side holds huge symbolism. Huge! I think it has an impact on the psychology of the community, and I think it's something I want to accomplish at this institution. We certainly do it during *Eid* prayers at larger venues.

"Honestly, I look forward to the time when a woman is leading the *Jum'ah* (Friday) prayer. We had a woman up on the *minbar* (pulpit) last night. She was leading our spiritual night. However, our spiritual night is different from leading a Friday *Jum'ah* prayer. It's something I wanted to do in 2015. In 2016, I pushed the idea forward, but you have to be very careful. I would like to think in the next ten years we could do it. Again, this is rooted in our faith because the Qur'an clearly states that men and women are equal in working for God's cause. The idea of what you see in other parts of the 'so-called Muslim world' speaks more of cultural backwardness than Islam.

"Unmosqued is a movement of young people around the nation who don't find spirituality in their mosques. They find harshness. They find rules and regulations. They don't go to the mosque anymore, that's why they call it unmosqued. As far as they are concerned, Muslim women in mosques are not welcome. I would not say that's the case here. At the same time, I would love to go to an all-female mosque for *Jum'ah* (mid-day Friday) prayer. They declined my request because I was a man. 'Wait a minute, that's interesting! As much as I want to support you, and I want to participate, you're telling me I must wait on the sidewalk?' Again, I can understand the reason why the all-female mosque came to be; however, men who want to support all-female mosques should be included."

We sat for a moment of silence, taking in what he just said. Miriam asked, "Did you start with the Islamic Center of San Rico in the previous building?"

"No, I started coming in 1975."

"We used to pray side-by-side. Do you remember that?"

"Oh really? I don't remember that."

"You were probably too little to remember."

"I was too little, yeah."

"As soon as the lecture was over, everybody would help put the chairs up, and then that aisle would just be an aisle, but men would be on one side and women would be on the other. It's when we moved to this building that it changed."

"Really?" asked Mr. Bianchi.

"Yeah. When we moved to this building, I wondered, 'Why did they change the way we were praying?' I didn't say anything because I was a kid."

"We could do that for every day except Friday. On Fridays, we have too many people."

"What are you most scared about in terms of women leading prayer?"

"That's a good question," replied Mr. Bianchi.

"The reaction is one thing. Women are at the forefront of resisting leading prayer. There's never a right time. When I brought this up at the Board meeting, the women looked like they were going to lambaste me. They were really upset about the idea and asked, 'Why do we need to do this? What are we talking about? What's the purpose?' It is not so much the fear of controversy per se, it is more that it could lead to divisiveness and what we would call *fitnah* (behavior that causes a state of trouble or chaos) in the center. It could lead to a lot of anger that could take away from other things that we want to do. Timing is everything. Even though I said there's no good or bad time, the timing has got to be right. I'm hoping we can get there."

We wrapped up the interview and decided to walk to the award-winning Kogi Gogi Korean Restaurant. It was only two blocks away from the Islamic Center. "What did you think about his take on the all-female mosque, Miriam?"

Miriam rolled her eyes. "Oh, brother. This is an endemic problem for women all over the world. Women and men praying side-by-side was interesting, but actually, that's how we prayed when the center was initially formed! In some ways, the center is far ahead of the curve. In other ways, there is a long way to go to achieve gender equality."

2

Freedom of Identity

> By fostering freedom of identity, students are guided to become confident and courageous American Muslims who uphold their ethical and moral principles.

We arrived at the upper campus just before 4:30 Tuesday afternoon. The corridors were absent of students. It was quiet. We peered into empty classrooms as we walked toward the conference room. We saw a few teachers tidying up and preparing their lessons for the next day, but we didn't stop to chat. We walked briskly in anticipation of the alumni arriving at 5:00 that evening to talk about their experiences at North Star Academy. We had some preparation yet to do and didn't want to be scrambling when the young people arrived. We found our way to the conference room. It was a white windowless room with two blue rectangular doors at each end. Each door had similarly shaped narrow perpendicular windows that offered a small view of an office on one end and a hallway at the other. In the middle of the room was an expansive rectangular boardroom table surrounded by twelve high-back ergonomic executive chairs. The furniture filled the room. We placed our bags on the far end of the table: one travel purse, one black backpack, a leather top-handle work bag, and three plastic shopping bags filled with recently purchased snacks and drinks for the alumni.

Dr. Muna Ramsey walked into the conference room just as we were setting down our bags. She stood with the warmth and attentiveness of a host preparing for a special event. "Hey there! It's so good to see you. The alumni should be arriving soon. Do you want me to order pizza now? We usually order from a local restaurant that serves *halal*."

"That sounds wonderful. Please do," said Melanie.

"They'll arrive hungry, so eight large pizzas will be enough. I'll order an assortment. I'll be back to greet them." Dr. Ramsey turned and walked back to her office. We opened our bags and unpacked plates, napkins, potato chips, water bottles, and chocolate chip cookies and set them on the credenza near the door leading to the hallway.

"You know, it'll be interesting to hear what the alumni have to say given the post 9-11 climate," commented Melanie.

Miriam thought for a moment, "It'll be a good discussion. I know from conversations with my nieces and nephew that Islam and Muslims are misrepresented in textbooks and curricula. I'll be surprised if their experiences aren't similar."

While unpacking laptops and placing two voice recorders at both ends of the long table, Miriam said, "Hey, look at this. They have a North Star Academy pledge that incorporates the US Pledge of Allegiance."

> As an American Muslim, I pledge allegiance to God and His prophets. I respect and love my family and my community, and I dedicate my life to serving the cause of truth and justice. As an American citizen, with rights and responsibilities, I pledge allegiance to the flag of the United States of America, and to the Republic for which it stands, one nation, under God, indivisible, with liberty and justice for all.

"I wonder if they say this every morning. I was watching a documentary about Senator Joseph McCarthy not too long ago that centered on his crusade against the communists. Did you know that before 1954, there was no 'under God' in the pledge of allegiance?"

"I had no idea," said Miriam.

"The pledge is steeped in White nationalism. I wonder how the alumni feel about pledging allegiance to an America that often demonizes Islam and Muslims. The pledge is thoughtfully crafted, though."

Miriam walked around the table and set water bottles in front of each seat. "I agree. It's also interesting that the student's faith identity comes first. First, they pledge allegiance to God, the prophets, family, and community. The second half is the pledge—." Miriam's thought was cut short as a line of students entered the room. The alumni took over the room, hugging, laughing, and checking in with one another.

Dr. Ramsey heard the noise and walked from her office to the conference room. She drew the attention of everyone in the room. The students greeted her with hugs. She wore a black sweater set and dangling pearl earrings that accentuated her curly textured salt and pepper hair. There was a flurry of chatter. While some alumni were setting down their backpacks, others fell into the executive chairs, creating a wave of movement. The energy was palpable as they all stopped talking and turned their attention to Dr. Ramsey, who stood at the head of the table. She had a commanding presence. Her smile was gentle and welcoming.

"Thank you for coming this evening. It's wonderful to see you after such a long time. Please keep the following in mind. I want you to answer all the questions honestly. Don't worry about saying negative things. You may not want to hurt our feelings. The truth of the matter is, you're not hurting our feelings. We want to hear everything, the good and the things that weren't so good because that helps us to do a better job for the kids that are here now and hopefully future generations, including maybe someday your kids." She smiled. "This is an opportunity for you to help us. I know you're all curious, the pizza will arrive soon!" With that statement, Dr. Ramsey turned and left the room. The students stole glances, and we heard a few giggles. Miriam turned toward the students.

"Welcome and thank you for being with us this evening! I'm Miriam Ezzani, and I'm a university professor. I was actually born and raised in California. I've lived in Texas for eight years. It's good to be home! I have kids who went to North Star Academy, and I was also affiliated with the Islamic Center of San Rico. I'm happy to be here and glad to meet all of you."

"I'm Miriam's colleague. My name's Melanie Brooks and I live in Australia and work at a university too. I've studied Islamic schooling for the past decade. I've learned so much, but there's always more to learn. I want to thank you again for spending your evening with us."

"Cool," said a few students. The students' heads turned in unison toward the door leading to the hallway, and we realized that the pizza had arrived. "Please grab pizza while it's hot," Melanie said to the group. The students jumped up, grabbed boxes, pulled out pieces of pizza, and opened their water. Once everyone had what they needed, Miriam asked, "When you answer, it would be great if you would tell us your age, your grade, the name of your school, and how long you attended North Star Academy."

The students sat with full plates of pizza, and the room was quiet. Miriam saw this as a good time to begin and nodded to Melanie, who sat on the opposite side of the room. "I'll begin the conversation," said Melanie. "What are your best memories from your time at North Star Academy?" There was a pause, and the alumni looked at each other, smiling.

Ali swallowed his bite of pizza and said, "I'll jump in. Hi everyone. My name is Ali. I'm a senior at Cleveland High School. I'm eighteen as of last week." Ali shook his head of big curly dark-brown hair as if to settle himself. He gave off a casual vibe with his black T-shirt, blue jeans, and Converse sneakers. "What comes to mind for me is the fact that North Star Academy offered music. Miss Allison was my music teacher. I have very fond memories of that time. She taught me how to play the piano. It's fair to say had I not had music and the arts integrated into my academics, I wouldn't be the leader of my school's marching band. I remember Miss Allison telling us that arts and being creative is just as important as academics."

The young female to Ali's right straightened her posture. "Hi. My name is Maysa. I'm seventeen. I go to Cleveland High School too. I'm a senior. I went to North Star from kindergarten to sixth grade, so seven years. I remember the plays we did! I believe we started in third or fourth grade. It was fun and something different. You got to be with your friends, and do silly things, but you're also super serious about it."

A hand shot up into the air, and a young woman was eager to speak. She had thick, black wavy hair, full eyebrows, and an oval face. She wore silver-rimmed glasses. Miriam nodded, giving her the floor. "I agree with Maysa. I was going to say plays were my best memories, but the science fairs were great because our teachers made them fun instead of stressing us out. Oh, by the way, my name is Ava. I went to North Star Academy from preschool to sixth grade, and I am a freshman at Lakewood High School." She gave a little wave to the group.

"Yes, please go ahead," said Miriam, noticing a small-statured young male with carefully coiffed black spiky hair waving his hand to get her attention. "My name is Ahmed. I'm a sophomore at Cleveland High School. I went to North Star Academy from preschool to sixth grade." He leaned back in his chair. "Hearing everyone makes me feel nostalgic. I miss the good old days. For me, the best part of North Star was just hanging out each day at lunch, playing soccer and handball, whatever. You could always rely on having a great time with the people you're around, which is something I loved." Ahmed's comment sparked a flurry of responses.

"I remember Catalina Island as being my favorite activity. It was a dream come true! It's a two-day sleepover with all your best friends. You're swimming, snorkeling, and just having fun! Oh, for those who don't know me, I'm Rayan, currently seventeen years old and a senior at Mission Hills High School. I went to North Star from preschool to sixth grade—so about nine years." Rayan finished and took a bite of pizza.

"I agree with Rayan. We were a tight-knit group. It was like hanging out with your family for seventy-two hours!" Large silver-hooped earrings swung back and forth. "Oh, before I forget, my name is Wafa. I went to North Star for nine years, from preschool to sixth grade. I'm fourteen years old and a freshman at Pinewood High School."

"My name is Hana. I am in eleventh grade at Lakewood High School. I went to North Star Academy from preschool to sixth grade." Hana wore a sky-blue *hijab* and had dark piercing eyes. "The jogathon was my favorite. There'd be popsicles at the end. It was something I looked forward to!"

Miriam smiled. "The bond you describe at North Star made me think about my time in the youth group at the Islamic Center of San Rico. It was a unique space in comparison to other centers that segregated youth by gender. Our Islamic Center was different. As a youth, we felt accepted and valued. We were born in America, and our parents wanted to make sure that we didn't lose our faith tradition. The youth group was every Sunday, and once a month, a family hosted a potluck at their home. We developed community and love for one another through conversations and sharing of meals, and the best part was when we held hands and danced the *dabka* (Palestinian folk dance). I went to public school—so it felt like I lived two different lives—one in my community and the other at school, where I only connected with a few students. Having said that, "Why do you think your parents enrolled you at North Star Academy?"

Maysa and Ahmed began to speak at the same time. Ahmed gestured for Maysa to speak. She apologized to Ahmed and said, "I think my parents wanted me to have an Islamic and Arabic education. Obviously, you can have tutoring, but it's pushed to the side. If you're in an environment where it's happening every day, then you build language, knowledge, and a basis for your faith, which is really important."

Rayan added, "I agree with Maysa. My parents wanted me to be rooted in Islam. Having this foundation is important, especially with the challenges of public school. No matter what, I can connect my faith to whatever issues I deal with in life."

Wafa raised her hand to speak. Miriam nodded, and the group turned to listen. "This isn't a memory per se, but something I remember about North Star. My mom is a convert and her whole family is not Muslim. I remember my mom's family visited North Star on numerous occasions for several different reasons. My grandparents, aunts, and uncles were always in awe, not only because of North Star but because they loved how it shaped our identity. They loved the fact that we have religion in our lives, and they're proud that North

Star was a part of that. Sometimes one interaction with someone from North Star, a faculty member or a teacher, can change someone's whole perspective on Islam."

A young woman walked into the room and appeared confused. "Is this the place for the alumni discussion?" she asked. She recognized the faces and smiled.

"Welcome! Please take a seat and introduce yourself," said Melanie.

"I'm Jasmine. I attend Marina High School, and I'm in the ninth grade." Jasmine looked around and sat in the empty seat next to Rayan. She had blondish-brown wavy hair, green eyes and wore a stylish dress and leggings.

"Thank you, Jasmine. Feel free to jump in and contribute to the discussion," said Melanie.

"Wafa—I bet the support you've received from your family has given you a lot of confidence. I'll pose this next question to the group. Do you feel that North Star Academy taught you self-confidence?" asked Melanie.

Hana raised her hand. "I'd like to respond to that. I want to share a pivotal moment when I realized that I'm different from other people. I had the unique experience of putting on the *hijab*. It was hard. I put it on the second year of high school, so everyone already knew me the first year without it. But I also love visual and performing arts. I'm the only one at my high school wearing a *hijab* in dance, drama, and choir. This can be a struggle. It is hard to be that one person, singled out and different, but I always reflect on the strength I received from North Star Academy. It was my decision to wear the *hijab*. I'm confident with that decision. When I dance, though, all the outfits are very revealing, because choreographers want to show the lines of the dancers. This year the girl who choreographed the dance chose a tight short dress to wear. I couldn't wear it. In the end, she had to change the outfit. She decided to make them all long dresses. Same with the musical; they had to change everyone's costumes three or four times to work around me. At times this can make me feel really insecure like I'm a burden. But it's also slightly empowering because I have a support system. People are accommodating, and I can still do what I love without sacrificing my religious beliefs. North Star gave me the confidence to advocate for myself without having to apologize."

"Thank you, Hana. Can any of you think of examples of how the teachers at North Star Academy helped you develop confidence?" Miriam asked the group.

Jasmine looked around the room and said, "I have an example. At North Star Academy, there's a real sense that teachers care about our success. My mom told me something when she returned home after a parent-teacher conference. 'Your teacher literally came to tears because she wants you to reach your potential.'

I was taken aback. This was the first time that I realized my teachers put in effort, time, and heart to help me find myself and succeed. It was empowering. I couldn't let my teachers down." The room was quiet.

Ahmed broke the silence by reaching toward the middle of the table and grabbing another slice of the deep-dish chicken barbeque, red onions, and mozzarella pizza. Several unopened pizzas sat on the credenza, and the rest were open and getting cold on the boardroom table. Miriam pointed to the pizza boxes, "Please feel free to get up during our conversation and help yourself to more pizza, drinks, chips, and cookies." A couple of students stood up and brought several pizzas to the table. They opened the boxes, took some, and passed them around. When the pizza came full circle, Melanie brought everyone back to the discussion. She asked the group, "So Jasmine, the high expectations of your teacher really impacted your confidence in being a successful student. Did anyone else have a similar experience at North Star that shaped them?"

Maysa wiped her hands to remove pizza crumbs, leaned in, and said, "I never called myself American before attending North Star Academy. I never said, 'Oh, I'm also American.' When I first heard, 'You're an American Muslim,' it made me feel emboldened. I learned that I never have to apologize for being Muslim or being in a vulnerable place where I have to say, 'Oh, I'm Muslim. I'm sorry.' I'm confident to say, 'Yeah, I'm Muslim. This is who I am.'"

Wafa brushed back a brownish-red ringlet of hair that was dangling in front of her right eye and looked at the group. "I think there are extremely high expectations, but not in a way that causes pressure. I think it's more of a sense that they have faith in you. They take comfort knowing they've done a good job providing the knowledge for us to go out into the world and make it a better place."

"I agree with Wafa. I feel like the pressure came from high expectations. We grew up with a strong sense of integrity. I knew right from wrong. That goes back to our roots, what we were initially taught."

"And you are . . ." asked Miriam.

"Oh! Ava. I went to North Star on and off. I spent three years in preschool and stayed until second grade. I left and came back in sixth grade."

"Thank you," said Miriam.

Ali covered his mouth with a small cough and waited until the room was quiet before speaking. "When a baby bird is leaving the nest, the mother bird expects it to fly. When we left, we also had strong academics, but we also had confidence. As Ava said earlier, the school trained us to know right from wrong, to know our faith, to know who we are, and to create ideas for ourselves. I think what's especially important is that lots of private schools have this focus on developing each student to be the same—like printouts. I think what's important about North Star is that students aren't designed to be exactly the same. In fact, they are helping us to learn how to change. As soon as we left the school, we were put on a path that allowed us to become our own person right from the start.

"I went to a private girls' school, and I felt that there were common expectations for all of us, such as going to a good university, getting married, and having a family," commented Melanie. "When you left North Star Academy, you all moved on to high school. Did the education you received at North Star help you to say no to peer pressure? Often there is a lot of pressure to conform."

Ava responded first. "Well, yeah. Just knowing what's right from wrong. Obviously, I'm not going to go out and date, smoke, or drink. I think we've just grown up at North Star Academy with strong morals and values."

Hana straightened up, swallowed her bite of pizza, and added, "I agree with Ava. They expected the best morals. We weren't exposed to that kind of stuff in elementary school, and so when I was older, that desire wasn't there. I believe that if you've had nine years where you didn't need to find an escape, you felt content to be good, to have fun in traditional ways with your friends, then there's no need to go down another path."

"I'd like to add to that," said Jasmine. "We grew up understanding that we were not the only ones to say no. We had peers around us with similar morals and values. This made it easier. At North Star, everyone was unique, but we also had the same grounding. So when we left and were exposed to different values, we had a sense of 'this is what I believe is correct.' It wasn't like, 'Oh, I feel pressure.' I knew from the beginning what I was and wasn't supposed to do."

"I'd like to add something about the experience of moving from North Star to public school," Ahmed said. "Unlike some of us here, who moved to public school with a friend or two from North Star, I went to middle school and high school on my own. It was an interesting experience. When I first started getting to know people, they were different from everyone here. They had different moral compasses, different belief systems, and different everything. That was okay, but it was jarring. I found it difficult to connect and make friends. It was eye-opening to see the different ways people grew up and the different struggles they experienced."

"I bet it was an eye-opening experience, Ahmed. May I ask a follow-up question to the group?" asked Melanie. Everyone nodded. "How would you say your faith was different from those you met as you moved through public school?"

Ali responded first. "When I interact with people, there is a general sense that when things get difficult, people fall apart. There's no rope for them to grab onto. They don't have a raft to cling to when the waters get rough. When stress comes up, I think to myself, 'Well, I have justification for this. Maybe I'll just go to the mosque, I'll pray. I'll reflect on this. Maybe this is part of the plan.' It's humbling. Thinking about faith helps minimize my stress and anxiety and makes it easier to approach my challenges head-on. Whereas lots of my peers who are agnostic or atheist do not have justification for why they're feeling the way they do. It's always, 'Well, I'm stressed because of this science test. I didn't study.' Sometimes their stress just spirals out of control. There is nothing for them to hold on to."

Melanie asked the group, "Do you agree with what Ali said?"

Hana straightened her *hijab* and replied, "I actually had a unique situation with a close friend who doesn't have a particular faith. We were doing an English project on satire, and we chose religion. We actually talked until two in the morning while working on this project. He was constantly doubting himself. He would say, 'Christians and Muslims believe in God. What do you think will happen when I die since I don't believe in God?' The conversation went to a very deep place, but it goes to show that people without faith have to constantly ask themselves if their lack of faith is accurate or not. I don't have that issue. Like Ali said, anytime I'm stressed, I can just think about the bigger picture, and that calms me down and grounds me. I can go pray. I can sit for a little bit and just relax. But I feel that people who don't have the belief that there's a greater being don't have anything to relieve their worry and stress."

"I'm curious. Do you think you are more mature than your peers?" asked Melanie.

"Well, some kids went through life experiences that required them to grow up fast. I've gone through things that have made life hard, but I can't say that school was the deciding factor," responded Ahmed.

Ali cleared his throat to gain the group's attention. "I'd like to say something about that. I have a different perspective. Maysa and I go to the same school, along with six people who are alumni of North Star. I don't hang out with Maysa every day. I think that's the point, isn't it? I don't want to bash other private Muslim schools, but their students stick together. I feel like this mob mentality results in bad decision-making. There is definitely evidence to prove that the people who graduated from North Star have built strong character and not strong reliance. I think that's a very important distinction. Oftentimes, private Muslim schools don't prepare students for the real world, and they crumble. North Star taught us that you are strong enough to rely on yourself when things get tough. I think that was the most powerful tool we were given when we left. North Star gave us a strong moral compass that allows us to make our decisions without a need for mob reassurance."

"It sounds like you're very resilient," said Melanie.

"Self-resilience," Ali corrected.

Jasmine raised her hand to speak next. "Please," said Miriam with a nod.

"After North Star, I went to another Islamic private school until eighth grade. What Ali said is very true. Many of those students attend my current high school. There was a young teacher at my school who became completely involved with a particular Muslim group's problems and issues. The vibe was, 'We have a close-knit community, and we can rely on each other.' That's good, of course, but it's also important to be independent and not rely on someone else to help you with everything. Of course, you have people you do rely on, but you also should be able to rely on yourself and be confident that you can have trust in yourself."

Miriam asked the group, "Where did that come from? How did you learn to be independent and trust in yourself?"

Hana answered, "I had a great sense that someone believed in me. It's not that you're hearing 'good job' for everything, just to say, 'good job.' There were times when I needed to work hard to get the grade I wanted, but my teachers were proud of the work I did. They were invested in my learning. You can totally tell when a teacher cares and when they don't care. I have a teacher now that sits at his desk for the entire class. We teach ourselves the content. At North Star, teachers made me feel I was worth their effort. Having someone believe in you allows you to believe in yourself. You begin to think, 'I can do this!' Not in a prideful sense, but in a gratifying way."

Wafa raised her hand slightly to indicate she wanted to speak next. Miriam nodded. "I want to comment on what Ali and Jasmine said a second ago. I go to a high school that actually has a lot of people who went to North Star. North Star does give you a huge sense of self-worth and knowledge. My mom says that the friends I met at North Star are going to last a lifetime. I think that's important. I have an army behind me, supporting and boosting me up to be the best version of myself."

"I'm curious, do you share with other people that you're Muslim? Is it an issue? Does it come up? Is it uncomfortable or not?" asked Melanie.

"I feel like I have a pretty unique experience as far as that question goes," said Ali. "To start off, I was in third grade when I left North Star and went to public school. There were no other Muslims in my class. There was never a point where I felt ashamed. In fact, I quite vividly remember that I advocated for a place to pray. The teachers were confused. I was so confident I prayed outside next to the playground on the dodgeball courts for everyone to see. I would never do that now. I'm not that bold! But I remember there were two other kids in the elementary school who were Muslim. Eventually, we prayed together at lunch on the dodgeball courts. I was like, 'This is who I am. I don't really care what you're saying.' I had a friend named John. Every day after lunch, he would ask me questions about Islam. I was not the most educated Islamic scholar of my time, but I would try. I shared with him the prophets' stories and things I learned in my Islamic studies classes. He asked hard questions, questions that would normally break a kid! I remember that it only made my faith stronger because I thought, 'Well if this is something that I really believe in, I need to know everything about it.'

"Fast forward to after sixth grade. I went to public school in the United Arab Emirates. I can say with certainty that seventh grade was when I realized I was a confident Muslim, but I wasn't a confident American. I think my time in the United Arab Emirates actually developed the American side of my identity. When I returned to the United States, I felt like I could fully call myself American and Muslim. I had both of those identities challenged, and I had to back them up.

"Fast forward to high school. I had such a strong identity that the first thing I did was introduce myself to the principal and the assistant principal. I asked them to help me figure out where I was going to pray. I will not call myself the most religious person. I was very respectful and shared that this is something that's important to me, and I think it's important to other people too. After the school gave me a place to pray, I decided to find other Muslims on campus. There were twenty people who I knew were Muslim. I've taken around forty classes, and there were at least five Muslims in every class. I will talk to somebody I've literally known for the entire year, and then something will come up, and I'll say, 'Wait a second, you're Muslim? Are you kidding me?' I call them spies. It drives me insane! When I talk to them, I'm like, 'Oh, do you know we have a Muslim Student Association on campus?' They say, 'You mean the Muslim club?' I say, 'Yeah.' They say, 'Oh, no. I didn't know.' Then they say, 'I'm not very public about it.' I get it. I never try to impose the idea that someone should be more overt about their Islam, but nine times out of ten, it's always because they don't feel like they'll be accepted in their community.

"I would say they haven't been given the same platform as us. It wasn't built into their character. You asked earlier what created that moral compass. I think there's setting up a moral compass, and there's keeping a moral compass. Setting it up is the easy part, and North Star does that, but keeping it is in our hands for us to say, 'Well, this is the wonderful gift I've been given. What am I going to do with it?'"

Maysa raised her hand to speak. "In my first year in middle school, there was another Muslim kid in my class. He was making controversial jokes about himself. I think he just wanted to assimilate. In my head, I was like, 'Dude, what are you doing? You're giving us a bad rap! Come on! Bomb jokes?' His friends were laughing. I was like, 'I know that this is not okay.' In America, there's so much that makes me angry. But knowing who you are and knowing how to advocate for yourself is so important. I feel North Star helped with my identity, and who I could be—a proud Muslim. This is important to me."

Miriam asked the alumni, "Some of you gave examples of how you advocated for yourself with peers. Do you have other examples of how you advocated for yourself with teachers or curriculum issues?"

Ahmed said, "All of us have had to."

Ava said, "I'll go if that's okay Ahmed."

Ahmed nodded.

"This is probably not the best story, but two things happened quite recently. My classmate made a joke about the word *jihad*, meaning Muslims want to bomb things. He sits across the classroom from me. I said to him, 'That is literally not what it means. *Jihad* means your internal struggle to pursue your religion.' I talked about it with him for the rest of the period. He said, 'Oh, but it can still mean war, right?' I was like, 'You're just not getting it.' He just kept on thinking that *jihad* meant Muslims were terrorists. It's sometimes good to teach people because you know there are so many assumptions out there. Being open to talking about it helps. Then last Friday, a girl at school said, 'I don't understand why you don't date. Just go behind your parents' back.' I told her, 'No, you don't understand. It's not my parents. It's me, my religion, and my beliefs that make me not want to do that stuff.' Then she said, 'Oh yeah, you know what? I respect that.' Then she backed off."

"Yes, I feel like we're always having to explain that to people over and over again," said Jasmine.

"You're so right!" said Hana. "If you don't mind, Jasmine, I'd like to jump in and give some examples."

"Please, go ahead!"

"I've had to advocate on numerous occasions. A lot of times, I get innocent questions. Other times I feel people are afraid to ask questions. When I know they're going to ask me a question that starts with . . . 'I don't know if it's rude,

I'm just really curious . . .' I say back to them, 'I love questions. Ask me any question you want.' I want to educate people, and I want them to understand me and to be open to ideas. For example, about fasting, 'Not even water?' These are innocent questions. I answer them because it means that people are opening up to acceptance. They're trying to understand." Hana raised her eyebrows and pointed to her *hijab*. "I also get, 'Oh do you shower with that?' These types of questions are interesting, but they may also not be so innocent . . ."

Several students nodded their heads in agreement.

Ali responded, "I'll be honest. Being a very tall and potentially intimidating man, I don't often run into people who come up and say [wagging his finger], 'How dare you, you Muslim!' I've never been attacked or harassed. I'm blessed for that. I feel like my experience has given me a responsibility to advocate for those who are not in my situation. I attended a girls' soccer game two years ago because one of our Muslim Student Association members was playing on the Varsity team. There was a freshman girl wearing a *hijab* on the team, and there was a referee who was insisting she couldn't play unless she took it off."

Ava whispered, "Oh my God."

Ali continued, "She was crying. There was nobody advocating for her. I went down to the field, and I talked to the referee, and I explained to him, 'Listen, no disrespect. I know the league standards do not restrict headwear, especially a religious garment.' I didn't necessarily put him in his place, but I held my ground against this elderly man. In the end, he apologized.

"I also have another story to share. A group of Muslim parents wanted to ban *Persepolis* because it portrayed Islamic characteristics and ideologies 'poorly.' At least, that's the way they put it. This was at a high school in another city. Sometimes I'm asked to go to other areas to speak. So, the parents started a petition. They came to the Muslim Student Association to ask for our support. This was a very rough time for me because I was the association's president. I went to the administration and said, 'Do not listen to the parents. What they're arguing for is not true. Just because there are people who practice our religion in a poor way does not mean it is okay to have the book censored.' When I read the book, I could not identify any anti-Muslim sentiment. Because of this, the Muslim Student Association lost a lot of support from the parents. We still struggle because parents still feel that we're rebellious and we don't conform to their traditional conservative views. *Persepolis* is still taught at Cleveland High School, much to the parents' chagrin and much to our joy. Defending this book was quite difficult. I had to be in a room with the principal and the school board, asking me why I am here and why they should listen to me. That was certainly a pivotal moment."

A few alumni around the table nodded their heads in agreement. Wafa looked at Miriam with hesitancy, "I would like to go back to your original question about teachers and curriculum. Is that okay?"

"Of course," said Miriam.

Wafa shared, "During seventh grade, my teacher had no idea what she was teaching. She read from the textbook, trying to get through the facts. You can tell she wanted to get to the next unit. She focused on the difference between Sunni and Shi'a (two main branches of Islam), their inability to coexist, and how they hate each other. She said, 'It's inevitable that war will happen.' There are so many beautiful things about Islam, why on earth would she focus on one negative thing? I raised my hand. I didn't want my classmates to get the wrong impression. I was extremely respectful. I said to her, 'Well, to be perfectly honest, that's not true. There are cases where Sunni and Shi'a people live together peacefully. It's not inevitable that war happens between two different people.' She shut me down and replied, 'No, I studied this and wrote an essay on it. You're wrong.' I said, 'Well, we can have different opinions.' I didn't want everyone to think that I came from a religion, or anyone came from a religion, based on the idea of war. At North Star, I was under the impression that I could change people's thinking about Islam. 'Everyone's going to love Muslims,' I thought. It didn't entirely turn out that way. I realized shortly after leaving North Star that you can't change everyone's ideas. I think that was a major moment for me. I put myself out there and tried to give this teacher information and help her learn. That's what I took pride in."

Without room for pause, Rayan said, "I remember this seventh-grade assignment. I go into class, and my teacher announces the chapter on Islam, and I'm thinking—'Yes, yes, yes!' Then a kid in front of me says, 'Okay, terrorist unit.' This is not what I expected. I was pretty upset, but I thought once they read the book, once our teacher talked about it, things would be fine. I remember opening the book and reading insane things about Prophet Muhammad, how he had seven wives, and how he chose which one he loved more. He was depicted as some lunatic in a cave that saw God. This contradicted everything that I learned and all that I valued. I thought, what are they going to do when they read this? They'll think, 'Okay, this explains what I'm seeing in the media.' That scared me. I went home and spoke with my mom. I was infuriated and ready to go into the principal's office, guns blazing."

Ali interjected, "Uh–poor choice of words, Rayan."

Rayan chuckled embarrassingly, "Sorry. Wow!"

Everyone laughed.

Ali continued, "My mom met with the principal the next day. She told him, 'Some content in the textbook is incorrect. We don't want students thinking something that isn't true about our religion.' The principal apologized. He was a history major, so we were confused that we had to explain the situation to him. He did get the textbook changed, which was awesome. I had an idea that I shared with my mom. I said to her, 'I think I'm equipped to teach the class. I want to put a presentation together.' We talked about what I'd say. I had a week to put a PowerPoint together, trying to make it perfect, trying to include everything I could. I remember it was like twenty or thirty slides. I wanted my classmates to say *Assalamu alaykum* correctly. I had on a slide a picture of a salami and a picture of bacon. I told them to say the names of the items on the slide fast, *asalamianbacon*, That was their way of getting it." Everyone in the room laughed. "After my presentation, my peers came up to me and said, 'Wow! That was cool. We had no idea!' I felt good at that moment because I was able to show the true Islam that I knew and loved."

Hana gestured with a wave of her hand that she wanted to speak. "In seventh grade, we were playing *Jeopardy*, which we did before every test. Each table was a team, and my table was winning by a lot of points, like 1,000 points. Everyone was upset, accusing us of cheating and saying, 'Oh they have an advantage because they're Muslim.' I was angry. How many lessons are there on European culture and Christianity? The reason they're salty is because we were winning. People walked out of the class mumbling, 'That's not fair. They're Muslim. They know everything.' I ended up with 101/100 on the test. People were mad about that. If there's a Mormon or a Catholic student who knows the answers, gets a good grade on the test, or wins *Jeopardy*, no one says a thing. You see the difference in treatment."

"Even though Hana and I had the same teacher, our experiences were different," said Ava. "I'm a big, bold, obnoxious person. On the first day Mr. Rivers started teaching Islam, he laid down the basics. He said Muslims follow two books, the Qur'an and the *sunnah*. I questioned this. 'I don't think *sunnah* is a book. There are books with different *sunnah* and *hadith*, but it's not a book we follow.' He responded, 'You know how there's the Bible and the Torah? There's also the Qur'an and the *sunnah*.' I sat there confused. He said 'Gabriel was an angel who embodied God to talk to Muhammad in his cave where he went crazy.' He said all this in one sentence! I was just sitting in my seat trying not to scream. After class, I walked straight up to his desk, and I corrected him. 'There's no book called *sunnah*. *Sunnah* are the things that The Prophet did that we try to follow.' He got so angry. 'You're trying to tell me that the textbook is wrong?' I was like, 'You're trying to tell me that the religion I've followed for the past twelve years of my life is wrong?' I was so angry. He never called on me for *Jeopardy* even though he knew I was the only Muslim in class. I got the lowest grade on the test which was confusing because the questions were dumb, like what's the difference between Sunni and Shi'a, and what are the prayers? I was the only person who got the prayer question right. I was upset. I wanted to talk to him, but he just wouldn't take criticism. Here's the odd thing—the next year in eighth grade, during Ramadan, I asked him, 'Can I go pray?' He was so chill. He even suggested a special room for prayer and allowed me to find twenty other Muslim students from their classes and gave us all passes to go pray. It was a really weird change. I don't know what happened to him."

There was a long silence as if no one was sure what to say.

Ahmed spoke first. "I'll answer. I remember being taught how to act in a situation through the example of the prophets. How did the prophets act when confronted with questions, opposition, or anything that was troublesome? What drove them was educating the people around them and trying to spread the message. That includes trying your best not to be offended. People are trying to learn, although, sometimes, they may just be trying to offend."

"Yeah," said Jasmine. "Yet, our education is so Eurocentric. There is so much history that is not included in the history books. It seems to be written only by Europeans. It makes history seem White."

"I was hoping we would be moving past that by now. But I guess some of these textbooks aren't inclusive," commented Melanie.

"They're not updated. It just falls on us to talk about the history, and obviously, we don't always know," said Jasmine.

"My experience wasn't as extreme as Rayan's," said Hana. "My seventh-grade teacher, Mr. Fabrika, was known for being a really rigorous teacher. He wasn't very open or welcoming. He said something that was a mistake. He said, 'There's a book called *The Hadith*.' But that was completely incorrect! I talked to my Muslim friends in the class. 'Should we say anything? Is it our place?' But the unit was about Islam. We didn't want to be rude. I told him, '*Hadith* are the words and the actions of the Prophet.' He got mad. He said, 'No, it's not. I'm reading the textbook right now that says this.'"

"Did you ever feel that there was a silver lining when things like this happened?" asked Melanie.

Wafa raised her hand to speak. "Our North Star teachers provided us with scenarios and helped us understand what to do, how to be respectful, and how to accommodate people while still trying to share the right information. I became so confident. I knew what a Muslim was supposed to be, and I knew how to react when people made comments or asked questions that may or may not be rude. I have faith in myself, knowing that I'm prepared to answer questions with my own thoughts."

A man in his mid-forties quietly entered the room and stood against the wall under the clock, which read 6:30 p.m. Miriam and Melanie noticed others waiting outside the conference room.

Hana looked at the clock and said, "I think problems we encounter make us realize what great teachers we had at North Star. Situations like these also make me realize I can brush off one teacher's insignificant comment. I'm confident when I know that I'm right. This makes all the bad go away. Like what Wafa said, 'It's okay if they don't believe me.' It's okay if they don't want to change their mind. I'm secure with what I believe."

Miriam looked at the clock. "Is anybody being picked up? Do you have rides home? I just want to make sure we're not holding anybody up."

The students shook their heads.

"We have some time," said Ali.

"Let's conclude with a silly question. If you had a magic wand and you could change something about where you currently go to school, what would you change?" asked Melanie.

Rayan said, "I want my peers at school to be open to the opinions of others and not believe what their parents believe and who their parents vote for."

"That would be good," said Ali.

"Yeah, just poof," said Rayan, closing and opening his fists.

"Man, that's such an open-ended question. I struggle with it," said Ali. "If I had a magic wand, I would use it to build the self-confidence of those who can't form their own opinions. I think it would be cool to have 200 people in the Muslim Student Association. That would really change the environment on our campus."

Jasmine looked around the room to see if it was okay for her to share her thoughts. "I want equal treatment. If everyone could get rid of their stereotypes about Muslims and Islam and be open-minded, they could see the person in front of them for who they are rather than assuming, 'You're like this and I'm not going to talk to you.' If this would happen, there would be so much more acceptance and understanding. Of course, we're not all the same, but we should all be treated equally. I just think that would be really nice."

"I know we are running out of time, but I want to share what happened two weeks ago at my school," said Hana. "We had Human Rights Week, which

I was excited about. They took us out of class to watch a seminar, and the topic was LGBTQ+ rights. I was actually delighted that different people were getting representation because a bunch of students at my school align with that community. However, it was not what we thought it was going to be. It was extremely aggressive. The message I received was, 'If you're straight, you're not liberalizing yourself enough.' My mom always tells me, 'You don't have to apologize for being Muslim just as much as they don't have to apologize for being part of their community.' I wish the school would pay more attention to other communities. I wish that there would be that effort put forth for Muslims. There isn't anything other than the Muslim Student Association."

Ava added, "I'm obviously not out there yelling from the mountain tops, 'I'm Muslim!' But, I'm not closed about it. People know. I think it's just great because all my friends are accepting, and no one tries to push anything on me. They respect me, so I think that's really good. One thing I wish I could change is people not making assumptions based on a few people at the school and for them to actually know about the religion."

3

Freedom of Acceptance

> By advocating for freedom of acceptance, students learn the importance of cultivating positive relationships with individuals, regardless of their differences.

The Farewell Sermon (Khutbat al-Wada) was Prophet Muhammad's last religious speech and is considered by many to be one of his most significant. It was given just before his passing during his final pilgrimage to Mecca in 632 CE. The sermon offered the burgeoning Muslim community a comprehensive and timeless message that encapsulated many core principles of Islam, notably the importance of accepting others regardless of their differences. Prophet Muhammad stated:

> An Arab has no superiority over a non-Arab nor does a non-Arab have any superiority over an Arab; also, a White has no superiority over a Black nor does a Black have superiority over a White—except by piety and good action. (*Hadith* 19774)

While at North Star Academy, we observed students, teachers, and school leaders demonstrating acceptance of others through their practicing empathy, using inclusive language, celebrating differences, offering support, and challenging stereotypes. The vast majority of the North Star community reflected a freedom to unconditionally accept others. Yet, there were instances when we observed biases and stereotypes. These reflected societal and cultural influences and were often unconscious. Acceptance was on a continuum at North Star Academy. To this end, we present freedom of acceptance through five perspectives.

Kindergarten through Third-Grade Teachers

"Respect. I tell my students some people like celebrating Halloween, and others don't. If there's an event that night at the *masjid*, the Arabic word for mosque, then it is okay to go there in lieu of trick-or-treating. They have pizza, activities, and games. It's good for the kids to not feel left out. I don't want my students to be sheltered. I want them to discuss Christmas and different holidays. I want them to understand, respect, and value other belief systems. I like the idea of diversity. One of my students told me they celebrate Easter. One of her friends said, 'You don't really celebrate? It's supposed to be for Christians.' I replied, 'You know, Easter celebrates Christ being risen three days after he was crucified.' My students all said, 'Ooh!' and I said, 'Yes! I think if you do the fun stuff at Easter, that is okay. You're not really celebrating the true spirit of Easter.' The students agreed with what I said, 'Oh, Okay, Yeah.' When I talk with students, I tell them, 'Okay, Christmas. We need to respect their holiday. Hanukkah also needs to be respected. You even need to respect Hinduism,'" said Ms. Sheryl Carpenter, a North Star second-grade teacher for the past thirteen years.

"I had three kids tell me that they had Christmas trees," said Ms. Mary Flores, currently in her fourth year of teaching at North Star Academy.

"You know, it's funny because one of my kids was singing Jingle Bells. I said to her, 'You know that song?' She says, 'It's everywhere! Of course, we know it!' Then my students asked me if I could put on Christmas music so they could listen to it while they worked! I replied, 'I can't.' They argued back, 'We hear it on television!' I said, 'No. I can't do that because I don't want to get in trouble.' But, on the other hand, I don't want them to be sheltered. When they discuss Christmas or any holiday, I want them to understand, show respect, and value other beliefs. I teach them to be humble because they need to learn to do the right thing, such as not bragging or showing off. So far, I've gotten along well with my students' parents. Even though I'm Catholic, we believe the same things, such as doing the right thing. The parents are very happy. They even tell their kids, 'You listen to Mrs. Flores because she knows. We believe the same things—even though it's not the same religion.'"

Ms. Cindy McLean, a first-year teacher, replied to Ms. Flores, "Yeah, but that provides them an opportunity to check their ideas. The students will say, 'I celebrate Easter.' Then as a teacher, we can ask, 'What do you mean by that?' It offers an opportunity to teach them."

Ms. Flores extended the conversation, "They all go trick-or-treating! Have you noticed? It's so funny because on Halloween last year—I took the day off this year, that's my thing now—but last year, we noticed at dismissal they all got picked up early because they were going trick-or-treating!"

"Only half of my class did; the other half didn't," said Ms. Carpenter.

"Some of them don't celebrate, though. I don't even know what's behind Halloween! Really, they are just getting candy. I couldn't tell them about the history behind it if they asked. Yeah, I'll just ask my Alexa. . . . 'Alexa, what is Halloween?'" laughed Ms. Deanna Davis, a third-grade teacher in her second year of teaching at North Star.

Ms. Anne Mirza, the elementary Islamic studies teacher, commented, "Yes, there are differences. There is nothing wrong with that. I love teaching at North Star because I'm teaching kids to be at peace—which may help bring about future peace in the world, who knows! It's a big thing to be connected with—and to be okay with other people having other religions."

Ms. Carpenter responded, "It's almost like Martin Luther King Jr.'s skin color doesn't matter. We're all people. We're all here on Earth. God put us all here. We need to be loving to our neighbors. Just being aware. Choosing to be around different cultures and different religions helps you. Just like when our upper school Islamic studies director, Farah Rafiq, Skyped the group in Nebraska. You realize that there are different people in the world, but you can share one common goal. They are kind. You are kind. You work together respectfully—no matter what religion or what culture, you learn new things! These opportunities help us learn about different cultures, such as the food they eat, what they believe in, and so on and so forth. Engaging with others helps our students become more well-rounded citizens of the world."

Ms. Camdyn Winter, new to the school this year, added, "True. But it's important to be aware of the fact that the relationships between parents and teachers are different from what I've experienced in public schools. North Star parents are paying for staff to work here. So, parents think, 'Okay, I want to be a little closer to the teacher.' They want to have a say in what you're doing. Which is awesome! They are invested in their children's education. They are also just lovely. My experiences so far have been really great. The parents here are just wonderful. They're just so kind and understanding. I told them straight off the bat, 'I'm not Muslim, I'm sorry if I don't understand everything—all your culture. I'm learning. But, if I do something wrong, please let me know.' I've told the kids that too, but the parents have just been understanding and kind—and very accepting."

Lower School Parent Association

"My husband and I are both immigrants. We first immigrated to Canada, and of course, part of the immigration process is a lot of identity searching and a lot of questions that you ask yourself, such as 'What are you going to be?' and 'Who am I?' When we were in Canada, we met a lot of people who were first-generation Canadians. We saw a lot of disconnect between parents and their kids. There was not a lot of shared identity, and many of the kids rejected their Muslim and Arab identities. This was a concern to us as new parents. We asked ourselves, 'How can we foster their identity?' We wanted them to have a chance to actually learn about themselves before they get bombarded with ideas and stereotypes. We moved from Canada to California four years ago, and we were looking for an Islamic school. Somebody mentioned North Star Academy, and we viewed a video about the school. As I listened to the teachers talking, I started crying. I said, 'This is what we want!' This is our fourth year at North Star and my first year in the Parent Association. My son is in third grade, and he started when he was in kindergarten. My daughter is in kindergarten, and she also attended two years of preschool at North Star. Having teachers of other faiths is awesome. We are impressed by the diversity of the community," said Ms. Bibi Abadi.

"My name is Alice Tilki, and I'm very new to the North Star Parent Association. This is my first year participating. I have one daughter, who just turned six, and she's in kindergarten. So, besides the quality education, North Star is providing a great Islamic education, which we're all here for. I think the number one priority is for our kids to learn Islam and find themselves. In many ways, diversity helps with this. Sometimes there is a fear that going to a religious school will expose your child to only people from your faith or from your community. In my opinion, this doesn't prepare your child to interact with people from outside of your community. At North Star, children are equipped to interact with people of all faiths because they form relationships with people from all different backgrounds."

"I'd like to add," said Ms. Sophia Seedat, "that I'm from South Africa. I have no family here. So, the school is like our family. I am a third-generation Indian born in South Africa. My kids don't identify with being Indian. I've never been to India, and neither have they. My husband is half-Syrian, half-Malay, and I don't know what! He's mixed. So, my kids identify as Muslim, then American, and then South African, and then everything else."

Ms. Dahlia Abdallah added, "I once felt that being in an American public school was beautiful. I wanted my child to experience public school, but my faith is really important. I connected with the fact that North Star teachers are similar to public school teachers, yet my daughter still gets the religious part. The teachers of mixed faith embrace the children so well. One kindergarten teacher reads *surahs* (chapters) from the Qur'an with her students. She says she's of the Christian faith. So, the children have this unbelievable sense of true acceptance. This school doesn't send the message that 'everyone here is from one faith.' You know what I mean? At most schools, you have to pretend you are like everyone else. Nobody knows anyone's faith. So, no one can embrace faith. Here, you can be Christian if you want and Muslim if you want. Whatever you are, you are."

"My two older kids are in public school. My daughter is in eighth grade, and my son is in fifth grade. I was worried about how they were going to adjust to a public school after being at North Star Academy their whole school life. I was really surprised that within the first week, most of their friends were not Muslim," shared Ms. Abdallah.

"My son's closest friend is a pastor's son," said Sophia. And my daughter is very comfortable sharing that she's Muslim or speaking about things she can and can't do. I think they're proud to be Muslim. She got that here."

"My name is Salma Cassiem. I have surprisingly been a part of the Islamic Center of San Rico community since it began in the late 1950s. I have two little boys. This is our third year at North Star and my first year in the Parent Association. This will come as a shock to you, but North Star was not our first choice for our children. Our family is very involved in the Islamic Center of San Rico. Islam is a big part of my family's life, but I was concerned about the shift in ideas, such as 'If you don't wear your scarf, you're not a Muslim. If you don't pray five times a day, you're not a Muslim. If you talk to boys,' just crazy stuff like that. To me, conservatism is taking over, and I did not want them to go to any Islamic school to learn these ideas. One of my boys started in a Montessori school. The other was in a STEM school. We got to a point where we weren't happy. We said, 'Let's give it a shot. Let's go to North Star Academy. Let's sit down and talk with the leadership. Let's go through all our fears, all our concerns.'

"I have to say, I feel like it was probably the best decision we've made. The love that my son has, and . . . I don't know why I'm getting emotional . . . sorry everybody, ...it's just the strength and courage they have and how everyone belongs here. It's helped them identify as Muslims, and it's something that I haven't been able to provide to them. I want them to have the strength and the courage to be Muslims in America, to be leaders of our religion. I want them to never feel like they have to cower or hide who they really are. I feel that North Star really prepares our children. I see how proud the alumni are . . . some are Muslim Student Association presidents at their college. My hope for my children is that they take it to the next level and make everybody realize how great Islam is and how they can live and be a part of this country as Muslim Americans."

"I'm Dhalia Abdallah. I'm relatively new. It's my first year in the North Star Parent Association. I have two kids, one in preschool and one in first grade. My daughter plays soccer. Even though we live in a city that's diverse, my daughter's team is mostly White. She sees herself as different. Her name is Qadira—she finds that her name is hard. She says, 'I don't want to tell them my name because it's different. I want to use another name.'"

Ms. Alice Tilki replied, "There's lots of Emmas. There's a lot of Emilys . . ."

Ms. Abdallah nodded in agreement and continued, "Qadira asked me, 'Can I give myself a different name when I play soccer, so they know how to say it?' I said, "Qadira has an Arabic meaning to it and an English meaning. So you can just tell them. You can spell it out.' She's like, 'But my name, you spell it differently than the way the other people spell it, it's not K-A-D-I-R-A.' I don't know. She's confident, but she still feels like she's different around certain people, which I think is okay. It may not be political, but just the climate, I guess."

"There is a climate that our kids are picking up on. My third grader came home one day and said, 'Oh, Trump doesn't like us. He hates Muslims.' We had to have a conversation because he brought it home. Maybe I'm in a bubble and not ready to expose him to the prejudice that we as adults sometimes have to navigate. . . We're still learning how to do that! I don't have an answer. I have a lady who helps me at home. She comes every couple of weeks. It was around Christmas, and she was talking about Christmas. My son pulled me aside and asked, 'Does she know we're Muslim?' I said, 'I think so. I don't know.' He said, 'Maybe you don't have to tell her.' That was the first time he told me, 'If they ask, maybe we should tell them, but sometimes you don't have to bring it up,'" shared Ms. Abadi.

Ms. Seedat commented on Bibi's story, "That's really funny but at the same time quite poignant. It's kind of cute. I could see a little kid doing that. But, if we dig deeper, it seems your son understands that he sometimes needs to hide part of his identity. He is learning to judge when it is good and when it might be bad to make his faith known. That's interesting to think about for a child in third grade at age eight."

Mr. Anwar Hasan, School Board Chair

"I think the biggest challenge is the isolationist versus inclusionist focus that is typical of Islamic schools. We are not trying to take anyone away from the community. We want to create students to be leaders within the wider community. Yes, we do charge high tuition. Most Islamic schools are part of a *masjid*, so they're subsidized. People see this school and say, 'Hey, this is too expensive for me,' and that's it. They draw that quick conclusion. Whereas, if they applied for the tuition adjustment program, it would be an affordable option. Most people don't know this option exists. About five years ago, we thought, 'How would someone apply for a program called tuition assistance?' There's a stigma with the phrase 'tuition assistance.' Many people probably think to themselves, 'I don't need charity.' As a result, hardly anyone applied. We decided to make it easier for people by rebranding 'tuition assistance' to 'tuition adjustment.'"

Another way we are different is our diverse school board. I've been the board chair for the last thirteen years. During this time, the board has expanded to fourteen members, and we make sure we have female representation. If we need new members, it's normal for someone to say, 'Who are some women we can add?' We look at gender and also profession. We may want an attorney or someone in real estate. Another consideration is financial status, not only wealthy people because they could potentially donate, but someone on the other end of the spectrum so they can have input on the tuition increase discussions. Also, from a religious standpoint, we include members who are very conservative and very liberal. We won't necessarily have conversations that say, 'We need to find someone that fits this.' But we'll look around the table, and we'll say 'Hey, you know what? We have too many liberal people,' or 'We're all too conservative.' We're pretty sensitive to maintaining diversity.

However, we definitely have parents whose highest priority is Quranic memorization. That's not necessarily a priority at North Star. There are other families where Islam is not a part of their family life, and the school serves that Islamic purpose and makes parents feel a little less guilty. Those examples don't necessarily reflect the ideology, but parents know what they're getting into by having their kids at North Star. We've never looked at it in numbers, but every year we're conscious of having diversity. For example, if you combine the two campuses, it's pretty common that we have at least one non-Muslim student. There is always a non-Muslim teacher that has her child in this school. But then occasionally, we'll have one in addition to that. Like last year, there was a Chinese kid that enrolled in our school. I think that's going to change. Most

Islamic schools have not crossed the barrier with staffing. They hire only Muslim teachers. We dealt with that a long time ago. Most of our staff is non-Muslim. We hope to be able to attract more non-Muslim teachers and students. We're not trying to market to non-Muslims just yet; but, if they come, we wouldn't turn them away. To me, that's almost like a badge of honor, 'This school is so good that non-Muslims want to go here.'

In terms of the school board, we used to allow parents to twist some arms. That created some commotion, and there was influence exerted. We've matured organizationally, and we don't have those issues anymore. I feel like the school has evolved significantly to become a leader in its own right. We now rent out this campus and have an endowment. The board now thinks strategically, especially on how to make things sustainable. As we achieve in this area, we are able to hire additional staff. In fact, our school's budget is bigger than the Islamic Center of San Rico's budget.

For example, we were talking about how to generate revenue for this facility, right? So, naturally, renting out the gym and the field comes up. A board member's daughter plays volleyball. Her daughter's league needed a place to practice. I'm thinking, 'Oh, God. The first time we rent the gym, there will be twenty girls in tight shorts.' I don't want that to happen. But again, we want to provide a school that's for the broader community. That means being flexible to the different interpretations present in our community. You even see it at morning drop-off. In one car there will be a mother dressed very conservatively. In the car behind her is a mother in a halter top ready to go to the gym. This can create challenges. When parents are thinking about their kids, they can become judgmental of others, right? 'The school is for the rich,' or 'It's a school for the less religious,' or 'It's too liberal,' or whatever.

Most enrollment is through word of mouth. Over the past few years, our marketing staff has done a great job putting things online and using social media. Every day there's an Instagram or a Facebook post or a Snapchat. All of this helps. As a result, every year or two, there will inevitably be a family that says, 'Oh, we just moved here from Switzerland because we saw your school,' or 'We chose the City of Springwater just because of the school.' Wow, that's amazing, right? We're blessed that way. Last year, we tried a more concerted marketing effort for the first time. We hired a marketing company that did a full mail campaign, specifically targeting families based on zip codes—not targeting only Muslims. I don't know how many thousands of dollars the social media campaign cost, but the hard part is not knowing what strategy is really effective. Right now, we are trying to gather data when people call in and express an interest in our school. We ask, 'Where did you hear about us?' and 'How did you get here?' There's not a direct link with the money spent, which is why we haven't paid for advertising this year. But we need to find something to do because there's still a lot of misinformation out there about our school.

For example, one group doesn't know about our school. The second group heard, 'Hey, that's just a school for rich people,' or 'That school is $20,000 a year.' The cost alone can scare people, and they never learn more about the school. There's a lot of room for improvement in how we market our school and how we make decisions. We no longer compare ourselves to other Islamic schools. We now compare ourselves to independent schools. We see ourselves as a peer with independent schools. We've accomplished a lot and are well beyond them in certain facets. We like to think, 'Yes, we're part of this community. There's something to learn from independent schools. At the same time, we're also providing things that they can learn. The fact that Muna was recruited to join the Independent Schools Association strongly signals that we are in a different tier than other Islamic schools."

Upper School Parent Association

"Sitting at this table, you can just see that there's so much diversity on this campus. I love that. In the upper school, there are first-generation and second-generation Muslim students. There are different cultures, different ethnicities, and different faith groups. I think that's what really makes North Star so unique. Especially as a second-generation or as an in-between generation, it becomes really important that North Star serves as an example of what an integrated community looks like and how it functions. I think we talked about this before—with other Islamic schools . . . sometimes you feel like it is ghettoized . . . that everybody is Arab. It just becomes this attitude, 'We stick together, right?' The diversity of thought, the diversity of cultural practices, and different Islamic practices are welcoming. It creates an atmosphere where anybody can feel comfortable being themselves. There isn't this awkward feeling of 'Where do I fit?' 'How am I supposed to be?' You just be. That is what sets North Star apart. This doesn't exist in a lot of places. I don't even think it exists in a lot of *mosques*, either. There's something unique here that we're creating and modeling for our kids," said Ms. Amira El-Hadary.

"Yes, I totally agree, and Amira makes a very good point. There are non-Muslims and Muslims at this school. I remember when we were in Chicago,

Muslims were fighting each other over how to be Muslim. 'This is not *halal*. How do you feed your kids?' Comments like this. My God, you don't need to be one way or the other! At North Star, we respect each other even if you eat or don't eat *halal*. It's a respectful atmosphere. The kids are learning this—to respect each other even if they don't agree. They are taught to have their faith, their beliefs, and be okay with differences," added Ms. Lena Morsy.

Ms. El-Hadary replied, "I think it's empowering for students to have non-Muslim teachers who understand their traditions and particular views. At this school, a child can actually go up to that teacher and talk to them about things. This primes them when they're in public high school and when they have a question for a non-Muslim teacher. North Star is modeling for them that a non-Muslim teacher can get you, right? That just makes it much easier for them to continue their education. They learn that they can be comfortable engaging and sharing views with any teacher."

Ms. Angelica Khan added, "I am Catholic, and my husband is Muslim from Pakistan. During the early part of my son's life, we were actually on the East Coast, and he was enrolled in a Catholic school. There wasn't an Islamic school near where we lived. I don't think there's an issue with introducing your child to people of different backgrounds. Introducing your child to diversity adds value to the school and shows them how integration should be. My son had the perspective of having Catholic teachers, and now he has some Muslim teachers. Each teacher has their own experiences, whether they were raised abroad or here, and how well they've integrated their own lives. That also adds to how my son views the world."

"Angelica, what you are saying reminds me of a school experience in Chicago and Boston, where I used to live twenty years ago. In both cities, Islamic schools were of poor quality. I'm sorry to say the ideas they would teach were that we're the good ones. It's very destructive to make kids think they're better than others. After all, they're going to be with them one day, in college and in the workplace. The students felt disconnected from their community and from the society in which they were born. A gap emerged. This was because the schools hired immigrant teachers and immigrant school leaders who brought their beliefs and ideology with them to the school. For example, schools only hired teachers who wore *hijab*. How well they could teach was a secondary concern. Now, the law won't let you hire just anyone to teach in school. You have to be accredited at something. Twenty years ago, education wasn't good in Islamic schools. When the students moved to high school, they thought, 'Oh my God, is this the real world?'"

Ms. Morsy replied, "That's why I was against enrolling my children into most of the Islamic schools. When I came to California and saw North Star Academy, my mind changed completely. We are American. All of the kids are American and American Muslim. We can be Muslim, respect our identity as Muslims, and still be American and faithful to the country we live in. All of us live in this country. If this is a shit country, why do you live in it? Go find another place to live. This is a great country! We have the freedom to express ourselves as Muslims in this country. Other countries don't have this much freedom. So, I respect North Star a lot. I know that the kids are going to have a balance here. They are Muslim. They are in control of their identity but can still be part of the larger community and be productive human beings. That's why I love North Star."

Fifth and Sixth-Grade Students

Jana spoke first: "There are people who pray at different times. There are also people who pray with their hands on their sides. There are other people who can't eat certain things. I feel that even though a person can't do certain things, we can still relate to each other and still interact."

Sara added, "My friend prays differently, and she is so kind. She is the other kind of Muslim. Even if someone is different, you can still be friends."

"There are different groups of people in Islam. There are some things, like, 'Do you pray with your hands like this [holding them beneath her chest], or with your hands like this to your sides?' Those are the religious differences I see in this school. Some people have different beliefs because they learned them from their families. Others have different beliefs because they heard it from another person. Some people are stricter when they eat meat. It's called *zabiha*. Either they are okay with eating any meat—but not pork because everybody has to follow that rule—or they have their meat Islamically slaughtered. It doesn't matter. When meat is Islamically slaughtered, the butcher says something over the animal, and they kill the animal in a way that doesn't hurt the animal," explained Joury.

Zikri said, "I'm not from a *zabiha* family, so I eat any meat. Not pork. But I still give respect to the people that are *zabiha*. We give respect to one another in this whole school—*zabiha* or no-*zabiha*. For example, I have a friend who is *zabiha*. He's in fourth grade. I don't make fun of him because he's *zabiha*, and I'm not *zabiha*."

Jana added, "When we pray, we have to clean ourselves. It's called *wudu*. Some people think that when someone has done *wudu* and a dog—or animal—

touches them with their saliva, then they are dirty. They have to do *wudu* again. Some people dis others about this, but that's one of the things you have to deal with when having a dog or maybe a cat. Most of the time, it's a dog because dogs are messy. Cats do little baths. I want to add to what Joury said about *zabiha*. In the Qur'an, it says that you're allowed to eat animals from the ocean that do not eat other animals. Some people will remind others of this rule. In my family, we eat things that other animals don't eat, like chicken."

Yasin replied to Jana, "My parents don't want to get a dog because they believe if a dog's in the room, the angels won't stay in the room. I never heard about the saliva part, though—that if saliva touches you, you have to do *wudu*, but I did hear that if a dog is in the room, all the angels leave."

Zikri added, "We all have a heart. We all have feelings and wants. We're all the same. We're all human beings, brothers, and sisters. My parents say, 'If it's okay with you and your family, then, of course, you can have a pet. But we are not a pet family.' I tell them, 'With all respect, I really need a dog.'"

"At this school, there are people from different places. Usually, most people around here are from Saudi Arabia, Egypt, Asia, and the top of Africa. There are also some Pakistani students. There are a lot of different people with different personalities. Some people are shy. Some people are annoying. Annoying people just follow you around. There are also some people who are really smart. There are other people who are really nice. There are funny people. In the wider world, there are people that think other religions are bad and you shouldn't believe in them, which is wrong because people who have faith are still human. They just have different beliefs," commented Sara.

Zikri added, "I feel like the Mexicans are going through a hard time because of what Trump is doing. He's building a wall so they can't get into America. When they arrive in America and get their passports checked, once they see that they're Mexican, the agents say, 'I'm sorry. We can't have you.' Then they have to go all the way back to Mexico. I feel bad for the Mexicans because I think America is a free country, and I think a free country should have everybody from every religion able to live in this country. But, with this president, I don't know. Mexicans are going through very hard times."

Joury replied to Zakri, "They are suffering. It's related to the suffering of the Jews. The Jewish people are also being oppressed. Their synagogues have been vandalized, and they're being persecuted. They can't pray in peace or do what their faith tells them to do in peace, so they have the same struggles as Muslims."

"The Jews are misunderstood. Our religion is kinda misunderstood too. In fact, a lot of other cultures and religions are misunderstood," added Daniel.

"I think the Jewish people are struggling because their population is decreasing. I saw from a presentation that the percentage of Jews is going down. Other religions, like Islam and Christianity, are going up in followers. I think synagogues might not be able to stay open if they don't have many donations," stated Yasin.

Jana replied, "There's a difference between equality and equity. If there are three boxes and there are three people trying to see over the fence, then it's fair that the shorter people get a crate or two to stand on. It would be equal if they all got one box, but that's not fair. You are equitable if the person who can see over the fence stands without a box. The medium person might have one box, and the shorter person would have two boxes to see over the fence. Islam says everybody should be fair to each other because it doesn't matter where you're from, your age, how you're raised, or anything like that. It says we should be fair to each other because we're all human and we're all equal. Someone may be better at something than somebody else. Everybody has a special talent or gift. Islam teaches us that everybody should be treated fairly."

"Our President Trump, he does not treat us fairly. He wants all the Muslims out of the country. That is unfair. But, there are other people who treat us very fairly. My mom has a friend. She used to be part of this interfaith organization. She is an evangelical Christian friend, and she is very nice. She invited us over for Christmas. She threw us a little Christmas party. She didn't judge us about our religion. She never said, 'Oh, you have to go pray. What's that you're doing?' She never laughed at my mom. I wish that all people would just focus on the good," said Joury.

"We can have more peace in the world without splitting everyone up into groups. It would be much better if everyone were kind to one another. I think our principal and teachers expect us not to be perfect but to try our best and not make fun of people, bully people, or hit others. They do not want us to do anything mean or unfair," concluded Sara.

Zikri added, "I think our principal and teachers expect us to be us. If you're creative, be creative. If you're sporty, be sporty. If you're smart, be smart. Be you."

4

Freedom of Pedagogy

> By supporting freedom of pedagogy, school leaders promote a reciprocal approach to teaching and learning that fosters the development of students' critical consciousness.

Like similar private independent schools in the region, North Star Academy taught the California state curriculum. This included subjects ranging from language arts, mathematics, science, and social studies to music, art, information technology, and physical education. As an Islamic school, students also attended classes in Islamic studies, Quranic recitation and memorization, and Arabic language. Maintaining a high standard of academic excellence was essential to Dr. Ramsey. She trusted her teachers to develop interesting and interactive learning environments and to use innovative instructional methodologies and materials. Teachers were required to uphold personal and professional courtesy. They were expected to be collegial and collaborative, and uphold the school's mission, vision, and values. The expectation placed upon teachers was to foster safe, predictable, and supportive learning environments.

Yet, the focus on progressive Islamic ideology distinguished North Star Academy from other Islamic schools in the area. Dr. Ramsey self-identified as a progressive Muslim. She referred to North Star Academy as a progressive Islamic school. In other words, the values explicitly taught at North Star Academy were aligned with progressive thought and action. Topics such as human rights, gender equality, LGBTQIA+ rights, women's rights, freedom of thought, freedom of expression, freedom of religion, interfaith marriage, and pluralism were incorporated as meaningful social justice issues, providing students with a humanizing curriculum (Wong & Mishra, 2021). For Dr. Ramsey, progressive values were Islamic values. Divergent interpretations of Islam that violated human rights and suppressed individual freedoms were expressly counter to progressive understandings of Islamic teachings and the lived example of Prophet Muhammad. To create a more humane world through education, Dr. Ramsey encouraged teachers to instill the universal notion of justice in their curricula and instruction. Teaching social justice was inseparable from God's divine nature: "Verily, God does not do even an atom's weight of injustice" (Qur'an, 4:40).

Dr. Ramsey referred to the school's pedagogical approach as a curriculum of resistance. She expected teachers to incorporate discussions of power and privilege in their lessons to intentionally create classroom communities of conscience. Dr. Ramsey explained, "Social justice is about critiquing current power structures. Critiquing is part of being a good Muslim. It is learning to look and see what is fair and what is not fair and speaking out when you don't see something happening that should be happening." Although discussions could be challenging, Dr. Ramsey saw this work as necessary—both for the development of students' American Muslim identity and for the formation of their critical consciousness.

Providing teachers with pedagogical freedom was foundational for this approach to teaching and learning. Dr. Ramsey encouraged her teachers to include issues of justice, equality, and freedom in their lesson plans as they saw fit. In doing so, teachers created an intentional process for identifying and discussing patterns of inequality, discrimination, and bigotry. Students learned not only about the issues studied but, more importantly, how to engage in productive dialogue about controversial and challenging topics. Dr. Ramsey provided an example: "If there was a crisis in the world, it would be discussed at school. It could be discussed in Islamic studies or maybe in social studies. It could be discussed in language arts class. We intentionally touch on issues of social justice so our kids become aware of injustice. For example, our middle school students participate annually in *The Global Read Aloud* project. This year our students read Alan Gratz's book *Refugee*. It is a book about survival and having the courage to be compassionate and choosing to do the right thing."

Dr. Ramsey valued Islam's tradition of critique and viewed it as essential to exposing, resisting, challenging, questioning, and ultimately overcoming injustice and oppression. She referred to the Qur'an to substantiate this perspective when she was speaking to us about her approach to developing critical thinking skills: "In *Surah al-Baqarah* 2:30-36, God shared with the angels that he is going to put Adam on Earth. In our tradition, the angels do what God commands. They do not have the freedom to choose. The first thing the angels do, who are just supposed to follow, is ask God, 'Why? Why would you put somebody on Earth who could spread corruption and shed blood when we extol your glory, your endless glory? Why didn't you just create creatures that can't make a decision between right and wrong?' In our tradition, the most obedient creature has the right to question the creator.

"The creator asked the angels the names of things on Earth. The angels said, 'We don't know.' The creator then turned to Adam and said, 'Okay, will you say what these things are called?' Adam named the objects. The angels responded, 'Wow! You know better than we know. Right?' Even in that exchange, we learned that Adam is a learning creature. As we progress, we add to our knowledge. Questioning and learning are completely tied together. It doesn't matter how young you are or how great you are, you can question and be questioned. That's powerful. That's the foundation for our faith. I understand this as meaning that we need answers, and it's not enough to say, 'It just is because.' Even if I don't have the answer, it's okay to say, 'I don't know, but I'm trying to figure it out.' It is important to be in that perpetual state of wanting to understand." Dr. Ramsey extended this thought by providing an example that often occurs between students, "If everyone's eating *zabiha* then there's no question. But, if your neighbor is eating something you want to eat, but can't, then you're going to ask why. Not being afraid of differences allows room for people to ask questions."

Ms. Rafiq, the upper school Islamic studies director, echoed Dr. Ramsey's thoughts concerning the importance of questioning. She said, "We are all unfinished, and being confused is okay. It's okay to not know. I want our students to feel comfortable asking questions. When I met students at the beginning of the year, I told them, 'This is a safe space. There's no judgment. You ask what you want to ask. If you want to submit a question privately, submit a question privately. If anybody ever tells you to not be curious or to not question, with all due respect to them, you take a different path.'"

The curriculum of resistance was scaffolded so that the upper primary and middle school students had the skills to activate their existing knowledge, examine their current understandings, and engage in questioning and dialogue with their teachers and peers on difficult and challenging topics. Dr. Ramsey wanted students to learn about power, privilege, injustice, and oppression; she procured three programs that created a fit-for-purpose framework of shared values, norms, and behavior expectations that guided this critical learning.

The Zones of Regulation

Dr. Ramsey adopted Kuypers' (2011) Zones of Regulation framework and curriculum to provide North Star Academy with simple language to help students articulate their thoughts and feelings. The specialized vocabulary was accompanied by color-coded "zones" that were arranged similarly to traffic signs. The Red Zone (stop) described a heightened sense of emotion, such as being elated, angry, panicked, or overjoyed. The Yellow Zone (caution) included feelings of stress, anxiety, frustration, silliness, or nervousness. The Green Zone (go) indicated calmness and being ready to learn. The Blue Zone (rest area) included low states of alertness and feelings of sadness, tiredness, sickness, or boredom. Students learned how to recognize and manage the zone they were in based on the environment and the expectations of that environment. Ms. Fatemi, the lower school director, explained the benefits of using The Zones of Regulation. "I've found that by using the framework and curriculum, students learn higher-level vocabulary and complex thinking skills. We don't brush off students' questions. We do not respond with an 'Oh, it doesn't matter. You don't need to know it.' We really go into depth because students need to know what the words mean."

Ms. Deanna Davis, a third-grade teacher, was in her second year of teaching at North Star Academy. She shared, "We spend a lot of time with The Zones of Regulation and developing the whole child. A lot of other schools say they foster the development of the whole child, but that is what this school's really about. Obviously, academics are huge here, but it's a lot more than that. This school really does develop the whole child. They take it seriously."

As we walked around the lower school, we noticed the majority of classrooms displaying child-friendly posters explaining The Zones of Regulation along with strategies students could use to manage their zone. For example, a second-grade classroom's poster included "What I can do?" alongside the zone. For the Red Zone (mad/angry, mean, yelling/hitting, out of control), student strategies included "walking away," "stop what I am doing," "be safe," "ask for a break," and "get help." We also noticed posters that showed pictures of strategies to help students get into the green zone. These included "drinking water," "counting to ten," "taking deep breaths," "doing wall push-ups," "using fidget toys," "drawing," "writing," "talking to an adult," and "self-talk."

We observed every student on task. We did not see any tantrums or outbursts, refusal to participate, or abusive behaviors, such as kicking, biting, or punching. We saw students working on different activities simultaneously while music was playing in the background. Neither of us was familiar with The Zones of Regulation prior to this study. However, from the observation data we gathered, it was clear that students were, by and large, in the green zone, attentive, calm, and learning.

Value of the Month

The Value of the Month program ran alongside the Zones of Regulation; however, this program was school-wide. A specific value was designated monthly throughout the school year. North Star Academy's monthly values were responsibility, honesty, thankfulness, self-restraint and control, fairness and justice, commitment, generosity, respect, and kindness and care. In practice, each month's value was integrated into the espoused curriculum and was the focus of day-to-day interactions. Students were reminded of the value through posters and wall displays. Co-curricular activities offered students the opportunity to learn about and discuss the month's value. For example, once a month, lower school teachers selected a student from their class to participate in the 'Lunch Bunch' program. Lunch Bunch students were asked to write and deliver a speech about the value of the month. More than a character-building program, the chosen values were expressly linked to Islam and marked North Star Academy as a rights-respecting school.

Ms. Sheryl Carpenter, a thirteen-year veteran teacher at North Star Academy, explained her approach to the value of the month: "Whenever I get an opportunity, such as when we read a book, I will bring Islam into the discussion. We will relate the character to Islam and to the value of the month. Social justice is a huge component of our faith, and social justice issues are salient within this environment." Yet, not all teachers were as confident as Ms. Carpenter in linking the values to Islam. Ms. Mary Flores was very happy at the school but shared, "I don't know much about Islam, so when I teach my students, I am more focused on American identity. I wish I knew more so I could incorporate more into my lessons. At times I'll ask my students to tell me what they know, but when we are doing our values of the month and leadership qualities, I take it from my point of view. I wish I had some different knowledge to incorporate."

Like Ms. Flores, other non-Muslim teachers asked their students about different aspects of Islam. These conversations occurred organically. Ms. Camdyn Winter was in her eighth year of teaching, but it was her first year at North Star Academy. She was a member of the Church of Jesus Christ of Latter-Day Saints and a Brigham Young University graduate. At North Star Academy, she taught first grade. She shared a spontaneous conversation: "I didn't bring up what religion I was, but my students see that I'm not Muslim. They perceive it in just the way I act or look. This was mentioned to the religious teacher. At one point, I heard, 'Oh, Mrs. Winter is Christian.' My students were so surprised that I was Christian. I thought, 'Oh, I don't know if we should talk about that.'

But it was interesting for them. It allowed them to reflect, 'Oh, but she's a good person.' Now that they do know what religion I follow, their religious teacher always points out, 'They believe this, and we believe that. But are we mean to that person? No! Are we kind to that person? Yes!' My students understand, and they are very respectful." Respectful relationships, acceptance of others, and learning about differences were values explicitly taught throughout the school and viewed as fundamental to being a sincere Muslim.

The Leader in Me

The lower school integrated the Leader in Me program throughout its curricula. This program is drawn from Covey's (1989) book, *7 Habits of Highly Effective People*, and was designed to transform a school's culture and raise student achievement by working in concert with the school's academic curriculum and behavioral structures to teach students the importance of personal responsibility, confidence, perseverance, and personal effectiveness. As part of the program, Covey's five paradigms guided North Star Academy's approach: (1) Everyone can be a leader; (2) everyone has genius; (3) change starts with me; (4) educators empower students to lead their own learning; and (5) educators develop the whole person. We noticed seven habit panels hanging from the ceiling in the main hallway during our first visit to the school. They said:

Habit 1: Be Proactive (You're in Charge)

Habit 2: Begin with the End in Mind (Have a Plan)

Habit 3: Put First Things First (Work First, Then Play)

Habit 4: Think Win-Win (Everyone Can Win)

Habit 5: Seek First to Understand, Then to Be Understood (Listen Before You Talk)

Habit 6: Synergize (Together Is Better)

Habit 7: Sharpen the Saw (Balance Feels Best)

Also in the main hallway was an "Acts of Kindness" bulletin board. Ms. Fatemi explained to us on our first tour of the lower school campus why the administration chose the Leader in Me program as part of their pedagogical approach. She said, "When we were evaluating different programs, we wanted to see how it connected with our school and how it could be added to our current programs. The Leader in Me program included staff professional training, on-site coaching, and tailored learning experiences. Each of these met the unique needs and goals of our school. We teach our kids the first three habits at the beginning of the year. This year we felt it appropriate to have service be our school-wide goal. We asked our students to do five random acts of kindness. We want to be a kind school. Sometimes students can spit out the value of the month and the seven habits, but the question remains if they are really embodying the principles. Are they being kind? In the first trimester, we said each child had to do five kindness acts within the school. Next trimester the students will be asked to do ten acts of kindness within their house."

Ms. Fatemi continued to explain the Leader in Me program in our one-to-one interview. She reflected on her goal of having the school be recognized as a model school or a Lighthouse Certified School. "When I really understood the depth of the Leader in Me program, I learned that we could become a certified Lighthouse School. And so, it was a natural journey. We didn't have to do this additional work. We could have stayed as a Leader in Me school. But when you work to get Lighthouse certification, you go very deep. You have to show sustainability. To be honest, it is now a language around here and a culture. We created a teacher-leader culture that didn't exist ten years back." North Star Academy became a Lighthouse Certified School seven years after starting the Leader in Me program. This certification commended the school's fidelity in implementing the program and its positive impact on staff, students, parents, and the wider community.

North Star Academy's *Leader in Me* program complemented the school's focus on developing students' Islamic values. Yet, connecting the seven habits to Islamic values was not automatic. Indeed, during the initial teacher training, teachers acknowledged the value of the program but questioned if the program was a fit for their Islamic school. Ms. Fatemi reflected on this challenge: "When we launched the program, we completed a two-day training session. It was so powerful. All the teachers remarked, 'Oh, this is so good for my own life.' After the training, some of our teachers asked how a habit connects with our monthly values. We didn't want to do away with our core values and principles that the North Star Academy was founded on, but we had to connect the dots."

Yet, linking Islam to the seven habits was left to the purview of each teacher in the beginning. In other words, Dr. Ramsey and Ms. Fatemi trusted their teachers to identify relevant ways to "connect the dots." For example, Ms. Carpenter was a lifelong Muslim. She found it easy to connect the seven habits to Islam. She explained, "I don't give my students direct lessons on the seven habits. Rather,

I integrate the habits into my lessons along with Islamic teachings. I just see the connection to the habit." Ms. Carpenter then provided an example: "I often refer my students to look at the seven-habit tree in our classroom. The first three habits are the roots of the tree. I refer to the roots as the foundation of the tree. I explain that they are now building their foundation. So, just like the tree needs to have strong roots to survive, they need to have a strong foundation. I use the concept of a mirror to impart the importance of developing their Islamic values and character, 'If you don't have the values now, as you grow older, you will bring darkness into your lives. Because of this darkness, you have to keep cleaning the mirror so you are always shiny.' These little examples really resonate with the kids, they get it somehow."

Connecting the dots was more difficult for non-Muslim teachers. Ms. Flores, a Catholic, was in her fourth year of teaching second grade at North Star Academy. She expressed her support for the program, "I really like this school because it's the first school that I've taught in that really believes in what they teach. I'm sure all parents teach their kids first things first, like first you work, then celebrate. But here, it is part of our curriculum and our lessons. I really like that because it's what I believe in."

It was clear to us that the Leader in Me was accepted as a core component of the curriculum and had buy-in from the teachers. Ms. Fatemi shared how impactful it had been for the school community. "They [FranklinCovey Education] come to our school every four years to do a formal visit. It's like accreditation. Every two years, we submit a virtual profile and a portfolio. We share the new initiatives that we've done. So, it's deep. I feel like it's impacted how we do goal setting because they [FranklinCovey Education] keep adding layers."

Tripartite Framework Underpinning the Curriculum of Resistance

Over time, Dr. Ramsey aligned the seven habits with the Values of the Month and Islamic teachings. Although supporting a progressive gender-affirming and gender-justice position, we noticed the frequent use of the masculine *He* when we reviewed the *hadith* and *ayat* included in the framework. We also noticed parenthetical female pronouns to the *hadith* for the month of December: "The strong person is not he (she) who has physical strength, but he (she) that can control his (her) anger." This modification showed an effort to promote gender inclusivity; however, this change was not made to all the aligned religious texts.

The Islamic texts, by and large, retained their historical heteronormativity and did not move beyond binary views of gender. We wondered if the insertion of female pronouns was an attempt to promote gender equality. We knew that the Qur'an referred to Allah using the masculine pronoun, *huwa*, a grammatically male word in Arabic. However, we also understood that Allah transcended gender, as the Qur'an says, "There is nothing whatsoever like unto Him" (42:11). In other words, in Islam, Allah has not ascribed a gender, and the use of male pronouns is a grammatical masculine construct and not meant to anthropomorphize or ascribe masculinity to God. These observations led us to consider the challenges associated with teaching progressive Islam through centuries-long paternalistic interpretations and understandings of the faith. We decided to look for examples of teaching progressivism through the curriculum of resistance to better understand this approach.

Examples of Learning a Curriculum of Resistance

In learning through a curriculum of resistance, North Star Academy students were made aware of the ideologies and assumptions underlying long-standing sociopolitical, economic, legal, and historical hegemonies in their community, society, and the wider world. School curricula incorporated real-world examples to teach students about power and privilege in a wide variety of sociocultural contexts to cultivate their critical consciousness regarding oppressive systems, structures, and practices. Through this learning, students developed their critical thinking skills and became aware of their agency to affect change. This learning was a process, as most teachers and school leaders were not trained to view teaching and learning as inherently political. When teachers were uncomfortable discussing difficult topics with students, Dr. Ramsey modeled this teaching for teachers and students.

Example 1: Challenging Patriarchy

Dr. Ramsey acknowledged that the Qur'an established the equality of men and women and called for society to uphold women's God-given rights. She also viewed current Western discourses about Muslim women to be one-dimensional, misrepresentative, and reductionist and was prepared to discuss

Table 1 Tripartite Framework

Month	Value	Habit	Examples	Link to Islam
September	Responsibility	Habits 1, 3	Start the year being proactive and know what you are responsible for. By Putting First Things First, you focus on the important tasks you are responsible for as a student, like finishing your classwork at school and homework at home.	*Hadith*: "Every one of you is a shepherd and is responsible for his flock. The leader of the people is a guardian and is responsible for his subjects. A man is the guardian of his family, and he is responsible for them. A woman is the guardian of her husband's home and his children, and she is responsible for them. The servant of a man is a guardian of the property of his master, and he is responsible for it. No doubt, every one of you is a shepherd and is responsible for his flock."
October	Honesty	Habit 2	Being honest about what you can and cannot do when planning. Sometimes, it means saying "no" to some things that do not fit with your big goals and plans.	*Hadith*: "Say the truth even if it is bitter." *Hadith*: "Verily, truthfulness leads to righteousness, and righteousness leads to Paradise." "A man may speak the truth until he is recorded with Allah as truthful."
November	Thankfulness	Habit 7	Being aware and thankful for your physical and mental health, so it is important to Sharpen the Saw.	*Hadith*: "He who does not thank people does not thank Allah." *Hadith*: "There are two blessings that people lose, they are health and free time for doing good."

December	Self-Restraint and Control	Habit 6	Take responsibility for yourself, so you can work together. When we synergize, we have to practice self-control and work in harmony.	*Hadith*: "The strong person is not he (she) who has physical strength, but he (she) that can control his (her) anger." *Hadith*: "Faithful are the believers to each other as the bricks of a wall, supporting and reinforcing each other. The Prophet then interlocked his fingers to gesticulate the meaning." Qur'an: And hold fast to the rope of Allah and be not divided among yourselves; and remember with gratitude Allah's favor and remember with gratitude Allah's favor on you; for you were enemies and He joined your hearts in love so that by his grace you became brethren. – Al Imran, 3:103
January	Fairness and Justice	Habit 4	Sometimes being fair is looking at a 3rd alternative creating a win-win over a win-lose way of thinking. Fair does not always mean equal.	*Hadith*: "If anyone wrongs a person protected by covenant, violates his rights, burdens him with more work than he is able to do, or takes something from him without his consent, then I will be his advocate on the day of Resurrection." Islamic Scholarship: Allah blesses a nation that practices justice, regardless of their faith. - Ibn Taymiah
February	Commitment	Habit 1	Being proactive means being committed to your goals and taking action. I'm committed to doing the right thing, even when no one is looking. I choose my actions, attitudes, and my moods.	*Hadith*: Mus'ab ibn Sa'eed reported: His father asked, "O Messenger of Allah, which people go through calamity most severely?" The messenger of Allah, peace and blessings be upon him said, "They are the prophets, then the next best, then the next best. A man is tried according to his religion. If he is firm in his religion, then his trials will be more severe. If he is weak in his religion, then he is tried according to his strength in religion. The servant will continue to be tried until he is left walking on the earth without any sin."

(*Continued*)

Table 1 (Continued)

Month	Value	Habit	Examples	Link to Islam
March	Generosity	Habit 4	Give of yourself, your time, and your energy. If I help others win, I win as well.	*Hadith*: "The Generosity is near to Allah, near to Paradise, near to the people, and far from the Hellfire. The Miser is far from Allah, far from Paradise, far from the people, and near to the Hellfire. An ignorant generous person is more beloved to Allah the Exalted than a stingy scholar."
April	Respect	Habit 5	We show respect to others when we listen first before sharing our point.	*Hadith*: "He who does not show mercy to our young ones or recognize the rights of our elders is not one of us." *Hadith*: "Who is most deserving of my good company?" The Prophet said, "Your mother." The man asked, "Then who?" The Prophet said, "Your mother." The man asked again, "Then who?" The Prophet said, "Your mother." The man asked again, "Then who?" The Prophet said, "Your father."
May–June	Kindness and Care	Habits 4, 5	When we practice Habits 4 and 5, we are showing kindness and care to others because we are not only thinking of ourselves but thinking of others.	*Hadith*: "Whoever has the quality of kindness has been given his portion of goodness. And whoever is deprived of the quality of kindness has been deprived of his portion of goodness." *Hadith*: "Verily, kindness is not found in anything except that it beautifies it, and it is not removed from anything except that it disgraces it." *Hadith*: "The one who cares for an orphan and me will be together in paradise like this," and he held his two fingers together to illustrate.

misogyny, sexism, and patriarchy with students, teachers, and parents as required. She did not want teachers to avoid these important discussions; however, not all teachers were comfortable discussing these subjects in the classroom.

Dr. Ramsey shared a recent event: "A middle school student asked his teacher about the legal problems of R. Kelly, the singer, songwriter, and record producer. The teacher told the class, 'Well, I used to like his music, but he was arrested for sexual assault.' One of the boys in the class said, 'She deserved it' or 'She was asking for it!' This angered the teacher. She shared with the class that this was personal to her and that blaming women for sexual violence was inappropriate. I learned about the incident the following day. I asked the teacher, 'Why didn't you tell me? Why didn't you come forward?' She was a brand-new teacher. She didn't know my style. She said, 'I just wanted to close the subject. I realized that it had opened up and gotten into a place, and I just wanted to end it.' I said, 'Yes, but what he said was so wrong and pervasive in male thinking. This needs to be a topic of discussion.'

"The students are like my kids. How would I want it handled if that was my son or my daughter in that classroom? I just went from there. I went to the classroom and tried to be honest with students that this type of thinking and behavior was a reality. I talked about how 25 percent of women are sexually molested or assaulted by the time they're fifteen and sixteen years old. I pointed out that in this room, there would be two of us that were victims of sexual assault. The bottom line is that she's a new teacher who knows how the story could get twisted, and she's not Muslim. I talked to the students about gender and male privilege, what women have to deal with, and the Me-Too movement. I said to the students, 'Even if she wore nothing walking down the street, it's not an invitation to be touched.' I had to be very clear about what was okay and what was not okay. I allowed this space to be a space for us to talk. I said to the student who made the comment, 'Look, it's not about you because what you said reflects society. So, thank you for saying it because it opened this conversation. You'll never step into that mistake again. Right? Maybe you can stop others from stepping into the same mistake.' I expect in this environment that we're going to have the diversity of behaviors and the diversity of values that you would find anywhere. Our kids need to be discerning, even in this environment."

As we continued with our fieldwork and interviews, we learned that freedom of pedagogy was not taken in a lighthearted manner. Challenging subjects had to be broached and teachers had to be willing to open spaces for dialogue. The lower school Islamic studies teacher, Ms. Shireen Elmohamady, shared a question she received from a parent. She explained, "A parent approached me after school earlier this week. She asked, 'Why do you keep talking about current events?' I had to explain. I said, 'Well, part of our identity and our role as Muslims is to be concerned for humanity, to be concerned about social justice issues.'" Communication with parents created opportunities to share that schooling embodies formal and informal ways of acquiring knowledge and skills.

Example 2: Challenging Economic Injustice

For the older primary and middle school students, North Star Academy integrated service learning and community outreach projects into the curricula. Ms. Fatemi mentioned the primary school's project of collecting and providing food for individuals experiencing housing insecurity in San Rico. She explained, "It is important that our students learn what is going on in their local community. These experiences teach not only restorative justice but also the actual language of justice." We felt it important to talk with the fifth and sixth-grade students about how they learned about fairness and justice. We asked Joury, a fifth-grade student, her thoughts, "Our teachers want us to be good Muslims. But they also want us to be overall good human beings. They take us places, such as when they took us to feed the homeless." Working and contributing to a social cause taught students to be civically minded, engaged, and in this case, aware of poverty in their community.

Dr. Ramsey explained their volunteer activities: "During Ramadan, we do canned food drives in the younger grades. The older students help *Uplift Charity*, a Muslim organization that boxes and delivers food to thousands of Muslims the Saturday before Ramadan. The students package rice, oil, a box of dates, and things families need for Ramadan. It's like a starter kit for Ramadan. Our older kids help with boxing."

Mr. Anwar Hassan, North Star Academy's board chair, proudly spoke of the school's engagement programs with the community. He listed a few off the top of his head: "For our local community, we volunteer at Harvest Food Bank and Second Harvest. We've raised money for the *Great Bedtime Story Pajama Drive*. Our older students made and donated hygiene kits. We do quite a few things. We have an *Eid* toy drive. We ask parents that when shopping for *Eid*, to buy a toy for a Muslim in need who won't get a present." He also discussed passion projects, which he described as "taking your passion and paying it forward." He spoke to us about a unique opportunity that students used for their passion project: "We had an alumna come back and visit North Star Academy. She founded an organization that helps refugees in Syria. She said, 'I want to partner with you.' We asked students to write a proposal for their passion project and consider donating to this alumna's organization. Then, we put students into groups based on their interests. Each group had to design their own flyers and develop a marketing plan. They had to contact affiliate organizations that could support their project. All of this was student-driven.

"Students decided which organization their work would benefit from. One group worked with the alumna. Another loved baking, and they helped through a bake sale to support a senior center. The boys hosted a basketball tournament and sold food. The money earned went to a youth basketball club. I do remember that one organization that we work with, *Tia*, helps refugees. It's a local organization. Another group did a book drive. And then, another group did a wardrobe drive. Through these various opportunities, students learned about economic justice and the importance of working to reduce poverty."

Example 3: Challenging Discourses

While walking around the school, we noticed three photocopied black-and-white pictures of Malcolm X taped onto a classroom whiteboard. When we spoke to the seventh- and eighth-grade students later that day, we asked them about the pictures of Malcolm X. Zayn, who had attended North Star Academy since grade four, explained, "We just had a conversation about Black rights and how neither a Black is better than a White and a White's no better than a Black. But Malcolm X believed that Blacks were supposed to be better than Whites, but then he found Islam and realized this was wrong, and that everybody is equal."

Joury added, "I think it honestly goes both ways, I know some people, even Muslims, who are stereotypical about Christians and Jews. I know Jews and Christians who are stereotypical about Muslims and other religions. They probably don't even know because they haven't had any experiences with either religion. North Star Academy teachers teach us to not be biased or stereotypical. We are to talk to the person and get to know their faith. They teach us not to judge others or group them together and think, 'I don't like any of the Jews.'"

Ms. Barbara Street, the seventh-grade English teacher, shared, "I don't hide information from them. That's why I like teaching older grades. I'm real with them. For example, if a terrorist attack happened, we would talk about it. I would say to them, 'This is not Islam.' I would emphasize to my students why it's so important for us to be excellent in our ways and in the practice of our faith. I always share the quote by Dr. Salah, 'Excellence can't be discriminated against.'

I don't say that the terrorists are not Muslims. What I do say is that this is not Islam. There is no benefit in focusing on the terrorists. That is a waste. My reply was, 'No, this is not Islam, period—done.' I'm always thinking about what is right, but I don't think there is always a right answer. It depends on the situation. I say to my students, 'You know what? I don't know.' I have to be okay with that answer. When I'm okay with that answer, my students will hopefully see that it is okay to not know."

Joury also shared a discussion held in her seventh-grade Islamic studies class. "We were talking about the football player Colin Kaepernick. He was the guy who kneeled when the national anthem was sung before the start of football games to protest injustice and police brutality. I think it was courageous of him, but there are a lot of different opinions about him kneeling. We discussed the different opinions. We also discussed Nike's decision to continue sponsoring him. Kaepernick's decision to protest cost him his career and a lot of money. But he protested anyway." Daniel, Joury's classmate, added, "I agree with Joury. Nike lost a lot of money, but they did the right thing supporting Colin Kaepernick."

Guns, gun ownership, and gun violence were also critical discourses. Ms. Farah Rafiq, the upper school Islamic studies director, shared her thoughts about an incursion her students attended about guns. She spoke of the event: "We had 'Every Town for Gun Safety' come and speak to our students. We talked about gun laws, gun safety, and gun sense. They gave a whole presentation, and the kids' questions were surprising. I was thinking, 'Oh my gosh! They are thinking!' It made me realize that the thoughts they have are so deep. I said to myself, 'Why don't we give them more opportunities to talk and ask questions?' Every single time we have a presentation, I always think, 'Gosh! I just wish families could be a fly on the wall here because they'd be blown away.' Really, it's powerful."

Amir, whose favorite subject was history, said, "In history, our teacher really likes talking about politics. She likes having discussions with us about what we think about certain people in politics." Amariyah added, "We talk about Trump and current events. About a month ago, when the elections were coming, we talked about all the people that were running for office and the Muslim women that were running too." Current events were often the entré to analyzing challenging discourses. Jana, a grade five student, shared, "One of the current issues we just learned about is the Guatemalan people in South America trying to come into the United States. Donald Trump allowed the border patrol to use teargas on them. Two children were killed. We discussed how these actions are unacceptable and that Trump is not considering their situation. We should always care and be active in our community and watch the news."

Daniel, a student at North Star Academy for eight years, added, "Also, in Islamic studies, we learned about the Muslims in China. They are being put into concentration camps and are being tortured. China is basically trying to brainwash them to reduce the amount of Islam in China." Ms. Street mentioned how important it was to teach students media literacy in order for them to become critical consumers of information. "I tell my students that the news might look at certain people and say, 'These people aren't good people.' We discuss the issue in class. I feel connected when I teach them about current events. I feel that it changes their opinion and their point of view, both on different people and on how they perceive what society says about them as Muslims."

From our interviews with teachers and students, it was clear to us that the students were eager to discuss challenging subjects. They wanted to know about the world in which they lived and understand the myriad injustices they observed daily. Yet, not all lessons and class discussions were problem-free. Politics, on occasion, caused friction and complications between parents and teachers.

Resisting the Curriculum of Resistance

North Star Academy's curriculum of resistance was not consistently implemented by teachers. Ms. Davis, who was in her second year of teaching at North Star Academy, shared, "I taught in first grade last year. I planned for the students to write a letter to President Trump. That did not go over well. It became this huge discussion in my classroom of first graders. 'You know he hates Muslims, and he doesn't like us.' I didn't know what to say. I eventually told my students, 'You don't have to be nice. You can tell him what you don't like in a polite way.' One of my female students said, 'What if he reads my letter and tears it up because I'm Muslim?' I had to pinch myself. I was going to cry. I thought, she's six, and this is the beginning of the year. We always write a letter as part of our curriculum. For years I've had students write the president. I reflected on this and said to myself, 'Wow, at this age, this is what she feels?' I jumped ship. We did not write to the president. There was just too much emotion. They were six years old. I didn't want to have to draft a letter explaining. In the end, I decided to have the students write to Kids Bop. We love Kids Bop, and that went over great. We just switched paths. Now I am teaching third grade, and the students and I have had lots of conversations about character traits. My students always bring up Trump and how they think he feels about Muslims. They always say that Trump sees them negatively. As for the letter writing, it was awkward for me. I see where they're coming from and agree in ways, but I don't want to start a big political battle in my classroom. When the issue comes up, I change the subject and let the topic fizzle out. I don't know how to address it correctly. I've never thought about bringing it to the leadership of our school. I did find that my students raised these issues over the last few years. They broke into a lot of 'boo Trump, boo Trump' in my classroom."

Ms. McLean, the third-grade teacher, reflected, "I tell my students that everyone is entitled to their own opinion. You may not agree, but to a certain extent, Trump is our commander-in-chief. He is the president of our country. We need to show some sort of respect toward that and then move on, focus on what we're learning." Ms. Davis replied, "Cindy, you are better than me. I never said we should respect the president. I was like, 'I agree with you.' Then I said, 'Okay, let's get back to our vocabulary words.'"

Toward a Pedagogy of Freedom

At North Star Academy, not all teachers were comfortable or had the skills to undertake pedagogical freedom. For example, Ms. Davis did not create space for the students to express their thoughts through letter writing, especially when she knew her students had strong feelings about Trump and the injustices of his presidency. Instead, she chose to redirect students to the "safer" learning of the California state curriculum and letter writing to Kids Bop. It was easier to ignore the issue and choose the path of least resistance to avoid discomfort. Teacher resistance to broaching uncomfortable topics did not always reach Dr. Ramsey's desk, but when it did, Dr. Ramsey was forthright in coaching leaders and/or modeling pedagogical freedom for teachers and students. Dr. Ramsey shared that she wanted teachers to engage students in authentic discussions to help them understand what it means to be American and to "navigate those parts of American culture that may push against what it means to be Muslim."

Dr. Ramsey acknowledged that the school was on a pedagogical journey. At the heart of this journey was a profound and all-encompassing focus on justice and freedom. Dr. Ramsey trusted her teachers to make the right decisions but also acknowledged that it was difficult for them to be leaders in their own right, leaders in their classrooms. She supported their pedagogical freedom to create meaningful, authentic, and spiritually linked learning opportunities for students to understand and learn how to confront injustice (*zulm*). Yet, to achieve this, students, along with the whole school community, needed opportunities to critically examine and question. Trusting teachers with pedagogical freedom was Dr. Ramsey's approach to developing fully engaged and socially just American Muslims—Dr. Ramsey just needed all teachers to trust the journey.

5

Freedom for Conflict

By facilitating freedom for conflict, the school community creates valuable opportunities to address challenges through accountability, open dialogue, empathy, and forgiveness.

Conflict is present in Islamic schools. In the near decade of empirical research, we've conducted in Islamic schools worldwide, we've found that conflict arises from inter/intra-religious divisions in the school and the wider Muslim community (*ummah*). These ideological divisions manifest in schools as diverging perceptions of right and wrong, differing interpretations of gendered behavior, conflicting goals, opposing interests, and the perpetuation of intragroup racism. In addition, the existence of intentional and unintentional microaggressions, the subtle slights that communicate social exclusion or oppression to a marginalized group or an individual, are also present in Islamic schools and affect individuals psychologically, socially, pedagogically, and physically. These disagreements, arguments, clashes, and disputes are further compounded by inadequate communication, poor staff selection, cultural and linguistic differences, lack of planning, and inequitable resourcing of schools and classrooms. If left unaddressed, extant conflict creates toxic Islamic school cultures that inordinately focus on rules, punishment, and compliance at the expense of enacting a global faith founded on Prophet Muhammad's teachings of kindness, forgiveness, altruism, and compassion.

The Qur'an asserts the importance of resolving conflict peacefully, no matter the cause: the recompense for an injury is an injury equal thereto (in degree); but if a person forgives and makes reconciliation, his reward is due from Allah: for (Allah) loveth not those who do wrong (Qur'an, 42:40). Reconciliation, and the re-establishment of harmonious relationships, is the preferred approach to resolving conflicts between individuals and their families in Islam. In Islamic schools, however, the ability for school leaders to develop and sustain positive school cultures requires both the understanding and the ability to enact the prophetic tradition of resolving conflicts through patience, deep listening, honest dialogue, mediation and/or arbitration, accountability, and forgiveness. At North Star Academy, conflict is viewed as an avenue for socio-emotional learning, the re/establishment of community, and oftentimes, necessary change. This chapter presents conflict ir/resolution from the perspectives of North Star Academy's leaders, teachers, and students.

Laying the Foundational Skills for Conflict Resolution

Ms. Fatemi, the lower school director, met us at the front door. As we followed Ms. Fatemi to her office, we said a quick hello to Wendy, sitting at her desk sorting papers. Ms. Fatemi offered us tea and coffee, and we both agreed that coffee sounded good. It was cold, overcast, and drizzling. Ms. Fatemi's office was at the end of a long hallway. The one window looked out onto the parking lot. The room was dark. We stood quietly and looked around the room. She had several plants on the windowsill, a large desk, and a tall filing cabinet. A picture of her two children sat on her desk. There was a stained whiteboard behind her desk that looked well-used. Ms. Fatemi returned with two coffees and turned on the light. The fluorescent lights flickered and buzzed as if they too were affected by the gloomy day. We took a seat in the two chairs facing her desk. As we sat down, we noticed another Zones of Regulation poster. This poster was larger than the ones hanging in the classrooms. Miriam asked, "How do you use this poster?"

"We brought in the zones program two years ago, and this gives our younger students the language to communicate their thoughts and feelings. For instance, if you're in the red zone, you are angry. You might be aggressive. You might be mad and want to yell. In the yellow zone, you might be silly. You might be frustrated, or you might be excited. I think this poster helps students build empathy. Our kinder and first-grade teams have been diving deep into this learning. In fact, this is their social studies curriculum.

"Kids need to learn social skills and develop emotional intelligence. These posters help our children develop an awareness of what they are feeling, but the kids are not free to just have that feeling either. How they feel and behave has consequences. If you push somebody, you'll hurt their feelings. How are you going to fix it? That's the big question. If it's an emotional issue, a lot of times our students will say, 'I'm sorry.' But our teachers push students a bit further. They will say, 'Okay. Now let's talk on a deeper level about giving an apology.' 'I'm sorry because' . . . 'I did it because' . . . 'Next time I will' . . . and . . . 'What can I do to make it better now?' That's the key part. The kids know to say sorry, but we want students to ask, 'What can I do now?' It's nice with the younger set because often their answer is, 'I just want a hug, or a thank you note would be nice.'

We're trying to teach our kids how to be leaders. We're also trying to teach them how to practice our faith in a very organic way. This morning, Muna and I were meeting about re-enrollment. For the families leaving, we hear all kinds of feedback—all the negative comments, not the positive—because they need to justify why they've decided to leave. We often have families say they are leaving because there is not enough focus on Islamic studies. Yet, socio-emotional learning is the core of Islam to me! Islamic studies include teaching about justice, injustice, conflict, being nice, and being kind. That's what we're pushing."

"What is the Wheel of Choice poster hanging opposite The Zones of Regulation poster?" asked Miriam while taking a sip of coffee.

"We started with the Wheel of Choice ten years ago. It is related to Positive Discipline. We notice that the parents are still having trouble with the concept. They don't understand it to this day. We've had it for ten years! Parents don't understand not having consequences for bad behavior. That's not the case though. It just means we are not going to punish a child for the sake of getting even. We are going to give a student a logical consequence. It's a hard program to implement because it's done on a case-by-case basis. It's not a formulaic system. It has to be led by teachers who are trained in Positive Discipline. We try to teach our teachers, but they struggle. If a teacher has been in the public school system, they are taught a rewards-based behavior program. They are told to use rewards in their classrooms. Token economies! Clip charts! To take all those tools away from a teacher and say, 'Just talk to the students.' Even our teachers are like, 'Are you crazy?' There are some who've done it, and those teachers are the ones who have the best outcomes with the students."

Looking at the Wheel of Choice poster, it was quite simple. In the center was a large pie chart with specific behaviors in each pie piece accompanied by a picture. The choices on the poster in Ms. Fatemi's office were to apologize, walk away, have a class meeting, use an I message, tell them to stop, count to ten to cool off, go to another game, and shake hands and take turns. The Wheel of Choice focused on solutions to conflict and seemed simple. We wondered why there was trouble with its implementation and parental support and understanding.

Ms. Fatemi continued, "Our students generate the choices. The focus then becomes, 'What's your solution?' If a student is having an argument with another student about who gets the ball, our teachers will ask them, 'What's your solution? What do you want to do?' For me, I'm not going to give students the answers. They have to come up with something, and we try it. That's restorative justice. If you've been wronged, the person who did the wrong has to take responsibility. By and large, kids don't take responsibility because of the fear of punishment. They don't want to get busted.

"I believe in restorative justice. I've been reading a little bit about it, and I think our Positive Discipline program is a solution-based conflict resolution approach. When a kid does something wrong, I can't just give him or her a consequence and sit down. You're punished! You get detention! When you commit a mistake, you have to fix it. How are you going to fix it if you don't have awareness? Our discipline philosophy is that the child will do something right. Either we'll catch them making a mistake and have a conversation with them right then and there or a child will come up to a teacher and say, 'So and so pushed me. So and so grabbed my ball' . . . or whatever their problem is, right? We will sit down. The pushing is a little sensitive because, again, if it's a pattern, if it's aggressive, it is hurtful. That I can't ignore. But if it's playground stuff and they grab the ball, or they push another kid, I'm not going to detain the kid or give them detention at their grade level. We want both sides to talk about what happened. We will ask the wrongdoer, 'Why did you do this?' More than half the time, they'll have a reason: 'You took my ball! Because you weren't listening! Because I used my words, and you ignored me!'

"A scenario played out this year that I'll share. In a kindergarten class, the teacher was leading a lesson on Martin Luther King Jr. and Rosa Parks. The teacher also presented the story of Bilal from our history. Bilal was a Black slave, and he was freed by our Prophet. Even though he was freed, he refused to leave the Prophet's side. He ended up being a leader within the community of early Islam. Now, this teacher told the students about Bilal being treated unjustly and being freed by the compassion of our Prophet. Well, it's a kinder lesson, so I don't know how much she said . . . but one of the children said to another, 'You're brown!' That child went home and told her parents, 'So and so called me brown and ugly!' He didn't call her ugly, but the child felt that way. The parents took it to the ninth degree and went a little crazy. We thought, 'We can't believe this is happening!' The parents contacted the teacher that taught the lesson. They also contacted the other kindergarten teacher. They contacted me. Then, they went straight to Muna. It was like, 'Wow, this is an out-of-control situation.' Why? Because the child is feeling hurt and the parents are protecting their child."

"Was the child African American?" inquired Miriam.

"No. My shade. They were of some Asian background," Ms. Fatemi said, pointing to her arm. "The parents went to the WhatsApp parent group and wrote, 'The school needs to provide . . .' We did, in that case. We said to the parents, 'Children are curious.' In response to this event, I read *The Color of Us* to the students and brought multicolored crayons to represent our skin. We talked about how we're all different shades. That was a way to show the parents that we were not ignoring their concerns."

Ms. Fatemi leaned back in her chair. She looked to the ceiling as if considering what to say next. She continued, "I've had different parents who've been angry over the years. It's hard for me. I am a people pleaser. I've had to work on how not to jump into rescue mode. Even now, with all my years of sitting in this office, it's tough. I think I am getting better every year. Just last week, I had to call a parent and say, 'Sorry to inform you, your child caused injury. I need your help and support. I could punish them here, but it's not going to go very far. I need your help.' The mom, thankfully, was very understanding. She said, 'That's not acceptable. I'm going to punish him! He did this because he's in Tae Kwon Do! Maybe I'll pull him out of the class.' I replied, 'You don't have to pull him out of Tae Kwon Do. But, he needs to understand that he can't kick and hit people at school.'

"The mom got on board. She said, 'I'm going to create a behavior chart for him.' I said, 'Okay. We don't do a behavior chart unless it's needed because we're trying to give a child room to grow.' Then the mom wanted to know the name of the child who was hurt. She said, 'I'll call the parents. Can you tell me who?' Now, I can't tell them because it's confidential. I said, 'I can't tell you, but your child can. If you don't have their number, let me know. I'll be happy to pass your information on to them.' In the end, the parents knew each other and talked over the weekend.

"Now comes Monday. I thought, 'Everything fell into place, and the other parent hasn't contacted Muna to complain.' All weekend long, I was expecting an email. However, Monday afternoon, the dad of the boy who caused the injury called me. Now, I've already dealt with his wife, who gave me the impression that they were very supportive. Yet, the dad said to me, 'Thank you. I understand we already took care of the situation, but I want to talk to you about a pattern I'm noticing. You need to do more. You need to offer students rewards for good behavior.' He was instructing me on behavior management! That's a tricky situation. It was nice that he took the time to call, but I'm not going to change my approach because he wants a different method. I thanked him and said, 'I understand your concern. Patterns are really good to observe. What I need the most from you, though, is for you to attend to your child rather than attending to me and calling a parent meeting and raising the alarm.' I talked to the child, and he was remorseful. I'm not going to suspend a second grader! That's what the parents were probably expecting. I stood my ground.

"Education is the only field where every parent feels like an expert. They feel free to give advice—not recognizing that we are experts. We know more because we stay up to date. I respect parents and never make them feel like they're stupid or dumb. They have the right to express their thoughts and opinions. But just because they share an opinion does not mean that I'm going to switch everything . . . but sometimes I do. I'll give you an example of a parent who was dissatisfied with the Arabic and Qur'an classes.

"Arabic and Qur'an classes were aligned with each child's level of understanding. This year, we couldn't provide that leveling because we've split into two campuses. We felt the students were young enough, but the demographics and dynamics of this particular child's class prevented the group from doing well. I said to the concerned parent, 'I understand your frustration, and I'll look into it.' I was able to fix the situation. We needed to improve how we were teaching Arabic. In the end, we have to take each issue individually.

"I learned that from Muna. She's a great role model. Too many staff would come to Muna with a problem and ask her to solve it. I follow Muna's style and ask, 'Do you want help with this, or do you have an idea?' Sometimes, staff just need help. When I was a new leader, I recognized that when I asked my staff, 'What's your idea?' They became annoyed! 'I came to you with a problem, and you are supposed to help me!' Now, I typically respond to teachers' questions with, 'Do you have any ideas on how you want to solve the problem? I want to hear from you first.' When I was a teacher, I listened to the concerns of the parents. I didn't argue my point. I think I've always been a contemplative person. My family would say, 'You listen well, and for a leader, that's very important. A teacher is a leader, Layla.' Teaching was where I gained my initial experiences in leadership. I'd listen to parents, and then I would give my take on whatever it was they were saying. When I stepped into formal leadership, I put myself in their shoes. In fact, now that I am a mother, I walk in their shoes, too."

Seeing Conflict as an Opportunity

"There is a belief that I'm a dictator," commented Dr. Ramsey. "I hear conflicting stories all of the time. I'm not a dictator. I'm just trying to identify a solution that is balanced and in the best interest of the kids in the long run. That's my central focus."

We sat in Dr. Ramsey's office later that same morning. She sat at her desk, and we sat opposite her in two chairs. A computer monitor blocked Melanie's view, so she moved her chair closer to Miriam. "That's better," said Melanie while reaching into her backpack for her notebook. Concerned for time, Miriam asked Dr. Ramsey to continue.

"I know that some people say, 'Oh when you go into Muna's office, you will walk out happy.' Others have said, 'It doesn't matter what you say to Muna; she's going to do what she wants to do.' I often have parents who come to me with their concerns, such as, "We want more Arabic. You need to dedicate more time to Arabic and less to art!' I'll have another group of parents who say the opposite, 'Please, less Arabic! I feel like Arabic is useless. They've read the Qur'an. That's enough! If children have enough Arabic to decode the words, why are we still teaching them Arabic?' My approach is to listen and take into consideration what they are saying. For example, maybe Arabic doesn't have to be ten hours a week. Maybe four hours is enough. In this case, I need to identify a happy medium and try to stay in that groove. Not to please everybody—because both sides are not pleased. But the solution I arrive at is typically in the middle of the road. I want to give kids something unique while, at the same time, not taking away from what is valuable. Most schools will dictate right and wrong without giving any kind of flexibility. It is really hard. I'm an educator, so I see everything as an opportunity to learn."

Dr. Ramsey's tone was serious. Miriam asked, "How do you make decisions? Do you have something like a 'kitchen cabinet' that you consult?"

"Yes. We have the North Star Academy Parent Association for the upper school. The president and a few of the members are trusted parents that have been around for a while and are part of the association. I listen to them. They are a microcosm of the greater school. When I ask them a question, I might get two different responses. But, at least, it is an opportunity to engage and share what I am thinking. It allows me to reflect on my thinking and identify if I might have missed something. I also reach out to a couple of staff members because they are parents too. They might have a pulse on what is happening or what people are thinking. Then there is the school board and the board chairman, in particular. I meet regularly with him."

"So when you are trying to balance all of this stuff, where does the idea of social justice play in all of that?" asked Miriam.

"I see it with the kids more than anything else. The kids know they can access me when things go wrong. In fact, there were two students who wanted to meet with me yesterday, and I promised I would call them into my office today. I'll listen to what they have to say, and then I'll ask them questions. Usually, I don't deal with problems globally. Maybe I could do a better job of that. I deal with problems and conflicts individually. I'll listen to what the student has to say, and I'll ask him or her questions. 'You know, is this something you just want to share with me? Or is this something you want to be solved?' If the student says they want it solved, I ask, 'Would it help if I called that other person in and you guys worked it out together?' They might say, 'Yes,' or 'No.' If it is a no, I ask the student if they want to practice what they would say or do if the problem happened again. I try to go through a process of not taking over."

"It sounds a bit like the Socratic Method, where you focus on asking questions," commented Melanie.

"Yes," said Dr. Ramsey. "However, I do need to offer things sometimes. It depends on the circumstance. It depends on the conflict. If a student says to me, 'So-and-so called me a name,' I bring the two students into my office. My office provides them privacy to talk about their disagreement. Each child is given the time to speak about what they didn't like or why they are upset or hurt. I want to give students a voice, and I'll open the space for them to talk. Sometimes, though, students come in wanting to use my power. Does that make sense? I don't let this happen. I do this by not taking over the conversation. I inherently know that there are always two sides to a story. Something might have happened right before the name-calling incident that shaped the way something was said or understood. It's believing in the humanity of the kids and bringing them together."

Dr. Ramsey continued without pausing. "Parents. I have a hard time with parents. Parents are very protective and emotionally engaged. They are paying the school money, and they have a tendency to think, 'I'm paying, and you need to do what I say.' I think it's harder to have that . . . I don't know . . . I'm not as good with parents because they bring these elements into a space, and that almost forces me to posture a little bit. I don't have to do that with the kids. I wish I didn't have to do that with the parents. I wish I could do the same thing with the parents where I provide a space to allow them to talk an issue through, making it a reflective conversation."

"But they might not be reflective," commented Melanie.

"Right. They come into my office wanting something. They believe that I owe it to them because they are paying for it, right? So, I just absorb what they are saying, and if I find an opening, then I'm able to maneuver and impart some other ideas . . . but not always. That's the truth. It depends on what is going on."

"One of the issues that come to mind as I listen to you talk is the challenge of interfaith activities. Does this cause problems with some of the parents?" asked Melanie.

"I don't think so," answered Dr. Ramsey. "We are a unique school. We are not going to take every—" Dr. Ramsey corrected herself. "Not every kid is going to come here. Parents who choose to enroll their student at North Star are parents with a particular slant. A parent who expects a more cocooned environment is going to find a school that offers that type of atmosphere. That type of parent wouldn't be okay with more than half of our staff being of another faith tradition if religious diversity is an issue. They would want a school that only hires Muslims."

"Do you participate in activities with other schools, like a Jewish school or a—"

Dr. Ramsey interjected, "We used to. I hate to say that I don't know how much value those activities have, to be honest with you. I feel they got more out of it than we did because we acknowledge their faith already. We recognize them as brothers and sisters in faith, so to speak. Or cousins in faith. They don't see us in that way, though. It's been very interesting, our experiences with interfaith issues. We are not always the same size school, so sometimes we are not well matched in terms of class size. For one interfaith program, we combined our fifth and sixth grades. Yet, the other school had hundreds of kids in the fifth and sixth grades. We had only thirty-five kids combined. Our work with the Jewish school tends to be more engaging because we can relate with them on a lot of different things. Even in terms of religious practices, I think we align closely. But then you have the political tension. We did experience that with one school. The one Jewish school we had a great relationship with, well, they ended up closing down, but they were similar to us. Progressive. Then we went to a more Zionist school that is nearby. We tried to do the same activities, but we could tell that there was a little bit of tension coming from their side, not from ours. It was not us."

"So, you put that on hold for now?" asked Melanie.

"I think so. Our kids have interfaith experiences all the time. Every day, in this environment, and for the rest of their lives."

Miriam replied, "So, you're saying that the school doesn't need to look outward, that the school's got it here?"

"We've got it here, and that is serving a good purpose. Our kids already know. They live in the world. They know about Easter and Christmas. No one needs to teach them about that. On the converse side, most people don't know about

Eid. They don't understand Ramadan. They know there is fasting, but they don't really know what that entails. If we are coming together to do something, I need to know that our kids are getting something out of it too. In the past, I questioned if interfaith activities were worth our time. I'd rather the time be spent on teaching. Just to be clear—that doesn't mean that I don't value diversity. They are just getting it already."

"Can I circle back and ask about how you handle conflict with a parent?" asked Miriam.

If I have a parent who comes forward and says, 'This girl is exposing my child to blah . . . blah . . . blah,' I say, 'Well, great. That girl is actually gifting you with the knowledge that your daughter is a follower. So, what are you going to do to fortify your kid? How are you going to teach her so that she doesn't get easily sucked in? She's going to be! Not in this environment but in other environments. She's going to be exposed to things that don't align with your belief system.' These are very hard conversations. There are some parents who respond, 'This isn't what I signed up for, I'm out.' I'm okay with that. I understand. It's literally holding the families' hands through these points of conflict. It's not always successful, but I think I see the end game.

"Parents are so focused on the here and now. I'm more future-oriented, 'Oh my gosh, in five years, they'll be in college, and you'll have no control. You have five years to teach them this! I see conflict resolution as informing their life trajectory. Parents often want me to separate kids who are in conflict. They might say, 'I want them away from that today!' My response is no. Conflict gives you an opportunity to teach your child something. This even happens with teachers. I had a teacher who said, 'Oh, that has gelatin in it! She can't eat it!' I replied, 'Her parent packed that lunch. It's not on you to say what they're allowed to eat and what they're not allowed to eat.'

"Many of our kids have visited me after they've left North Star Academy for middle school or high school. Often, they tell me about a time one of their teachers said something wrong about Islam. Our kids have had to face telling the teacher and correcting them on Islam: 'No, that's not right.' Even my daughter at university was taking a religion class where the instructor said that a requirement for being Muslim is that you have to know Arabic! I guess, amidst all the misinformation, assumptions, and the media, our kids are finding themselves having to make the choice between speaking up or just shaking their heads. To help prepare them to speak up, I'll listen to what they say. Then, I'll ask questions. 'Is this something you want to share with me so that only I know?' 'Is this something that you want to be solved?' If they say they want it solved, my response is typically, 'Would it help if I called that other person into my office and you guys worked it out together?' They might say, 'yes,' 'no,' or 'I'm afraid.' Depending on their response, I ask, 'Then, how can I help? Do you want to practice what you would say if they said something like that to you again? I could pretend to be you, and you could pretend to be me.'

"It's important that the teachers have a space to talk about issues that come up. So, we do Monday huddles. All of the teachers come together to connect for about fifteen minutes every Monday. We cover anything that is happening that week, any announcements, clarifications, or reminders for our faculty and staff. The Monday huddles serve as a platform for teachers to raise issues or problems. For example, during lunchtime, the kids were saving balls while they would eat lunch. Someone else would be done with lunch and want the ball. The person saving the ball would not give it to their classmate. These little things pop up. During the Monday huddle, we sit together and problem-solve. This prevents one person from fighting the fight by themselves. We collectively decide on a solution. 'If it's their ball from home, it's their ball. We can't force students to share. Okay, do we all agree? We agree, right? All right. If it's a school ball, we need a bin where the balls are placed. We created a new rule that says balls are not to be touched until students are finished eating.' An issue like this would not normally be on my radar.

—"Monday huddles provide opportunities for faculty and staff to be on the same page. It's also an opportunity for us to celebrate with each other too. Monday huddles are open to anyone who wants to say something. Sometimes people share family information, 'My daughter just got accepted to Stanford.' It has become a space where we build community. I make it as short as possible, so people don't feel burdened. I used to be part of a school where they would make you stay for an hour and a half once a month and that was painful. Now I'm getting them for more than an hour and a half in a month if you add them up, right? But somehow they don't feel it and actually look forward to Monday huddles."

Dr. Ramsey was starting to look tired. Melanie asked, "Maybe one last question for the day?"

"Sure."

"This idea of individual differences, how does that affect your leadership style?"

"I'm not sure what you mean?"

"Let me restate the question," said Melanie. "As a leader, how do you handle diversity within your community that might cause conflict? Such as a grandmother who insists her grandchild prays with socks on."

"Well, that goes back to what I said about making space for the home to dictate what is and is not okay for each individual student. Simple things, such as *zabiha*. 'Oh, they are eating something they are not supposed to eat.' We reply, 'If your mom said you can't eat that, then you can't. But if her mom said she could eat it, then she can. It allows space for those differences. There are a lot of little examples. Halloween. Some people don't believe in celebrating Halloween because you are threatening your neighbors by doing a trick or a treat. That's not aligned with our faith. Having a dog as a pet. It's not on me or the teachers to say what students are allowed to eat or how to practice their faith. We have to grab these teachable moments and be very clear about what is okay and what is not. The key is having the space to talk about it."

Learning to Live with Conflict

That afternoon, we ate lunch with the seventh- and eighth-grade students. The hallways were noisy. Students entered the boardroom, threw their lunch bags on the table, and hurled their bodies into the seats. Students arrived out of breath. A wave of mixed food smell penetrated the room as they unzipped and opened their sack lunches. We had met the students earlier in the week and so jumped right into our first question. Miriam asked, "What current issues do you talk about in school?"

Amir raised his hand. Miriam nodded, giving him the signal that he had the floor. "We learned from Shaykh Tarek that the Guatemalan people in South America are trying to come to our country. Donald Trump used teargas on them and killed two children. Shaykh was telling us how those actions aren't acceptable and how Trump is not looking at the situation from the perspective of the Guatemalan people. He also said that we should always care about and be active in our community, telling us to watch the news because then we can stay informed."

Zain spoke next. "There are different perspectives. There is disagreement about the Guatemalan people at the border of Mexico. Many people agree to keep them out of the US. They want to protect their American jobs and children. They could also be agreeing with Donald Trump, who is spreading the stereotype that all Mexicans are rapists, or all Mexicans are going to steal our jobs, or all Mexicans are going to ruin our country. Then there is the other side that sees the importance of human rights. Where there are two sides, one side might be right, and one side might be wrong. But everybody always thinks . . . or mostly thinks . . . that their side is right. So that's where the problem lies."

"Can I add one more example?" asked Zain. Miriam nodded again. "In Islamic studies, we learned about the Muslims in China being detained. I think they are being put into concentration camps and tortured. The Chinese are basically trying to brainwash the Muslims to reduce the amount of Islam in China."

Amir swallowed a large bite of his sandwich. He started talking while taking a drink from his juice box, "Yeah . . . and when there are terrorist attacks and the terrorists actually kill someone, they're not Muslim anymore. Terrorists don't follow the Muslim rules, so they are automatically not Muslim—even though they say they're Muslim." Amir took a deep breath. "I had this great idea. When I was about to sleep, I called my parents into my bedroom to share this idea. I really wanted to do it, and I told Zain about it and asked him to join me. My idea is to audition for *America's Got Talent*. I know it's a talent show, but in our audition, we will start off with funny things, like pretending we have talent, and we perform, but then we'd tell them the true story about Islam and the 9/11 attacks. We'd explain that the terrorists are not Muslims. Because *America's Got Talent* auditions are on television around the world, we want to express that Muslims would never do that sort of thing. It even states specifically in the Qur'an that Muslims are not allowed to physically hurt people just for fun."

Musa added, "Like Amir said about *America's Got Talent*, my concern is that the people watching won't believe him. So, maybe he could get a well-known person to speak about this with him. Maybe people will think, 'Oh, this person is saying something. They're obviously famous, so maybe they know what's right.' It's sometimes scary because people might believe what the terrorists say and want to retaliate against all Muslims out there."

Sidra raised her hand but didn't wait to be called on. She reflected, "I think there are good actions taken by Muslims, and these are talked about in the media. But sometimes Muslims get frowned upon because there are people claiming to be Muslim who are *haram*, which means forbidden and you're not allowed to do it. On the news a few years ago, there was a man who claimed to be Muslim, but he ran with a bomb into a car and killed a bunch of people. It was reported as a suicide, which is actually *haram*. He was called a Muslim, and that was on the news."

"So, what do you think needs to happen in order for Islam and Muslims to be treated fairly in society?" asked Melanie.

Malik raised his hand to speak. "I think that everyone should get the full story. For example, the news might talk about the ISIS terrorist group. People associate ISIS with Muslims. But the news would never say, 'A Muslim lady just saved a dog.' The news just shows the bad parts. It would help if the news would not be so controversial."

"I agree with Malik," said Aziza. "People should know that Muslims who do bad things are only a fraction of the population. I think there are more than a billion Muslims around the world, and the only thing that gets on the news is Muslims who are bad. The good things that happen are unknown, and the bad things are the only things exposed."

"How does that make you feel?" asked Miriam.

"It feels disappointing. Everyone should be treated equally, and everyone should get the full story."

"What subjects tend to upset students at your school?" asked Melanie.

Zain answered, "People argue about pets."

"Yeah, people argue about that with their parents," echoed Amariyah.

Zain sent an annoyed look to Amariyah. He continued, "Some people say no, you cannot have pets because it's . . . I can't remember the word . . . ah . . . *najis* (ritually unclean), yeah, that's it. You're not allowed to have a pet around while you pray. Some people say it's okay because the pet could be put in another room. Others say no because it goes to the bathroom everywhere."

Amariyah replied, "We have two pets in our family. We went to a Shaykh before we got them to see if it was okay to have dogs because their spit is *najis*, and you're not allowed to have it on you while you're praying. That's why we do *wudu*, where we clean ourselves before prayer. The Shaykh said we can have pets outside but can't have them where we pray or inside the house."

Aydin added, "Once or twice we've talked to our Qur'an teacher about having pets because it's more of a religious problem than our parents saying, 'yes' or 'no.' There is *najis* to consider and dogs being dirty. Some people say it's acceptable. Some people say it's unacceptable to have a dog in your home because your house couldn't be a place of worship. That's basically it. Our teacher, Shaykh Tarek, said that it's okay to have a dog outside and in parts of the house where there are no people praying, and you never worship in those areas."

"I've gone to Dr. Ramsey for many problems. She is very calm and very loving. She always tries to help fix the problem. She's not just like, 'Go fix it yourself!' But she wants us to try to fix it ourselves first. If that doesn't work, then she comes and helps us," said Amariyah.

"Yeah," added Zain, "She helps us understand how other people are feeling. She wants us to look at the situation from the other person's shoes. She teaches us that we can solve problems without yelling or getting physical." Aydin spoke next. He said, "To add to Zain's comment, I agree. She always wants us to look at the problem from the other person's side. That's probably one of the biggest lessons she's taught us. She says, 'Don't try and solve a problem or turn it into a big fight without seeing the other person's side. Looking at it from their point of view can do so much to help rectify the situation.' Today I had a disagreement with my teacher. She thought I was messing around even though I was just disposing of something in the trash can. She wouldn't listen to my side, so we really couldn't come to a resolution."

Reya, a new student at the school, reflected, "North Star Academy isn't as strict as the previous private school that I went to. They were really harsh on everyone. They were so strict about uniforms. I didn't like that because that just made us hate it more. But, here, they give you a chance." Mousa added, "I think our teachers teach us about problem-solving skills and not to start a fight with people. They want us to take everyone's point of view and make sure everyone gets to say what they want to say. When everyone gets to say what they want to say, it becomes easier, and problems get solved."

Navigating Gossiping, Bullying, and Passive-Aggressive Behaviors

We sat with the primary school teachers one afternoon. The interview provided a much-needed outlet for newer teachers to talk about the challenges with students' parents and to reconcile the ups and downs of being a teacher at a private school. Ms. Deanna Davis, a third-grade teacher in her second year of teaching at North Star Academy, started the conversation. She said, "I told the administration last year that they need to have a conversation with parents about WhatsApp and tell them either to remove it or to use it appropriately. I wasn't heard as a parent or a teacher. I was part of the parents' WhatsApp group because my daughter is in first grade. WhatsApp has become a forum for parents to complain. My daughter caught scabies from a hotel room last year. It's actually less contagious than lice. They don't jump; you have to actually have skin-to-skin contact to get scabies. Yet, on WhatsApp, the group of parents freaked out. They demanded to know which child had scabies. Parents called the front desk and harangued Wendy: 'Do they have other kids? What are the school rules about scabies? Is this student attending school with scabies?' I saw all of this happen in real time and found myself in the office bawling. The parents were just like a pack of wolves. They were awful. The same parents would approach me before and after school saying, 'We just love you. You are a fantastic teacher.' Yet, while they were saying this, I was thinking, 'I know what you are like on WhatsApp—the parent who threatened the scabies' mom to come forward.' I was so worried about what they would do to me once they knew it was my daughter. I'm actually leaving the school next year, not because of this situation. I just need to go.

"To give you another example, I friended a parent on Facebook. I never should have done that. That parent took a screenshot of a post I made that mentioned a new job I was going to have. That parent sent the screenshot to everybody, and it got to the administration. I wasn't able to tell them I was leaving in my own way. It was so disturbing to me. I felt violated. You're taking this small community as everybody's business is everybody's business too far. That woman had no right to take a screenshot of my personal message and send it to all the parents and administration."

Ms. Carpenter asked Ms. Davis, "Are private school parents different from public school parents?"

"Yeah, but they weren't like this," Ms. Davis said, shaking her head back and forth. "But I feel that in the public schools, the parents don't have that much voice. In private schools, parents pay tuition and are of the belief that they should have a voice. I've removed myself from the WhatsApp group. I feel bad for my daughter at times. The parents plan activities, and she isn't invited. I couldn't handle the complaints, especially about other teachers, and other kids."

Ms. Mary Flores leaned in to speak, almost whispering. "This year, one of my friends enrolled her daughter in kindergarten. She told me that parents gossip, and she finds it inappropriate and offensive." Sticking up for her friend, Ms. Flores said to the group, "Not all parents are bullies."

Ms. Davis replied, "A parent of a third-grade student keeps me informed about what is going on. She disagrees with the parent WhatsApp group completely. The teachers sent home a survey. Surprisingly, this survey became a huge issue on WhatsApp. I wish the administration would step in a little bit. We are pushed around by our parents quite a bit. I'd like the administration to ask us, 'What do you need?' 'What can we do to support you?' I'd like for them to shut the parents' WhatsApp group down."

Ms. Flores concurred. "Yeah. I worked in a public school for thirteen years. There are so many students that you have to go by the book. I liked that about public school. Here, there is pressure to bend. It's okay because I'm flexible."

Ms. Carpenter nodded in agreement with what the other teachers were saying. She added, "I've worked at North Star for over a decade. In the first couple of years, parents test you. They want to see what kind of a teacher you are." She shared, "Once you build a reputation, you can have a straight conversation and say, 'If you have a problem, come and let's discuss it.'"

Getting On or Moving On

Dr. Ramsey pulled us into her office at the end of our day. "I forgot to mention something when we were talking this morning. I think it is important to share with you a pattern that I see over and over again with White teachers. When I hire a White teacher, they experience a pattern of feelings. In the first year, things are great. They act like tourists in a new country. During their second year, they start to experience a bit of discomfort in navigating the culture and the faith amidst their own personal views. During their third year, White teachers experience frustration that we do not do things the 'normal way.' They do not stick around beyond the third year. It is a pattern I have seen consistently in my twenty years. The only exceptions are those who themselves have experienced oppression or othering, such as Catholics or children of immigrants. These teachers get it and love what we are doing. They are the ones who stay. If a teacher chooses to leave, then I support them. This school isn't for everyone."

6

Freedom to Trust

By prioritizing freedom to trust, the school community emphasizes the importance of building relationships through openness, integrity, and personal regard.

Wednesday Morning, 6:50 A.M.

We woke up early and headed to a nearby café overlooking Sea Star Beach. It was a cold morning, and the sun was low on the horizon, hiding behind a haze of clouds. As we sat at a table set for two, our eyes caught the early morning news. On the television that hung from a corner of the room, Rashida Tlaib was front and center, proclaiming: "We're going to impeach the motherf-—r." As the news replayed it a second time, "impeach the motherf—-r," we noticed a silence in the dining room. A White man at the bar and a woman sitting alone stopped eating and looked up at the television. Two male millennials seated in the center of the room nodded and smiled at each other, sending a nonverbal message of support.

Miriam stated, as she sipped on her coffee. "I totally get it, but I wonder if she could have chosen better words to convey her sentiments." Melanie whispered, "I agree, but if she used nicer language, would she be getting this airtime now? I doubt it. Look at how divided this room became when she said that."

"I'm wondering if Rashida Tlaib and Ilhan Omar are classroom discussion topics at North Star? I think they are. They were both elected in 2018, and it's a huge milestone for the Muslim community in the US. I mean, there's only one other Muslim, Keith Ellison, who was elected to Congress in 2006," reflected Miriam.

"Yup, let's ask. They probably do talk about them," replied Melanie. "We should think about going." Cautious about the weekday traffic in California, we finished breakfast, paid the bill, and walked to the car.

While heading toward the freeway, we couldn't help but notice the gift shops, grocery stores, resorts, and million-dollar homes in Sea Star. This part of the coastline had 20,000 acres of protected wilderness, dramatic vistas, tide pools, oceanside bluffs, and coves. Miriam rolled down her window. She took a deep breath of the ocean air. "We haven't enjoyed any of this scenery! We need to walk along the beach and take in the sites."

"I agree. But, it's been rainy and cold."

"Yes, but we must get to the beach before we leave," insisted Miriam. "Hey, can you please look up today's schedule and read it out loud so we can get an idea of how much time we have between sessions?"

"Let me bring it up on my phone. First, we meet with the middle schoolers. It'll be a mix of students from fifth through eighth grade. Then we have an hour's break, which will give us time to debrief. Then we will meet with the board chair, take another break for lunch and debrief, and at the end of the day, we will talk to the upper school parents."

"You Can Cry at This School"

We reached North Star at 7:20 a.m. for a thirty-minute catch-up with students. We were excited to engage in another round of discussion with them. We set up food and equipment, and shortly after that, Jeanine, the upper school's administrative assistant, walked in with hot coffee. We were grateful for one more cup. The students began to arrive. Over the next ten minutes, eight students trickled in and took a seat. Miriam opened the conversation, knowing they had to go to class when the first bell rang.

"The last time we met, we didn't have a chance to ask you about your school head, Dr. Muna Ramsey. Can you tell us what she's like?"

Khadija responded first. "Dr. Ramsey talks to you. She doesn't want to betray your trust and stays in contact often."

Laith spoke next. "She's not that strict, but she knows how to run a school."

Mousa then added, "She's a very hardworking person. It's amazing how she got this school up and running from the groundbreaking day—it took a little more than a year. Just the amount of work and hours she put into the process is unbelievable."

Laith interrupted, "For me, the main issue is just how some promises weren't kept. For example, at last year's gala, they said this campus would be done by September 5th. It was delayed until November. They said we would have a completed gym before our basketball season ends, but our last game is tomorrow. It's just the fact that some construction promises weren't kept."

Joury added, "Making this whole school takes a lot of courage and patience. The gym isn't ready yet, so it takes a lot of patience not to break down. She opened this school with construction still going on, which is amazing, and she's been a part of this school for a long time. She also comes up with many creative ideas for the students and makes us feel welcomed."

"I can relate to Joury," said Zikri. "There's actually an upstairs in this building just in case they decide to open a high school to allow people to stay in this environment so that they can continue to feel safe and welcomed . . . and, if anything bad ever happens . . . which is almost never, she always knows the right way to solve it!"

Daniel continued Zikri's train of thought. "I think that the school has a lot of nice people. You can also trust them. Everyone's just nice."

The students needed to be in class in about twenty minutes, and time was at a premium. Melanie moved the conversation along and asked, "What makes this school different?"

Daniel cleared his throat. "I feel at this school, you can learn and tell each other your feelings. You might need to hide your feelings in other schools because people can get mad. I can cry at this school because they're always nice about it."

"If I'm walking down the hall and I see a man wearing a *thobe* (ankle-length robe with long sleeves), I feel more comfortable," commented Jana. "If they say, *Assalamu alaykum*, I feel a connection. If I see a woman wearing a *hijab* or something like that, I feel more comfortable. It is what I know. I know they won't ask me anything weird. If they do ask me something, I know how to answer. It won't be awkward."

"I agree," said Ahmed. "At this school, everyone is connected, and we can tell everyone our feelings. If you have a problem with someone, you can always find a way to solve it." Jana then disrupted the feel-good stories with a dose of middle school reality.

"Sometimes people get into fights. If it's a big problem or someone feels hurt, they go to the principal. If it's something small, the teacher will come over and ask what happened, but she doesn't solve it. She would ask the two people in the fight to solve it." The bell rang, and as much as we wanted to remain in the room and further the conversation, we had to stop.

The First Debrief

We picked up our things, pushed in the chairs, and walked down the hall to a small windowless conference room next to Dr. Ramsey's office. We sat at a round table that could fit four comfortably and pulled out our laptops.

"So, how do you think that went?" Melanie asked.

"Well, I wish we had more time with the students," replied Miriam. "You know, where most middle schoolers are trying to figure out how to keep and maintain relationships, these students were comfortable learning, fighting, crying, and just being their authentic selves."

"Agreed. I was so touched when Daniel said he could cry here."

"I know, right? What vulnerability he showed. But what was equally powerful was the other students' responses when he said that. They were nodding and agreeing with what he was sharing."

"The school culture is warm and caring. The students were young—around ten to thirteen—yet they spoke as if they were much older and more mature. Darn! We forgot to ask them about Rashida Tlaib and Ilhan Omar!" exclaimed Miriam rolling her eyes.

"We Have to Bend"

Mr. Anwar Hassan, the board chair, entered the small conference room and cleared his throat to get our attention. He was wearing a dark suit and tie. "Hello! Good morning!" We stood and shook hands. He was headed to meet Ms. Fatemi, but Dr. Ramsey asked him to drop by the upper school to speak with us before his meeting. He sat across from us, folded his arms, and leaned back into the conference chair as if to size us up.

"Thank you for making time to meet with us this morning. We were just speaking with students about their experiences going to this school, and they gave us some positive perspectives of Muna. How would you characterize your relationship with her?" asked Miriam.

Mr. Hassan repositioned himself in the chair and replied, "I'm just trying to find the right words for this. I feel like we're a team. When it comes to important and strategic matters, we're always on the same page. It's a matter of me trying to enable her to do her job, and she plays a huge role also in enabling me to do my job better. So we support each other, and we push each other to do better. I think the advantage we have over, let's say, other Islamic institutions, like a mosque, is that everyone on the board is on the same page regarding the vision. There isn't disagreement around the vision. It's more a matter of, 'Okay, how do we get there? What should we focus on?' Every few years, a big global incident happens and triggers us to ask, 'Okay, what's the security situation? How are our cameras?' Muna does a great job in terms of the relationship with the police force. So, when an incident happens, we've got cop cars hanging out on both campuses to make people more comfortable.

But again, I have to move forward. It's a tug-of-war, you know? Do we want this to succeed? Well, then we have to bend."

Mr. Hassan crossed his legs and leaned back again. "It creates other challenges because people can become judgmental. At the end of the day, if we provide results, and our kids become great role models, contribute to the community, and become successful, then that will speak volumes - more than advertising."

Mr. Hassan looked at his watch. "Oops, it's time to go." We stood up with him. Miriam reached for a handshake without lingering too long and then placed her left hand over his to convey partnership.

The Second Debrief

"You know, despite the ongoing threats to American Muslims in the US, the leadership at North Star Academy seems to not be paralyzed by it," said Miriam.

Melanie responded, "You're right. There's a low level of trust right now in America, and the fear is warranted given news reports."

"The ACLU just reported that anti-Muslim sentiments have spiked with attacks on mosques. These are people directly taking aim at religious freedom. Also, Muslim communities proposing to build sites for their *masajid* have been targets for vandalism and other criminal acts. They're also trying to block or deny zoning permits for the construction or expansion of *masajid* around the country."

Jeanine peeked her head into the room. "I couldn't help overhearing your conversation. I do get worried, for example, our Facebook page. I think our Director of Marketing is on top of it. When somebody follows her, she tries to follow back. She does some due diligence to at least identify that person as a person. But then again, you never know on social media. There's that concern with our Facebook group, but we also have a very active social media platform. We talked about it earlier this year in terms of the website being password protected. Our website has the calendar of all our games. I feel like, God forbid, somebody who wants to hurt us can easily find where we're playing. I've got to run now, but I couldn't help adding to the conversation."

We had a reasonable amount of time before meeting with the upper school parents in the afternoon. We were curious about the social media postings and how trusting they were about the information posted on the web. We also had a hunch that Dr. Ramsey would not let fear be the basis of the school's security strategy. We also wondered how easily we could access information on North Star's social media accounts.

"How about you look at Facebook, and I'll check out Instagram?" Melanie unpacked the salads and sandwiches and set water bottles on the table.

"Hey, Melanie, this is interesting. I see that the lower school has its own Instagram account, and the upper school is named 'North Star Academy Community,' which suggests it's inclusive of the greater community. The upper school posts are varied—spanning basketball events, free concerts, an International Women's Day Banquet, to topics such as sexual harassment, grooming, abuse, recovering from disillusionment with the community, spiritual abuse, and secret marriages. Then there are pictures of students and families, youth reflection on a Friday night, and wellness workshops. There's also a post for the Super Bowl on the big screen. What eclectic postings!"

"On my end, it looks like there's one Facebook page for the lower and upper schools. There's no way to see who's following them or who the school is following—except for a few institutions, such as the Chamber of Commerce. The page is internal to the school, with pictures of students, an annual giving announcement, and a list of novels for second to eighth grades. Some of the novels on the list are *Flat Stanley, George's Marvelous Medicine, Amal Unbound, Esperanza Rising, The Giver, The Outsiders,* and *Home is Not a Country*. Look at this—pictures of students next to a school corridor with a street named after them. There's also an announcement for alumni to share updates, such as graduations, university acceptances, or if anyone landed an internship or new job."

"I appreciate how these social media sites chronicle the life of the school. It is interesting to see the wide variety of content included because that is not typical of other Islamic schools," reflected Miriam.

"Most People Don't Like Schools Affiliated with a Mosque"

We were becoming quite familiar with the upper school campus. We made our way down the corridor, turned the corner, and entered the conference room on the left. Three moms from the parent-teacher organization were waiting for us around the conference table.

"What hopes and dreams do you have for your children?" Melanie asked.

Ms. Khan spoke first, "I think what any parent wants for their child's education is for them to become well-developed. We hope that our kids integrate well into the community and that they are accepting of other people's beliefs. . . . Not accepting, sorry, that they respect other people's beliefs and can function well—not just academically but socially. My background is from a Catholic perspective, and my son's father is Muslim from Pakistan. During the early part of my son's educational years, we were on the East Coast, and we enrolled him in a Catholic school. There wasn't an Islamic school nearby. Growing up, I went to a Catholic private school, and because I was more focused on academics, that's what I stressed. When we moved to California, his father insisted he has more of an Islamic education to reinforce what he learns when he goes abroad every summer. North Star is close to our home and has a really good reputation in terms of academics, so we decided to enroll him here."

Ms. El-Hadary spoke next. "As Angelica said, the Catholic school model is about academics and small class sizes. I think that's an important piece that North Star offers. It isn't just jamming 30 Muslim kids in a room together and being like, okay, at least you're in an Islamic school. It's not about that. It's really about private school education, which I think is invaluable. As we see in public schools, classrooms are getting crowded and differentiated learning is difficult, especially when there are a lot of English language learners in the room."

"I'd like to add to that," said Ms. Lena Morsy, leaning forward to stress her point. "I'm not sure if the idea was made clear that the school is not affiliated. Many people don't want to send their kids to a school affiliated with a *masjid*. North Star is an independent school. I had a previous experience with an Islamic school in another state. I used to live in Chicago. Most people don't like schools affiliated with a mosque because there are ideas of control by a small group of people. They don't want that because they want to be free Muslims, not aligning themselves with this side or that side. They don't like to be connected . . . not connected, that's not the right word . . . controlled . . . by the *masjid*. I think that's the idea behind North Star." She reached toward her plate and took a bite of pineapple.

Ms. Khan stopped the conversation. "We hate to run so quickly, but we're meeting a speaker for a school event that's coming up next month. We have to go."

"Not a problem," said Miriam.

The Third Debrief

We were unsettled by the quick departure of the parent group. Dr. Ramsey's door stood ajar, and we recognized the 8th-grade student sitting in a chair across from her desk from one of our interviews. We quietly entered the room next door and unpacked our laptops. We could hear Dr. Ramsey speaking with the student, but the words were inaudible. Miriam whispered, "I wish we could hear the conversation."

Miriam closed the door. "The parents are quite invested in the success of the school, and they are such an eclectic group. One mom, an immigrant to the US, and another with a Catholic background," said Melanie.

"I sense a certain level of vulnerability with these women, a closeness not just as moms but as parents who want success for their children and the school. When I was looking through the North Star community website earlier, I saw some of the posters we passed near the front door. One poster advertised a session for Positive Discipline to help parents connect with their children. Another advertised a student performance. There was a third poster promoting a parent session on why play matters . . . and then there was yet another with an expert coming to discuss how to encourage a culture of open communication."

"It's clear that Muna is pulling families into the school. I wonder if families who speak English as a second language find coming to attend these events challenging?" asked Melanie.

"I'm not sure, but it might be worth asking her next time we see her," replied Miriam.

The next day, Thursday, 9:00 a.m.

We waited for Dr. Ramsey in the small conference room adjacent to her office. She popped her head into the doorway. "Come on in. I hope you've had a good morning?"

"We have!" We headed to the campus just in time to watch the students enter the building! There's something energizing about being on campus with students. It makes me miss my days as a school principal," Miriam reminisced. "I hear you," said Dr. Ramsey. "I rely on our Parent Association as a sounding board. I see them as a microcosm of the greater community. When I ask them a question, I might get two different responses. But that gives me an opportunity to engage and share back what I'm thinking. It also provides me with feedback to check to see if maybe I missed something. Within the school, I have a couple of staff members.. . . . they're also parents, so they might have a pulse on what's happening or what people are thinking. Asking parents questions also gives me a chance to reflect on my own thinking. And then the board . . . and the board chair in particular . . . we meet regularly, too."

"Does building these relationships with parents affect how you relate to students?" asked Miriam.

"In terms of the students, I see them as my own. For me, there was never a taboo topic with my daughter. We could talk about anything and everything. I either would have an answer for her, or I would say, 'I don't have the answer, let's figure it out together.' I probably need to give more thought to other things, but the kids know that they can access me when things go wrong. So, to answer your initial question, I listen to the president of the board and a few trusted parents that have been around for a while."

Melanie asked, "Have parents raised any issues about the curriculum?"

"I don't know, well I'm trying to think—can you give me an example?" asked Dr. Ramsey.

"Sure. Some parents might get angry at reading the *Refugee* book that you have as part of the curriculum. There are thousands of books . . . so they might ask you, 'Why that one?'"

Miriam added, "Or something that might be political. They might ask, 'Why did you discuss this current event in class? Why are you exposing our kids to that?' Do you experience pushback on anything like that?"

"No. I think parents understand that's part of the mission of the school. I think our families trust the school. They know that they have the freedom to share whatever concerns they have. I think that they see the school as co-parenting with them. They trust us enough. But, there are exceptions to everything."

"Can you give us an example?" asked Miriam.

"Other schools may feel more like us-versus-them, school-versus-family . . . you know, that kind of thing. I don't feel that with our parents as much, but of course, when they're mad at us, it feels like a divorce. You can't love something and then be ready to leave it without it feeling like a divorce. So when things don't go well, or we don't have alignment, then it can be uncomfortable."

Dr. Ramsey changed the subject to the future of the school and successive leadership—and who she might trust to take over.

"In terms of who could do the job, anyone could do the job. You could find anyone with an administrative credential or some administrative background. So at the front of my mind or maybe the back of my mind . . . I want to build this school with the next 100 years in mind. I'm anxious to find whoever the next person would be to take over my position. Do you remember that you asked me, 'Who do you work for?' Well, I'm not holding on to this job in that way. I'm ready to hand leadership over tomorrow if somebody steps in and is confident in doing it. But I don't think getting somebody from the outside would work unless they're really just a unique individual. I've thought about our alumni. I can't wait for them to come back as teachers, staff members, and administrators because they will have been raised in this environment and will know what feels right and what doesn't feel right. In the end, I want to spark that excitement in somebody young who says, 'Maybe someday I could be a leader of North Star Academy,' the executive director or the head of school."

Dr. Ramsey smiled at the thought of passing the torch. "I think the long answer has been in my head for a while. It could also be a faculty member or a staff member who has been part of the school long enough that they embody it and can lead the school. They need to have been soaked in that special sauce. I would be happy to pass the baton to somebody who can do the job better than me. Layla, to some extent, might be good. She has been seeped in the environment long enough. But, she's not us."

Miriam responded, "No, she's not."

"I mean, philosophically, she's not us. But she could do it. Her gut tells her what's right and what's not right because she's been a part of the school for so many years. But it's not . . . yeah . . . I think, if I disappeared completely, it would be hard for her because she doesn't have that Islamic Center philosophy."

Miriam added, "She's not anchored in that. It makes a difference. It definitely makes a difference."

Dr. Ramsey thought for a second and added, "The pressure socially is too great. You can't be frustrated by people saying, 'You're an Islam 'lite' school. Or be mad when they ask, 'Why do you call yourself an Islamic school?' The people who shop for Islamic schools are not shopping for a school like ours. We have to convince people that we're right."

"Yes, I hear you," said Miriam.

"So it's constant. You can't just sit and say, 'Okay, where's the market taking us today?'"

"If you're not steeped in it, you can waver," added Miriam.

"Easily."

"And you can give in."

"And then you lose it."

"And then it's gone."

We left Dr. Ramsey's office feeling the heaviness and responsibility that she bears. North Star was a product of the Islamic Center of San Rico, which had a very specific and unique ideology. Not all parents paid attention to or attended the center, but it was the school's foundation, and Dr. Ramsey clearly accepted the responsibility to safeguard the essence of the school.

Our next appointment was with lower school parents on the primary campus. We collected our things and walked out of the building and into an empty parking lot. Miriam's rental car looked as if it was abandoned at the far end of the lot.

"Do they have another parking lot for the teachers?" asked Melanie.

"They must. It is strange that it is so empty."

"No one would know this is a school, much less an Islamic school, especially since we are in a corporate park."

"I wonder why they chose this area?" replied Miriam.

"I'm used to seeing schools in neighborhoods, not next to manufacturers and distribution centers."

The drive took eight minutes between the two campuses. Miriam turned onto the I-10 highway. It was late morning, and traffic was light. As we entered North Star's lower school campus, the change in feel was noticeable. The landscaping was mature, and the buildings noticeably older. The parking lot was small but full. Miriam squeezed into one of the two empty parking spots.

"If You Say You Are Progressive . . ."

We walked down the hall to meet with a group of lower school mothers. Our thoughts were of Dr. Ramsey's concern over succession planning and protecting the school. We entered the multipurpose room and were welcomed by a group of mothers sitting at a U-shaped rectangular table. On the far end of the room was an accordion door that could be opened to expand the room into a gymnasium. The door was closed, which made the space feel cramped. We decided to open the conversation about holiday celebrations. We knew from our previous research that this topic was an easy question for parents to answer and would help make the mothers feel more at ease.

"I know that Christmas, Halloween, and Valentine's Day are big holidays in public schools, and they incorporate these holidays into their class activities. My first grader told me that her teachers told the students, 'We don't celebrate these holidays.' As parents, we tell her that we celebrate *with* others. We go trick-

or-treat with our friends and our neighbors because we live in a community with people who do these things. If someone wants to celebrate and eat with us, they'll come over, and we can celebrate together. The kids understand that 'We don't celebrate these holidays,' but they can participate in holiday activities with others. Of course, there are some children who don't participate at all. There was an incident at school where a child said, 'My dad said we don't trick-or-treat. Why are you guys trick-or-treating?' My answer is, 'We trick-or-treat with the friends who trick-or-treat, and that's why.' We are partaking in their celebrations because they partake in ours," explained Ms. Bibi Abadi.

"There is this perception that if you say you're progressive, it means you don't follow the religion. You're relaxed about following Islam. Yet, this isn't the case. There are rules that you must follow if that makes sense . . .," said Ms. Sophia Seedat.

"You're right," said Ms. Abadi. "It hurts when someone says, 'This is a progressive school. It's not that Islamic.' But that's not the case! Everyone here is Muslim. Faith is something you practice. It's between you and Allah. But, at the same time, there is respect. There are things that you have to do. So, when an issue that's very simple comes up, it's something that people debate. 'Should you eat it?' 'Should you not eat it?' 'Can you eat it?' Everyone knows faith is way more than these little things. This school is a combination of great leadership and parents who have a very strong faith beyond all the little things that we all argue over. I get a lot of judgment from my other Muslim friends that send their kids to other Islamic schools. These schools have the model that everyone is the same. All the girls have to wear the *hijab*. All the teachers are Muslim. They can't understand why we are paying so much more for an Islamic education that's not up to par, in their opinion."

Ms. Seedat, the Parent Association president, added, "And we end up arguing about why I choose to send my kids here. There are Islamic schools where everyone has to be Muslim. I'm asked, 'Oh, you have non-Muslim teachers? That's very interesting. So why would you even send your kid there?' This happens so much. I remember growing up feeling like all I heard was, 'Oh, you shouldn't do this, or you shouldn't do that.' This doesn't happen here because everyone is on a level higher . . ."

Ms. Seedat struggled to identify the word she wanted to say. Miriam asked her, "So how do you socialize new parents, who might be a little petty? Because not everybody is going to come in fully formed, right?"

Ms. Salma Cassiem answered, "I think people who find these things important do not come here . . . or . . ."

"Or they leave," said Ms. Seedat.

"It's not a match. I think it comes from the leadership. It comes from the core group who built the school. They created what they wanted. They had a vision and how they wanted the school to be. They've done a great job. The parents that attend the school are aligned with the ideology and the goals of the school. I've gotten to know the principal of the school, but she gets to know everyone. Every year she invites all of the new families to her house for a potluck dinner. She does this purposefully to send the message that we are a family and that new families will be supported."

"This is how it starts. You feel welcomed. I'm looking for a word, but it's not coming to mind . . ." commented Ms. Abadi.

Ms. Seedat said, "I'm thinking of a word. Embraced."

"Embraced! Yes!" replied Ms. Abadi.

"She's going to need a bigger home really soon!" laughed Ms. Cassiem.

"We've noticed that diversity is embraced and celebrated in the school. How do you like having teachers of different faiths teaching your children?" asked Melanie.

Ms. Dahlia Abdallah spoke first. "I grew up in the Middle East. My parents immigrated to America in my early teens, and we didn't stay. We only stayed four or five years, and then, my parents moved back. The reason my parents returned home was that they felt like they were losing us. It was the early 1990s. We were in Alabama. My family was very different. Looking back, my parents just felt that they couldn't raise us here. Moving to the US as an adult, though, I could relate to the idea of having an American identity. But, when I am back home in the Middle East, I feel comfortable there too. When my husband and I moved to California, we were looking for an Islamic school. But the idea of an Islamic school was always a small school next to a *masjid*. We didn't want this for our kids. We were concerned about the quality of education. Then, a colleague mentioned North Star Academy, and I went to the school's website. On the home screen was a video about the school. The teachers were talking, and I literally started crying." Tears began to fall on Ms. Abdallah's cheeks as she spoke. She looked in her purse for a tissue. "I'm so sorry about this!"

Farhana reached over and touched her arm for comfort and added, "I just feel this is a second home . . . or maybe my first home. I feel comfortable here. It is a relaxed environment. We know the teachers. We know what they are providing. We know what they are talking about. It's the same message that I am giving to my child at home. He is learning the same message here from different teachers. So, the same vision. That's the best part. I would like to say that North Star is a progressive school because of the diversity of the teachers. I grew up in Saudi

Arabia. Islam was imposed upon us, you know. Girls always had to wear a *hijab* at school. We are progressive in the sense that we are Muslims, but nothing is imposed on us. It's our choice how to present ourselves. So, a lot of people ask me, 'Oh, why would you send your child to an Islamic school?' They have this perception that Islamic schooling means . . . homogeneity . . . or everybody looking and thinking a certain way."

"Being progressive or not progressive does not change the religion. Religion is what it is. It's a certain set of rules and actions and things that nobody can change. No school can change this. North Star doesn't change this in any way. Everything that's taught is taught correctly," commented Ms. Abadi.

"As a parent group, we expect that if there are issues or complaints, parents will take it up directly with the school. The Parent Association is the spirit of the school. We help with fundraising. We help with creating a positive environment and a sense of community. The school does a good job of having events for parents when they first enroll their kids. There's a lot of interaction with other parents at the very beginning. This helps new families meet different people," explained Ms. Cassiem.

Ms. Hillary Myers spoke for the first time. "It's the culture. I think those events really help to educate new parents."

"And I didn't want my children to go to just any Islamic school. If it wasn't as good as other schools, then we would obviously take them to Saturday school or Sunday school instead," reflected Ms. Cassiem.

By this time, a couple of the other moms were tearful. They smiled and were somewhat embarrassed that they were crying while talking about the school. A tissue box was passed between them, and noses were blown, and eyes were wiped. Rarely had anyone cried in one of our interviews before. We were surprised but not surprised at the same time. There was a type of love that was present in that room.

7

Freedom to Love

By embracing the freedom to love, the school community fosters supportive relationships grounded in respect, compassion, and care.

Friday morning we visited classrooms in the upper school. As the building was new, the only splash of color was from two rows of blue classroom doors, three on the left and three on the right. The hallway was absent of awards, plaques, pictures, student art, and other paraphernalia usually found in a school. Our footsteps echoed down the hallway as we walked. Miriam's hurried clicking of the heels indicated we were running late.

Miriam arrived at the last door on the left. She gently opened the door and peeked in. The teacher stood up and smiled. She gestured with her hand for us to enter. We walked into the room and stood against the wall. The room looked disorganized, not ready to host a classroom of students. The four rectangular tables in the middle of the room held chairs that were placed haphazardly on top, with some chairs stacked upright and others flipped over on their bottoms and sides. Six backpacks on wheels stood in the middle of the room, where the students must have left them before taking their seats. One backpack had a basketball sticking out of the top and lime green hand sanitizer dangling from the handle. The other backpacks had lunch boxes clipped to their frames. The decorations on the backpacks included sunset beach scenes and pastel colors, and others were navy blue and black with orange trim. When we entered the classroom, everyone turned and looked at us. We smiled sheepishly and waved our hands.

The teacher gave off the impression of a conservative Arab mother. She wore a *hijab* and *abaya*, a loose-fitting, full-length robe worn by some Muslim women. She hovered over five students who squeezed around a small circular table. A sixth student sat in a chair and desk combo, facing away from the group. The placement of this student added to the haphazard feel of the classroom, as if they occupied the room as a temporary space for the lesson. We observed the other students wiggling and rocking on large colorful Ergerite flexi stools. One girl wore a light-pink *hijab*. The other three girls had long black hair tied back from their faces with barrettes and headbands. The two boys had similar California surfer-style haircuts. They turned back to their iPads.

The teacher picked up where she had left off. She was holding a MacBook Air and stood above the students. She spoke to the students in Arabic, and the students responded to her in English. Their task was to read Arabic sentences to each other, scaffolded with cartoon images. As the students worked in pairs, we slowly walked to the other side of the room and tried not to draw attention to ourselves. The room was named "The Thought Generator." We later learned that the focus of this room was for students to have a place to come together for projects based on significant issues, such as sustainability, human rights, and social justice. A cluster of student drawings hung between the windows on the far side of the room. Each picture had a word in the center decorated with drawings that students felt represented the word. We read the following: better, believe, strong, exceed, mindset, kind, positive, love, goofy, change, perseverance, hard work, worthy, simplify, peace, and improve. As we looked closer, we noticed that students embedded political messages in their art. We read "Black Lives Matter," "Don't be racist," "End gun violence," "Bring peace and diversity," "We don't want violence in our world," and "Positivity is key." We also saw the anarchy symbol, Yen and Yang, the Syrian, Iraqi, and Egyptian flags, soccer balls, dollar signs, and Disney characters. It was a curious display of innocence merged with political ethics.

We hoped to have an opportunity to observe the "Thought Generator" class before our departure. Feeling we had overstayed our welcome in Arabic class, we visited the room across the hallway. We whispered, "Thank you." The classroom opposite the "Thought Generator" was empty, and we went there to talk.

Unconditional Acceptance: Believing Every Human Is Worthy of Dignity and Respect

"That was interesting. What countries were the red, white, and black flags from?" asked Melanie. "I'm not sure, but I took a picture, and we can look it up later," replied Miriam. We walked to the front of the classroom to look at what was on the whiteboard. We saw a series of Malcolm X images taped at eye level with inscriptions underneath, representing phases in his life. Starting from the left hung a picture of Malcolm as a young boy, with "Malcolm Little" written in blue erasable marker. The second picture showed Malcolm in his youth with slicked-back hair. This picture was labeled "Detroit Red," his nickname because of his reddish hair at the time. The third picture tagged "Malcolm X," showed the well-known portrait of him smiling and wearing a suit and glasses. The label on the final image displayed "El-Hajj Malik El-Shabazz." This photo showed him wearing a *kufi*, a headdress worn by Muslim men, with a suit and glasses. The phrase, "We are having a party," was incongruent with these photos written above the images.

"They must be reading the Autobiography of Malcolm X," commented Melanie. "Have you read it?"

"No, I haven't," replied Miriam.

"It was good. It seems they had a class party. I wonder if it was for finishing the book?" said Melanie.

"Check out the progressive flag. In the blue square were the words, "In Our America." The red and white stripes read, "All People Are Equal; Love Wins; Black Lives Matter; Immigrants & Refugees Are Welcome; Disabilities Are Respected; Women Are In Charge of Their Bodies; People & Planet Are Valued Over Profit; Diversity Is Celebrated. I think this might be the only Islamic school in the country with this in a classroom," commented Miriam.

We heard a noise coming from the neighboring classroom and decided to look. The doors were open, and we walked in. There were fourteen students in small groups scattered throughout the room. It was a science room, with some students sitting on stools around raised lab tables while others sat on the floor in small circles. Along with general classroom supplies, we saw glass beakers, microscopes, magnifying glasses, molecular model sets, student-made science fair posters, wall posters of the element table, and a diagram identifying the parts of an atom. A large television screen hung catty-corner from the ceiling and displayed an outline for students to follow when writing their science report. Spanning the length of the far wall were glass cabinets and a long counter. The counter was completely covered with books, reusable shopping bags, some filled and others empty, and plastic containers. At the far end were a sink, Clorox wipes, and a bin with paper towels. Our eyes quickly turned toward the students, who were comfortably situated all over the classroom. Students worked with open laptops, notebooks, and pencils. At the front of the classroom, three students stood with the teacher at the whiteboard. They appeared to be seeking help in the design of their science fair poster. The other students worked in small groups, talking and laughing. We sensed authentic connections with the teacher and students and among students. The organized chaos indicated deep engagement with the work and a sense of camaraderie. We walked over to a group of students on the floor.

"What are you doing?" Melanie asked.

"We're putting together a compost bin. These are our worms!" a middle school student said as she juggled a red wiggler between her hands.

Miriam asked, "What are you learning?"

The girl responded, "Well, the worms eat the food we put in the bins, which becomes compost. The worm creates compost through its tail end. We then use the soil to feed our plants growing in our yards."

"What do you feed the worms?" asked Melanie.

"We feed them fruit and vegetable scraps," she said as she moved to pick up another red wiggler.

"How many worms do you have in your bin?" asked Miriam.

"Maybe around ten. When there are too many, we move them to the larger compost bin outside."

We watched the classroom for a few more minutes. The teacher worked with individual groups, visibly unbothered by the classroom noise.

It was almost 10:00 a.m. We needed to meet Dr. Muna Ramsey in an hour. We turned and left, making our way to the "Qur'an Studio." Outside the classroom, we removed our shoes and then entered quietly. Shaykh Tarek sat underneath the whiteboard with his back against the wall, with two girls and two boys facing him. One girl sat, looking disinterested, in the far-right corner. We read the week's agenda on the whiteboard:

Monday: Memorization

Tuesday: Reading Noraniya

Wednesday: Memorization

Thursday: Reading Noraniya

"What is Noraniya?" whispered Melanie.

"It is a method designed to simultaneously teach the Arabic alphabet, pronunciation, and the *tajweed*, rules governing how to pronounce the words of the Qur'an during recitation," answered Miriam. The students, facing Shaykh Tarek, sat in a lopsided circle. The Shaykh wore a black *kufi*, a tan blazer, and a black button-down shirt. The students had white plastic Qur'an stands that looked like TV trays. Students sat on the floor wearing sweatshirts, pants, and socks on soft, cushioned, green, cream, and maroon Islamic prayer mats. Neither the boys nor girls donned headwear. Each rug was for four people, as indicated by the *mihrab* design (arches that are niches in the wall of a mosque that indicate the direction of Mecca, which the congregation faces to pray). The rugs were spread across the room, with little to no space in between, intended to give the illusion of a seamless carpet, although some were cockeyed and off-kilter.

We had a full view of the room. We sat in the back on the floor with our backs against the wall. On the left side of the room were two students sitting against the wall, one unengaged with the lesson. The four students facing Shaykh Tarek practiced Quranic recitation aloud. Shaykh Tarek did not acknowledge us, and the students didn't look our way. Listening to the students recite the melodic Arabic verses in the Qur'an relaxed us. We could have easily laid down for a nap. Miriam put her hand on my knee and nodded toward the door. We got up and quietly left. We put on our shoes and headed outside to the yard. We found a small group of students enjoying their recess. We noticed some girls from the basketball team wearing their T-shirts that read "Falcons."

Mercy and Compassion: Caring for People in Need

The middle school students looked at one another as we approached them for a quick conversation. Miriam asked, "We want to ask you about Dr. Ramsey. How would you describe her?" asked Miriam.

Zain, who was outspoken, answered first. "Dr. Ramsey is calm, hardworking, and she is always loving towards us. She wants the best for us."

Amina agreed, "Dr. Ramsey is very loving towards us, and she's not just like, 'do this' and 'do that.' She talks to us, too. That's what I like about her!"

"Yeah," said Aziza. "She's loving and caring, but she also treats you like family ... not like she's the principal."

Daniel offered a bit more detail. "She does a lot for the school. She's really easygoing, and she cares about all of us. She doesn't try to get us suspended. She doesn't seem angry—even when she is."

Aydin answered, "Ms. Muna is a very forgiving person. She wants the best for all of us, and she treats us like her own children. In fact, I consider North Star as a second home. I think my parents enrolled me in this school because they love the environment. The teachers are here to support you, and they don't treat you like a number. They treat you like a real human being."

"I like Ms. Muna because she's always there for us. She is hardworking, and she wants the best for us," added Reya.

"Who are your favorite teachers?" asked Melanie.

Yasin answered, "Miss Feryal is really nice. She's funny, and she has her own way of making us quiet down. We're just really comfortable with her."

Sara added, "She's also nice, but she can be firm and fun. She isn't stern."

Amariyah commented, "Okay, so my favorite teacher is Ms. Street. She's my English teacher. She's my favorite teacher because she's helpful and explains things. It's different how she explains things. She doesn't explain things really fast, where we won't get it. She doesn't go at too slow a pace, either. It's in the middle. I don't know how to explain it, but she understands and gets our point of view. For example, I moved, and our printer broke. We couldn't go to Office Depot that day to print my paper. She helped me print my assignment at school."

Amina agreed with Amariyah. "Ms. Street is understanding about what we do after school. She tries to give us the bare minimum of homework. We can't do homework all the time, and we don't have enough time, so she gives us what we need to do, and she teaches us grammar. She teaches us in a way that we understand."

Adam said, "All of our teachers expect us to try our best to be as good as possible. They don't expect us to be perfect. They expect us to always try our best no matter what."

"That's great to know. What topics are you currently studying in your Islamic studies class?"

Joury answered first. "We are learning about how everyone should be treated fairly. Islam promotes fairness and equality—for example, the situation Mexicans currently face at the border or how Jews and Muslims are disrespected. Jews can't pray or do what their faith tells them to do in peace. They also struggle with the same issues we face."

"Yeah, non-Muslims should put themselves in our shoes. I think it would advance peace and understanding in the world. We should try and stop hate, but they should also learn. If they put themselves in our shoes, things might be different," reflected Adam.

Yasin commented, "I'm putting myself in their shoes. What if you're in the middle of praying, and somebody sees you? They call the police because they see you praying, and then the police catch you. What do you think they would do with you? It won't be good. I'm also putting myself in a Mexican's shoes. Let's say I'm Mexican and just got a job in the USA. I travel over the border for work, but one day the border patrol refuses to let me cross. I try to show them my passport, but they make me return to Mexico! Now I'm struggling. I quit my job in Mexico because of my new American job. You don't know what to do anymore."

"What you are talking about is social injustice," commented Joury.

Yasin added, "If someone were to trip you accidentally, you don't retaliate. Even if they tripped you on purpose, you still don't retaliate. You ask them why they did it, and you try to solve the problem. As a Muslim, you're supposed to request that you would like to make it right."

"Where did you learn this from?" asked Melanie, remembering the other lessons shared on the school's social media pages, such as their participation in *The World's Big Sleep Out: Ending Global Homelessness* program. Their Facebook page shared images of eighth-grade students building temporary shelters from cardboard boxes and sheets of plastic. They slept in the boxes and put themselves in the shoes of those who were homeless. Just then, the bell rang. We didn't get an answer, but we did learn that the students were processing their learning about justice, injustice, compassion, and mercy. We made our way to Dr. Ramsey's office.

Self-actualization: Realizing One's Full Potential

"Do you identify as a liberal-minded person?" asked Melanie.

Dr. Ramsey quickly responded, "Yes! I see God as the supreme judge."

"So you don't judge someone if they are gay or if they are this or that?" asked Miriam.

Dr. Ramsey reiterated with a direct and confident gaze, "I don't need to. God's the supreme judge. I don't know what was offered or taken away. That's God's realm. I try to have authentic conversations, and I value that. I want parents to have that with their kids, too. That goes back to what I originally said about us making space for families to dictate what is and is not okay for them. Simple things, such as the *zabiha* issue . . . 'Oh, they're eating something they're not supposed to eat . . .' and our response . . . 'If your mom said you can't eat that, then you can't. But if your mom said you can eat it, then you can.' That's it, end of story!" Dr. Ramsey said, leaning back in her chair.

"But what about things that might be more gray, such as homosexuality?"

Dr. Ramsey gave us a hard stare and said, "We've not faced that conversation explicitly."

"Okay," said Miriam. "That would be a tough one."

"Yes," said Dr. Ramsey, "And you know, I've talked to our board chair. I said, of all the Islamic schools that will eventually have a gay couple or student who comes out, it'll be us. Because we're the progressive ones."

Miriam remarked, "Or even a transgender child?"

"Or that," said Dr. Ramsey. "I think Muslim gay families would probably be too protective because of what they know exists within our cultural views. They probably wouldn't send a child to an Islamic school. But, if they did, it would be us over any other school. I said, there will be a day . . . so we need to give some thought to that. I don't know. I mean, again, I would open a space. I would do the same thing I've done with any other thing."

Miriam completed the thought, "and view it as a teachable moment?"

Dr. Ramsey paused for a minute and nodded. "That would be huge. I know that will make a huge wave. It will be like when you turn the direction of the bus or make it very clear where the bus is headed. Half the people will get off the bus because they don't want to go in that direction. But we get a whole other crew that joins the bus because they want to go in that direction. So, I think the day that this happens will be that bus-defining moment. Does that make sense? We will probably lose families as we move in that direction. I pray we gain families because we've decided to go in that direction."

"That leads me to ask, what type of a person do you hope this school produces?" asked Melanie.

"Somebody smart, compassionate, and kind. I want the best kind of human being. It's believing in the humanity of the kids and bringing them together. So, if I ask teachers to write report card comments, I expect the comments to indicate each child's skill set. For example, if a teacher only writes about a child's behavior or how many homework assignments he missed, that doesn't tell me anything about that kid. What it tells me is that this teacher doesn't know that kid. I'll continue to push. I'll talk with the teacher and tell him that he is just looking at the grade book. How is the child's writing? Is she illustrative in her writing? How are her reading and reading comprehension? Have you noticed that she can make connections between thoughts? Does she infer when you ask questions in class? When a teacher cannot answer these questions, this is a sign that they are not quite connecting. Or, they are just talking about what it is without being creative or inserting themselves or the things they love into the job. It becomes clear that they're not the right person. We end up having these tensions, right? I want to be able to sleep at night and feel like I've made a sound decision for the best of the community, which, to be honest with you, is a lot. It weighs heavily on me. I feel like the kids are my boss too. These things motivate me to decide one way or another on an issue. I try to put the kids in the center of what's best for them, even if it goes against the parents. It's tough when that happens because I've advised teachers that you can't care more than the parents do about their kids.

"I'm going to shift the conversation tangentially to describe what type of messages we want to send to the students so they understand the big picture. We've never done an eighth-grade graduation. I still have to figure out what that's going to look like. We may do some kind of senior superlative thing, such as acknowledging and recognizing their uniqueness. I think that would be special. I don't think that's competitive because each person can shine in their own way. To answer your question, we want our students to be good human beings. You know how you define good, right?"

Dr. Ramsey paused and looked at both of us. We shrugged our shoulders, not knowing where she was taking the conversation.

"You know how to define good, right?" Dr. Ramsey repeated. After a pause, she answered her own question. "Good means being independent, being self-sufficient, and being able to take care of oneself. Once they achieve this, we want them to look outside themselves and identify ways to contribute to their community, society, and the wider world. That is the simplest answer I can give. So, we're trying to build community. I believe a competitive environment is exactly the opposite of building a community. In the past, when we had a principal's honor roll, it didn't have much meaning because either everyone received an award or someone was left out. This caused unhealthy competition. Nothing good came of it except the parents liked it when their child won an award. Maybe that's another one of those things where parents like something, and I'm going against the bigger picture. How do you wish for your brother when you want to beat him?"

Dr. Ramsey stopped and took a drink of water. "So, with awards, we've really tried to minimize these as much as possible. We reintroduced awards a little bit this year with the Student Leadership Club. We have to choose representatives. Leaders are chosen democratically because their role is to speak on their classes' behalf. Students do throw their hats in, and some do want to be elected. We tolerate it. We also have the sixth-, seventh-, and eighth-grade science fairs. Students are judged, but we usually have outside judges. This helps avoid any feeling that we chose one student over another. We are part of the whole collective community, and we are trying to think of other rewards. But maintaining a cohesive community is more important.

"In the end, I want to be the one who lights a spark in students who might decide to return and be the next generation of leaders. Someone to take on the role of executive director of the lower school or the head of school. How do we support them in achieving this? I think the long answer has percolated in my head for a while. The individuals who take on the leadership of this school need to have been here long enough to have embodied our mission and vision. They feel like they've been soaked in that special sauce long enough. I don't think getting somebody from the outside, unless they're really just a very, very unique individual, will be our best way to go. I've thought about our alums. I can't wait for our alums to return as teachers, staff members, and administrators because they will have been raised in this environment and know what feels right and what doesn't. That's why we talk about it. We don't build it just for you. We build for the next 100 years. I'm anxious to find that next person. I'm not holding onto this job. I'm ready to leave tomorrow if somebody can confidently step in and lead."

Interconnectedness: Sharing a Bond, Being Linked, or Joined Together

We left Dr. Ramsey's office and walked to the conference room. Dr. Ramsey arranged for us to have a second meeting with a few upper school parents who are active members of the Parent Association.

"Hello! It's great to see you again!" commented Miriam. "This round, we'd like to ask about the work you do at North Star."

Ms. Amira El-Hadary, a mother of three children, two alumni of the school, and one in fifth grade, spoke first. "I've been a part of this school for fifteen years, and as mentioned before, I'm the current president of the Parent Association. One of our goals is to welcome new families. In a way, we could be called 'The Welcoming Committee!' When Dr. Ramsey created the Parent Association, she wanted diverse representation. I, too, wanted all different kinds of parents, different grades, and different traditions. I wanted the Parent Association to reflect our school. I didn't want it to be a clique of moms. In retrospect, I feel like we model that." Ms. El-Hadary glanced at Ms. Angelica Khan, hoping she would add to the conversation.

Ms. Khan spoke over Ms. El-Hadary, finishing her thought, "Her welcome..."

"Yes! The welcome breakfast," replied Ms. El-Hadary.

Ms. Khan interjected again, "Lunch, brunch, or something . . . Yes, so she does that every year, for all the new families, she brings them in, and we're there as ambassadors. So, we really put ourselves out to welcome new parents and get to know them so they recognize a friendly face when they come on campus. So, things are in place."

Ms. Lena Morsy added, "Yes, this is an introduction Dr. Ramsey hosts in her home. So, it's a really homey and nice gathering. At breakfast, parents meet the new Parent Association members. We socialize with them and talk to them about the school. When attending events, like my son's basketball games, I target new North Star parents to talk with them. I'll often invite them to do something together, especially if they have a son close to my son's age. Usually, I'm a shy person, but the Parent Association has changed me a lot. I'm not the kind of person who comes and says, 'Hi, my name is Lena!' But I'm more comfortable now approaching new parents."

"What is your perspective on the teachers?" asked Melanie.

"What's remarkable about North Star Academy is our non-Muslim teachers. When our students attend public school after leaving North Star, they experience real life. But because they've had good relationships with their non-Muslim teachers, they've learned how to respect people's differences and not to judge people because of their religion or skin color. Our kids have learned to love their non-Muslim teachers because they are great teachers and good human beings. It's very important for kids not to be hostile or be in a 'we versus them' space. This is what makes us human, our respect for one another. I think this is one of the great things about North Star Academy. But, on reflection, I think we insulate a bit, right?" asked Ms. Morsy.

Ms. Khan responded, "Yes, that's true, actually. This is my first year as a member of the Parent Association. My son has attended North Star since fourth grade, and now he's in seventh grade. Muna includes as many people as possible at events she hosts in her house. She makes you feel like you are part of a whole school community. It's like a family. In addition, the Parent Association hosts movie nights for students, and even some alumni return to participate. All the events we host allow people to congregate, which is important for Parent Association members and families new to the school."

Ms. El-Hadary added, "I want to circle back to what Lena said. I do think we are insulated. We don't feel discrimination here, and our kids don't experience harassment at this school. There's so much respect and love here that there isn't any need to get into anything political. The school has evolved from when my kids were in preschool. When my kids were younger, I felt families enrolled their children out of fear and a desire to protect them. They also wanted to send their kids to a school that felt like home. Over the years, it's been interesting to watch the change. Now kids tell me, 'I want to be at this school!' The kids are choosing this school, and it isn't coming from the parents, it's coming from the kids."

"True," commented Ms. Morsy. "We are in a very safe community. I believe Muna knows everyone in the school. Every kid. Every parent. I remember when I enrolled my son in second grade. I was planning on having him at the school for just a year. Muna treated me as if I was going to stay here forever! Maybe that is why I'm still here. Muna was on top of everything happening with my son's adjustment. My husband didn't live with us because he works outside the country. So, she would check in on Abdul and ask his teachers, 'Is Abdul adjusting well?' 'Is Abdul making friends?' 'Is Abdul still crying because his father isn't home?' I was shocked when after maybe three weeks, she said, 'Hi Lena, how are you doing?' My first thought was, 'How does she know my name?' Dr. Muna is an amazing person."

Ms. El-Hadary added, "The school provides good support. My primary role is being a parent. I don't outsource that to the school, but I feel like the school is a co-parent that knows what our family is trying to do for our kids. As I said before, the friendships kids develop here play a big role. Alumni come back, and they still feel connected to this space."

"Actually, North Star is our first home, not a second home," commented Ms. Morsy. She repeated, "It is our first home." Ms. Morsy looked up at the ceiling to gather her thoughts. "To show you how important North Star is to my son, I'll share a little story. When we were doing the fundraising for the upper campus last year, Abdul came to me and asked, 'Mom, could you give the school one million dollars?' In response, I laughed and joked, 'If I had one million dollars, I'd run away with my one million dollars!' Abdul was serious, though. He said, 'Mom, they need money, and they need to build the upper school. You know, if they can't raise the money in time, I will take a gap year and stay home and wait. Then, I will start upper school at North Star Academy.' So, that is how much North Star plays a role in my son's life. He is involved socially, academically, and spiritually. Last year Abdul had an English teacher he was particularly connected to. Mr. Chow was so connected to Abdul. It was amazing. He was like a father to Abdul, not just an English teacher. He was there for him not just religiously but emotionally. He was supportive and someone Abdul could talk to. Most of the teachers are like that. They are involved with the kids as if they were their own. So if anything happens, if a kid is not feeling well, they call home immediately. Yes, they are really involved in supporting us and contributing to my son's positive development."

Ms. Khan turned to Ms. Morsy and said, "I've only had really pleasant experiences with Dr. Muna. She always has really good things to say about the school. I know she was very involved, especially when the upper campus was being built. But, importantly, she's made me and Mohamed feel really welcome. This school is different. It makes you feel special—that you're known and accepted as part of the community. Everybody knows you and is invested in what happens to you, so I think that's the difference."

"My kids are older, and we're busier now. We're in a different stage of life. I feel a little more disconnected, but I definitely know when my kids were younger, the parents at the school were like family. Some of my best friends came out of the friendships of my kids. These friendships continue to grow. But, right now, at the upper school, we are still trying to build school culture because it is so new."

Altruism: Selfless Action for the Welfare of Others

That afternoon, we walked around the lower school campus. We happened to see a group of parents and teachers working in a classroom, preparing some items for a lower school event. We thought this might be a good chance to get their perspectives on the school's leadership. We walked into the room and asked if we could join them.

"We are making tissue paper flowers," said Ms. Morsy. "Do you remember how to do this? You fold the paper in an accordion style about one inch at a time. Fold the accordion in half and fold an inch and a half of a pipe cleaner around it. Then twist the pipe cleaner together to secure the flower to the stem. Then cut the paper, making rounded edges. Then Fluff and finish! No two flowers are alike!"

We decided to join them, even though it had been years since either of us made paper flowers. As Miriam started cutting her paper, she asked the group, "So, tell me a bit about your school leaders. What is your experience with them?"

Ms. Monica Hart spoke first. She was in her first year of teaching at North Star after graduating from a private college in the area. She was originally from New Mexico. "I worked at a public school teaching fifth- and sixth-grade students before starting here this year. What I can tell you about Muna is that she has an open-door policy. It is so hard for me to even wrap my head around that! I have to remind myself that I have an administrator who cares. I have an administrator that wants me to go talk to her. This is very different. I love it! Muna is there for you all of the time. Let me give you an example. I just had a hard time with one of the parents. The parent sent me an email, and in my reply, I didn't want to say the wrong thing and make matters worse. So, I emailed Muna. I didn't know if she'd respond because it was my first time interacting with her on an issue. She was amazing. She reviewed my draft and gave me suggestions, 'Say this. This will be better than saying that.' My response was, 'Oh my gosh! You're right! Oh, thank you!' I've been doing this for a while, so I know what to say to parents, but Muna just hit the right tone. She's really great."

Ms. Anne Mirza sat next to Ms. Hart. She was the primary Islamic education teacher and was in her seventeenth year of teaching at North Star. "You know, I'm a veteran teacher. I've been in the San Rico area for most of my life. I know the families. Our preschool director is a marvelous person. She takes everything to heart and doesn't hesitate to help out when needed. We also have a fantastic kindergarten through third-grade director. Both of them have become my friends. Sometimes that is difficult when you are a leader. But, they both can switch hats." Ms. Mirza pretended to put on a top hat and said, "Okay, I'm in my administrator hat." Then she removed it and put on a second hat, "Now, I'm wearing my friend's hat!" Everyone laughed at her antics. Ms. Mirza's voice rose in excitement, "You know how that goes! Both directors can sense things. Like today, the primary school director pulled me into the office to touch base with me because she knows it's been a rough year. A lot of things have happened in my personal life. She said, 'I want you to deal with the emotions because you might be holding them in.' She knows me. I hold everything in. She gave me that time to break down. I felt comfortable doing that. I live far from here, about an hour's drive. I couldn't do it unless I had a great place to work. So, this has been my second home."

The room was silent. Ms. Mirza didn't share her personal struggles, but others in the room seemed to know. Ms. Patricia Starr, a long-term substitute teacher for one of the kindergarten classes, said, "I agree. Muna is very warm and welcoming. When I started working here, I felt like, wow, this is a wonderful school to be at."

Ms. Dahlia Abdallah nodded her head in agreement. She was a parent of two children, one in preschool and the other in first grade. This was her fourth year at North Star and her first year as a member of the Parent Association. "I want to add that the teachers of other faiths embrace the children so well. One of the kindergarten teachers reads *surahs* of the Qur'an with them. She recites *surah al-Fatiha* with them but tells the kids that she is a Christian. I celebrate these different things! The children receive an unbelievable sense of true acceptance from everyone. I don't think you would have that if everyone were just one faith. Do you know what I mean? At other schools, you have to pretend you are like everyone else. But no one knows what people's faiths truly are. So, no one can embrace the differences. Here you can be Christian if you want and Muslim if you want. Whatever you are, you are. I feel that this is so important."

Ms. Sophia Seedat raised her hand to speak next. "I have an example of how great Muna is. My kids were following the last presidential election very closely. They went to bed at 9:00. When they woke up for school the next morning, and I told them Trump won, they both broke down into tears, and they were sobbing as if somebody had died. That's how much they were crying. We got to school, and Muna brought everyone together for an assembly. She reassured them, and it helped them so much. By the time they got home, they were so comfortable. They felt safe, I guess. I trust North Star as if it is my own family. Well, in most families, you are accepted for who you are. At North Star, your kids are accepted. Every parent is accepted. This makes it feel like a second home, as others have said. I went to an Islamic school in South Africa my whole life. That school also felt like a family. That is one of the reasons I chose North Star Academy. I wanted the same kind of experience for my kids. I wanted them to go to a school where everyone knows everyone. The difference was that I went to a very conservative school in South Africa. This school is more liberal and progressive."

"I think I have the letter Muna sent to the community after Trump was elected. Give me a second, and I'll go get my computer," said Ms. Abdallah. While we waited for Ms. Abdallah, Ms. Salma Cassiem reached for the tissue box and wrapped a tissue around her right index finger. She dabbed her eyes, "The love that my son has here . . . I don't know why I'm getting emotional. Sorry everybody. Just the strength and courage that the school leaders have . . . and the inclusion they foster have helped my kids identify as Muslims. It is something that I haven't been able to give them as much as I have wanted to. This school gives that to them and more."

Ms. Abdallah entered the room. Taking a seat, she read aloud the letter Dr. Ramsey sent to the community the day after the election.

November 10, 2016

Dear North Star Community,

Last night, our nation chose a new president in the most divisive election perhaps in this nation's history. The months that have led up to the election and last night's results have shaken many and have brought into question our core values as a nation. Many members of our community will be distraught today—many will be fearful and concerned about how they can possibly face the future—worried about personal and national safety. Nonetheless, our country will see a new president enter the White House as we enter the new year. And although our nation was split during the elections, I still believe in our democracy, and I am certain we will survive our divisions.

Having said that, I must also share our perspective as a school based on Islamic principles. Our expectations of behavior are very different from what we have seen throughout the public debates—and not just because of our values but because we work with children who are easily influenced and are much more vulnerable than adults. The current irony is that our President-elect has said and done disrespectful things that would have resulted in termination of an employee from just about any organization, including North Star Academy. Unfortunately, his words were part of an overall effective political strategy, but at North Star Academy, we explicitly reject his words and behavior because we believe that a leader is the people's servant and should exhibit the highest level of character.

We must make clear to our students in the days ahead that the values we teach—honesty, kindness, responsibility, generosity—are as true and valid as ever. Children may be confused and even hurting in this political climate - but they will continue to be strengthened by the smart, decent, and loving adults who surround them.

As many of you grapple with how to respond to your children's questions, teachers and administrators here at North Star will assure them that we will protect them, that bigotry is not acceptable, and that developing the skill of engaged discussion (Habit 5: Seek First to Understand, Then to be Understood) will give them the tools to heal whatever divides us as human beings. Here are some articles we use to guide our children/students:

- Ali Michael, Nov. 9, 2016, What do we tell the children? Huffpost.
- Lauryn Mascareñaz, Nov. 2, 2016, The day after. Southern Poverty Law Center, Learning for Justice.

I pray for our children, our families, our entire community, and our fellow citizens who are in disbelief and worried about the future. I pray for God to protect us all and guide our next President in his decision-making. Today, North Star's mission of raising proud American Muslims who will give back to their community and to humanity is all the more meaningful. We will remind our students and each other of our shared values. We are committed to honesty, justice, charity, and the pursuit of knowledge. We respect the dignity and worth of all human beings—their thoughts, their feelings, and their individuality. Today we will teach like we have never taught before. And tomorrow, we will teach again and again.

Most Sincerely,

Dr. Muna Ramsey

Head of School

The room was silent. Everyone's mind was in the past as they struggled to fold and cut the colored tissue papers. Ms. Seedat broke the silence by unfolding her flower, fluffing it with her hand several times, and holding it up to the light. "Beautiful!"

"I'm going to finish them with glitter spray. You won't believe how nice these are going to look hanging from the ceiling!" said Ms. Khan.

8

Five Years Later

In the five years that followed our visit to North Star Academy, the Trump presidency came to an end. Extreme far-right nationalism continued to harness alternative truths and fake news to advance their agendas. Ongoing disinformation and misinformation spread harmful conspiracy theories about Covid-19, which compounded extant hesitancies as to the efficacy of vaccinations. Widespread Black Lives Matter protests continued to demand justice for the murders of Black men, women, and youth at the hands of the police. Joe Biden was elected as the forty-sixth president of the United States. Yet, on January 6, 2021, a violent insurrection at the Capitol to halt the certification of Biden's electoral win revealed growing holes in the fabric of American democracy.

Authoritarian regimes continued to expand around the world, fostering anti-democratic alliances, attacking freedom of the press, undermining the rule of law, sabotaging elections, and discriminating against and mistreating migrants and refugees. The Taliban returned to power and reinstated oppressive policies. The Uyghurs continued to be held in Chinese detention centers and reeducation camps. Millions continued to starve in Yemen due to a near-decade-long civil war fomented by Saudi Arabia. The Syrian refugee crisis has left millions displaced since the fighting began in 2011. Russia invaded Ukraine, starting an unprovoked war.

Islamophobia, coupled with discriminatory and derogatory language, continued to fuel anti-Muslim hatred and violence. In 2019, an Australian far-right extremist murdered fifty-one Muslims in an attack on two mosques in Christchurch, New Zealand. Palestinian American Journalist Shireen Abu Akleh was shot in the head by Israeli forces while reporting from the occupied West Bank. Shootings, stabbings, melee attacks, arson, vandalism, and other crimes against Muslims bore witness to a rise in human rights abuses and anti-Muslim racism worldwide.

It was important to us that we returned to North Star Academy, as we, too, were delayed in writing this book because of Covid-19 and job changes. We specifically wanted to learn how the school changed and developed over the last five years, with particular attention to leadership. On Friday, March 10, 2023, Miriam returned to the school and spoke with the still-current head of school, Dr. Ramsey. On her drive to the school, Miriam noticed how pristine the buildings and landscape looked against the morning California sunrise. Manicured landscaping lined the city's streets. Bicycle corridors connected child-friendly parks. Well-kept houses reflected the city's wealth due mainly to high employment in the finance and insurance, real estate, pharmaceutical, and computer industries. Arriving at North Star Academy's upper school, the office park looked the same, although the trees had grown and matured. The school building remained in its original condition, yet, there was a new soccer field and outdoor basketball court located on the side of the school. The strategic placement of flood lights allowed for nighttime games, and four-level concrete steps served as event seating.

Miriam walked to the front door. Deborah, a new receptionist, escorted her down the hall to Dr. Ramsey's office. Dr. Ramsey looked up from her computer to see Miriam smiling. Miriam said, "*Assalamu alaykum*, stranger! It's so good to be back on campus!"

Dr. Ramsey stood up, reached out her arms for a hug, and replied, "*Wa-alaykum assalam!*"

"I've been out for a week with some kind of infection. Today's my first day back. The calendar is full! I'm afraid we will have a hard stop after ninety minutes," commented Dr. Ramsey.

"Let's get started, then." Miriam made sure that Zoom was recording the audio and transcribing the text. "I remember when we were here last time, some of the students shared with us how safe they felt in the school. They spoke about feeling welcomed and were excited to have extra space upstairs. So what are your current plans?"

Dr. Ramsey replied, "We're actually undergoing a strategic planning process right now. We would have done this in 2020, but Covid delayed us and pushed the timeline out. Part of this process includes surveying the parents, students, alumni, faculty, staff, and board members. And yes, there are still conversations about opening a high school. This is because they know there's a potential space upstairs for expansion, and to the students, it feels like the next step is opening a high school. Personally, philosophically, I don't think that we would be serving our community by opening a high school. This is controversial, but in the end, the strategic plan will be what it is. The stakeholders will ultimately make the decision. But as a school leader, everything we do in the school is intentionally designed to prepare kids to navigate the world beyond North Star. This is our foundation.

"I think a few things would happen if we were to open a high school. We are not a Catholic school that attracts kids from all backgrounds and faith traditions. We would create a cocoon where kids would stay at North Star until adulthood. If we had a high school, our kids would graduate as eighteen-year-olds, as adults. That's too late for them to test boundaries and figure out how to navigate the world. They're gonna make mistakes. That's part of growing up. Making a mistake as an adult is very different from making a mistake when you're fourteen and still have parents watching you and saying, 'That's not how you do it.' Personally, I think opening a high school will attract more conservative families that like the idea of a cocoon. Many students would stay here for their entire education and not have the opportunity to learn how to navigate the world. Questions such as, How are you going to keep your prayers? How are you going to ask for time and space to pray? With Ramadan, when everyone else is eating, how are you going to navigate being able to hold onto that fast? It's important that students learn how to do this in high school while they have the support of their families. They are still close to North Star and can connect with their friends. If they stay in a cocoon until university, they have no opportunity to practice navigating these issues. They will not have anyone watching. They may not be connected to any support system. They may be living in another state. So, in my mind, it would be much easier for an alum to slip," explained Dr. Ramsey.

"Are a majority of the stakeholders in agreement with you, or are they torn about the idea of opening a high school?"

"I have not openly shared my ideas because I want to honor the process of the strategic planning that we are currently doing. I've had a few conversations with people I trust, such as my board chair. But, with the strategic planning committee, I need them to come to that conclusion. When we came together to begin the strategic planning process, we agreed on what was non-negotiable, which was to ensure that we safeguard our mission of developing American Muslim identity in a progressive environment. All that needs to happen is to question how a high school would impact this non-negotiable. I think it will work itself out."

"That's right," Miriam whispered in agreement. "It's interesting that you're just letting the process unfold. I can imagine that being difficult for you. You are guided by a clear vision. You can see it, and you're hoping everybody else can see it too. But people are looking at things and making decisions from their own perspectives, right?"

"It's like the franchise model. Just because you have one good thing, the question remains, 'Can you replicate this twenty times?' It's not that easy. The answer is yes, you can, but it won't be exactly the same. So, what do you give up when you make decisions like that? I'm not concerned about it because they already agreed to the non-negotiables. If we were a franchise, we would lose our non-negotiables. The school would change. The question then becomes, 'Are we willing to lose who we are to grow?' Every decision has consequences."

"On that note—we noticed that the school changed its name to 'North Star Academy and Community Center.' Why did the name change?"

"We want the school to be used by the community. There's a lot of time when the building is unoccupied, whether it's the summer months when we are not in session or the evenings and weekends. The school could be used by the community during these off times. So, we decided to rent out the facility to sports teams and other religious groups. Muslim nonprofits use the space for fundraisers and banquets. This makes me happy. I enjoy seeing the space being utilized by the wider community. I don't see a distinction between the Academy and the Community Center."

"That's what we noticed when reviewing the social media sites," added Miriam.

"For me, it's a *dawah* (inviting people to embrace Islam) thing too. The greatest expression of *dawah* is the fact that we have sports teams that play other schools. When we have a home game, our gym is filled with people from other faith traditions. I think it demystifies who we are because our girls are playing soccer, basketball, and volleyball. You know all of the myths out there about girls and Islam. The families who come to our school to watch these events see our parents cheering for their kids the same way they do. How many people of other faith traditions ever enter Muslim spaces? Probably very few. Those that do are inclined toward interfaith work. Why would someone of another faith tradition come into a Muslim organization? Parents come because their kids play a sport. That's how we can get people to bend a little bit and see another point of view."

"In the last five years, a lot has happened. Covid-19. The murder of George Floyd. Mass gun shootings in schools. Fake news and a rise in extreme right politics. What's been going on in society that's impacted North Star?"

"Some of these issues are bigger than our youngest students can fully understand. Social justice is definitely a part of our curriculum, and we talk about it whenever there is an opportunity. We discuss right and wrong and ask,

'Can we help? In what ways can we help?' But it doesn't go very deep because they're young. More happens with our middle school students. We participate in the *Model United Nations* event. That is usually reserved for high schoolers, but we do that at the middle school level because we want to discuss global issues. For example, topics include sex trafficking, climate change, nuclear proliferation, and drug trafficking. The middle schoolers are mature enough to go deep, and they do. They do their research. They discuss the topics, and they generate ideas. Model UN is run by our social studies and Islamic studies teachers. For me as a school leader, I'm lucky. Although we are a very diverse school, we are monolithic politically to some degree. We all lean a little to the left. For other schools, that's not the case, and a school leader would need to stay very neutral when it comes to certain topics.

"After Trump was elected, I wrote a healing message to the school community because Muslims were used as a platform for his election. I know that our kids had questions about why the bully won the election. They asked questions, such as, 'What does this mean for me and my family? Are we going to have to go back to Lebanon or the country of our heritage?' There was a collective discomfort that I was able to address. You have that letter, right?"

"I do."

"The same with the murder of George Floyd. It was so important for me to say something and to share a perspective. I have the freedom and the ability to do that because our community members hold similar political values. I'm so lucky in that sense that I can voice my opinion. Let me share with you the letter I sent." Dr. Ramsey turned her computer for Miriam to see the screen. Dr. Ramsey began.

June 4, 2020

Assalamu Alaykum Dear Extended North Star Academy Family,

I can't breathe.

I have been wanting to address the numbingly familiar tragedy of the loss of our Black brothers and sisters to violence this past week—this past month—for my entire lifetime. The topic of race was an essential component of our beloved Prophet's (pbuh) last sermon given almost 1400 years ago. He stated:

> **You know that every Muslim is the brother of another Muslim. All mankind is from Adam and Eve, an Arab has no superiority over a non-Arab, nor a non-Arab has any superiority over an Arab; also, a white has no superiority over a black nor a black has any superiority over a white— except by piety and good action.**

What a sad reality that these words are a relevant guidance to those of us living in the 21st century despite being spoken the first time in 623 C.E. As Muslims and as brothers and sisters in humanity, we should all go beyond being horrified and do what we can to support the Black community. As members of a minority group, we should be the first to show our solidarity and stand up whenever we see an injustice towards any group. As a school, we should be committed to raising socially conscious and engaged young leaders who are eloquent and fearless. If we lead the charge today, I have faith that our youth - especially if they are grounded by the values of social justice within our faith - can fulfill the hopes for a better future through their knowledge, confidence, and compassion to serve others.

A high school friend of mine shared a poignant story about her own experience with White Privilege after being married to a Black man for five years. She always thought that "loving all people was enough" until they recently installed an alarm system in their home, and her husband shared his concern that sharing the code with too many people "increased the chances of the alarm going off by mistake, the police coming and [her husband] or his son getting shot by mistake." In that moment, she recognized her privilege and realized how different her husband's reality was simply due to the color of his skin. Like my friend recognized, I believe we all need to educate ourselves and others about our own privileges. With the privileges we have, we have an obligation to be a voice for justice and change.

Diverse communities are inherently stronger communities, and the more points of view, perspectives, lived experiences, cultures that come together, the better we are individually and collectively. North Star Academy aspires to attract, serve, and maintain a widely diverse community. Many of the programs adopted by our school, such as Positive Discipline and Leader in Me, train students to understand that it starts with them, each of them has a voice, and to use their voice to stand up and speak out when they see injustice. Having said that, there is still much more we can and need to do to educate ourselves, our students, and our community explicitly about racism and discrimination. We cannot passively watch as if this is outside of our community, but rather, we must recognize our own biases and work hard to do better.

Say their names. AHMAUD ARBERY. BREONNA TAYLOR. GEORGE FLOYD.

May God's Grace be upon these souls who were recently killed, and may His Grace be with each of their families and loved ones. May God spread His Mercy on all who face injustice and the multitude of innocent lives that have been lost to violence. #BlackLivesMatter

In Solidarity,

Dr. Muna Ramsey

Head of School

After Dr. Ramsey finished reading, Miriam sat in silence. "How did the community respond?"

"It was well received. We needed healing."

"You know, when we were here last time, we noticed social media posts on a wide range of challenging topics for parent night, such as mental health. Are you still continuing to host these events?"

"Yes. Most of the topics originate from conversations we have with parents. As you know, Covid was difficult to navigate. All of a sudden, this very open school with its active community was restricted. It felt so different. Everyone was in silos. If parents were able to drop off their kids, they would drop them off and run. Parents didn't hang around to chat. Before Covid, parents hanging out at school was part of our culture. To bridge this gap, we tried to bring people together through Zoom to discuss various topics, such as parenting. This year, I really feel the disconnect. Essentially, for the last three years, we didn't have a school community.

"At the beginning of this year, we decided to run some parenting classes where the parents attend in person. The response was, 'Can you broadcast this so we can do it from home?' Our whole intention was to rebuild the school community. We decided to run a parenting workshop for kindergarten and first-grade families. Second grade had its own event because they are preparing to transition to the upper campus next year. For the third-, fourth-, and fifth-grade families, we offered a parenting class that discussed physical and mental development. But there's more to be done. I think these events have just scratched the surface. We still have parents who don't fully understand our mission. We have parents who complain that there is too much homework. This is the same for Arabic. A parent will complain that their child is not speaking Arabic yet. But our Arabic is not designed for them to be fluent. Parents are in their own world. Now that we've come back to school, parents are asking, 'Why this? Why that?' So, there's some work to be done. We need to reset and remind people of our philosophy. We need to reclaim a collective understanding."

"Speaking of collective understanding, I know that many families in the school are unaware of the school's affiliation with the Islamic Center of San Rico. Are there any updates on the relationship between the school and the Center?"

"No," said Dr. Ramsey. "The relationship is a structural one, right? There's really no interference into the school from the Center because, philosophically, we are still aligned. I think the only time we would hit a snag is if some kind of intervention was needed from the Center. For example, if all of a sudden we said this is a Shi'a school, or if we took funding from the Saudi government, the center would intervene because those decisions are counter to American Muslim identity and the progressive view of Islam. Other than that, the relationship just exists. There isn't any involvement, although I get together with other heads of school. There's still that connection."

"So, it sounds like there is a loose connection between you and the center. Would you call it a relationship of checks and balances?"

"I think the check and balance are in the structure itself. For example, if we're going to change our mission, we have to go back to the center and get it ratified. So that's the check and balance. It's in the structure."

"So, it wouldn't be just the school board. It would be the Islamic Center's board, too?" questioned Miriam.

Dr. Ramsey clarified, "Yes, but it's not even the center. The center has delegated this responsibility to the Executive Council, which includes the board chairs and the heads of the four schools. It would be our peers who would identify if there was drift more quickly than the center."

The bell rang. Noise entered the hallway. Sounds of lockers opening, children talking, laughing, and the interruption of a teacher saying, "Slow down! No running, please!" reverberated throughout the school.

"The school has a different feel and energy than I remember," commented Miriam.

"Yes, the school has grown so much since you were here last. We have well over 300 students. I don't have as much direct contact with families as I used to, and I miss that. We now have a dean of students, an upper school director, a lower school director, and an associate director at the lower school. There is an extra layer that handles issues and problems now with the students, such as if a kiddo needs an intervention or a discussion."

"Are teachers empowered to take on a leadership role in problem-solving?" asked Miriam.

"I think no matter what, the teachers always feel stuck in the middle. That's really hard because I want the teachers to feel like they're administrators too. I want them to sit with parents and say, 'No, your child is struggling. I know you want to blame me, but it's not me. I don't think it's benefiting Ali to say I'm not giving him enough.' I don't know how to help teachers have that voice. I think a lot of our teachers are people pleasers. They work with kids. They are not used to having their ideas questioned. So, when a parent does question them, all of a sudden, they're like, 'It's so hard. My feelings are hurt.' They need to be in a place that allows them to take a leadership role and tell parents, 'Okay, let's work through this.' Many of my teachers are intimidated by our parents. Many of our parents feel entitled. In the public school system, the teacher says, 'That's how I do it. That's it.' But our parents demand more. It's my wish that every teacher could be a leader. It depends on the teacher and if they're comfortable enough to say, 'I'm nervous. I know these parents are gonna challenge me.' I wish a teacher would ask me to be present in the room with them when they talk with parents or allow me to help them practice their response to a worst-case scenario. I could pretend to be the parent, or they could pretend to be the parent. We could act out whatever their worst fear is about the meeting. The teachers would then see how I navigate these relationships. But this is very rare. Usually, the teachers just get nervous.

"I always say to parents, 'You're the expert on money because you do that, right? I'm an expert in education, and I can tell you how Ali behaves in a classroom setting, which is not his day-to-day experience with you.' When I talk to the parents about a problem their child is having at school, I'm gifting parents insights into their child within a classroom environment, an environment they don't see. I'm always on the side of the child. I am not against parents. I want what is best for every child. Parents often are mistaken about what is best, though. I feel it is my responsibility to make it clear to parents that if their child continues down the road they are traveling, they are going to lose their child. I'll ask parents to imagine this behavior at age fifteen. So, I'll stress the importance of handling it while he's seven."

Miriam replied, "It's easy for you to say that to parents. But you're right, it's hard for teachers to have these conversations."

Dr. Ramsey smiled and asked, "Do you know about research on the reasons why teachers go into the profession and how it's the same as that of the clergy?"

"No, I don't."

"There was a study that examined different fields and what inspires people to enter different professions. The study found that what inspires people to become teachers is the same thing that inspires people to become clergy. They both pursue their profession for a higher purpose. It's not about compensation; it's about giving back. So when you're entering a field where all you're doing is giving, you don't want to hear criticisms on how you do the job—because it's the source that feeds you—this ability to give and make a difference. So when someone says, 'You're not making a difference,' all of a sudden, teachers feel like they want to quit."

"What have parents criticized?"

"Well, there's always a question about rigor. Our parents' schooling experience, by and large, was much different. They would come home from school and study until midnight. The mom would bring in cookies and then tea. They would eat dinner while they were sitting and studying, fall asleep while working, and then get up early and do the same thing again the next day. They identify this rigor as quality schooling. Recently I had a parent who came in and said, 'We heard about the school's reputation and brought our kid here for that reputation. She's in middle school now, and all she does is projects and group work. She's done with her homework in forty-five minutes, and we just thought, with your reputation—'"

"What? That she'd be studying until one in the morning?" Miriam asked, laughing.

"Yes! I said to him, 'I know you are a successful businessman. What makes you successful in your work today? Is it that you memorize a lot of things? No, it's your ability to communicate and your ability to work with others. Our curriculum is designed to support your daughter's ability to communicate.' I gave him an example. 'My father is a pharmacist. Back then, the book of compounds for medication was this thick.'" Dr. Ramsey raised her hand and mimicked a six-inch book. "'If you have a sick patient, by the time you diagnose them and then go to the compound book to figure out what medicine to make for them, they could die. So, you needed to have everything memorized along with a good filing system so that you could diagnose their illness, figure out what they needed to get better, make it for them, and then give it to them. That's what made you the superior doctor over your neighbor. Today, you can put the symptoms into a computer and get the diagnosis and treatments within seconds. So, what is going to distinguish you from the doctor next door if they also use a computer? It's going to be your ability to communicate, your bedside manner, and your active listening skills. It's not going to be about how smart you are or if you've memorized a compound book.' We know the importance of emotional intelligence.

"Here is another example related to math. I don't need to calculate in my head or on paper. We have calculators. We have to push parents outside of what they believe an education looks like and then have them recognize that we are preparing kids for a future that doesn't yet exist. We don't even know what types of jobs there will be in the future. It makes me rethink our curriculum. Even writing, in the future, our students are going to have tools that will write for them. So how do you use that knowledge, such as ChatGPT? Do they use it to begin an outline or provide an overview? Is writing a skill that's going to be needed in the future? As an educational leader my focus is never on moving students from fourth to fifth grade. When a student comes in, I envision that student as someone who is fifteen, sixteen, or seventeen years old. I focus on what we can give that student to become a successful adult. What does this student need to prepare them for a career? What skills might they need in the future? What do they need to learn to be able to effectively navigate being a minority within a majority population? That's my focus. For parents, though, it's more narrow. They are concerned about their child being the top student in the fifth-grade class."

Miriam shifted the conversation: "How are the alums doing?"

"There was a time, especially when we were on one campus, that I had a connection with each one of them and their families. I felt like I had a positive influence on their lives. I was young and energetic. I was leaning in. I love them. They are a reflection of everything good about the school."

"Do you see an opportunity to bring them back into the fold? Do they come to visit?"

"Yes. They volunteer when they have time off from school. We don't have a formal process, but I think that's probably the next phase. We now have enough alumni that we could formalize some kind of programming. That's probably going to be in our strategic plan. Part of the community center concept is to be able to maintain a connection. We have a basketball gym. Alums can come back and play basketball after school or on the weekend. There's a sense that this is still their place. My dream of dreams is that eventually, our director of admissions and teachers will be alums of North Star. I'd love to see the school carried into the future by those who benefited from this schooling experience."

"What do you look for when hiring teachers?" asked Miriam.

"First, qualifications through paper screening. We look at how many years they have taught. We look to see what degree they have and if they have teaching credentials. After that, personality. I screen through a fifteen-minute Zoom conversation. Before, I used to do this screening on the phone because I thought I could get a sense of a person in five minutes. Now I do a fifteen-minute Zoom meeting. In the meeting, I ask three questions. What brought you to teaching? Why are you looking for a teaching position now? We're an Islamic school. How do you feel about working in an environment that may be different from your belief system? What I'm looking for is someone who almost tears up when talking about teaching because they love the profession and see it as a calling. I want to hear from them a certainty that teaching is what they were meant to do. If they happened to be let go from a previous school, then I want to understand why. If they moved from out of state, then that explains why they left their previous school. Sometimes they'll say it wasn't a good fit, and then I'll want to understand what that means. It could be they are running away from something that they may find at North Star. I don't want that. I really want to understand what it is they want. I also look for openness. I actually love it when someone says, 'I need to learn because I'm afraid that I might make a mistake.' This is somebody who's sensitive and isn't coming in with their own opinions. They're open to learning, and they're considerate of others. That's enough to get them in the door. Then we do a mock lesson. When I see them in person with the kids, I look for chemistry. How are they interacting with the kids? Are they firm but fair? Are the kids learning? Is learning fun?"

"What challenges do you face leading your teaching staff?" asked Miriam.

Dr. Ramsey laughed. "Well, we've just gone through a big teacher turnover. The school has grown quickly, and we hired the wrong people in some cases. We don't want to lose the teachers who we are in the process of growing. With the layer of Covid on top of this, my gosh! There was a lot of fear. As a leader, I had to try to push people through something that felt very scary. I remember initially that I thought this would blow over quickly. It would be a week or two of remote learning. Then we would be back. The day before we closed the school, I called for meetings with each teaching team. I told them, 'We're closing tomorrow. I'm going to send out an email. Tomorrow is going to be a faculty work day. We're going to need to change how we've been teaching because next week, and maybe for a couple of weeks, we're going to be teaching remotely. I want you to plan as if this is the new normal moving forward.' I didn't want a Band-Aid. I didn't want their lesson plans to be half done. I said, 'I want you to pretend this is our teaching approach for the remainder of the year.' I wanted them to really invest in the process. I did that with each group, not knowing if it would be a reality.

"I wanted to inspire them to dig in. I wanted this done with quality. All of the teachers stepped into it. We were lucky. We had a student teacher at the time who had previously done some online classes. She became our resource. 'Teach everyone how to do this!' I told her. It was crazy. But we all went into action. We literally only paused for a day. I sent out the announcement on Thursday that explained to families that Monday would be our first day of learning remotely. Parents contacted me, 'What are you doing? You're out of your mind!' Then, the next day, Governor Newsom made his announcement that we were going remote." Dr. Ramsey laughed.

Miriam laughed along. "I think it's a direct line. Oh my God!"

"So, we moved. We only paused for a day. On Monday, we went to remote learning. We spent the whole weekend redoing the schedule. We weren't going to have kids for seven hours on Zoom. We had to rethink everything. Preschool parents said, 'Zoom is not what we signed up for. We want childcare. I'm not sitting my three-year-old in front of the screen.' These families were in the worst situation, and many pulled their children out. We had to let preschool teachers go. It was hard. What's interesting is that parents began to notice that the public schools didn't have it together. It took public schools one month to transition. It took us one day to be ready! Families started to see that their kids were on track. They were making good progress. Parents began asking if the school would be open next year. What were we going to do? By May, I knew remote learning would continue for at least a year.

I told the families that the whole world was shut down. We were lucky to have this new building. It wasn't full because we were just starting our second year. We're going to spread the kids out, twelve students per class. We'll have morning sessions and afternoon sessions and require that a child attend one session in person. They would learn remotely for the other. We allowed parents to choose what arrangement worked best for them. Some kids stayed at home entirely because of health reasons. We had to apply for a waiver with the state of California and submit a plan. I told my teachers that none of us were going anywhere this summer and that we needed to return to work a month early with the hope that we could end a month earlier. Everyone was Zoomed out.

"The prediction was a surge, and then things would get better. Everyone was on board to start early. Parents were on board. Teachers thought the hybrid approach would work. We were the first school in the county to receive approval from the state to teach face-to-face classes. All the other schools were teaching remotely. Our preschool shrunk from eighty to twenty kids, with half attending in the morning and the other half attending in the afternoon. All of a sudden, our middle school enrollments grew because we were approved to hold face-to-face classes. This bounced our reputation. But this bounce occurred at the cost of the teachers. I had burned out teachers."

"Teachers were leaving the profession in droves," commented Miriam.

"So, you've got to imagine we're in this growth mode, and we're trying to create culture amid this trauma. So last year, I had teachers who left in the middle of the year. I had a director who left in the middle of the year. You could just feel it. No one was in a happy place. The kids were so used to being home in their pajamas during lessons that they came to school not knowing how to behave. Kids would roll around on the ground. Kids forgot how to interact with other kids. Last year was really hard, possibly the hardest year I've ever had.

"Then coming into this year, 2022–2023, there was a breath of fresh air. Covid is still there, but it's not materializing in the same way as before. We hired new teachers, and now it's a matter of socializing them into our culture. I brought on a great upper school director. She has really helped to hold the ship together. It feels like year one all over again, but a healthy year one. We're not coming out of a disastrous situation like last year where we lost a large number of teachers, had unmanageable and unruly kids, and had to deal with impatient parents. This year, we're in a better place."

"How do you empower teachers, especially those that are not Muslim?"

"We start with Islam 101. So, at the beginning of the year, we invite every teacher who's not Muslim and Muslim teachers, if they feel like they need it, to do an overview of the basics of the faith. Of course, not with the intent to convert. It's simply for information to make them feel comfortable. For teachers of other faith traditions, something happens to them. They find themselves supporting Islam when people react to where they work. 'What, you work in an Islamic school? That's crazy. What are you doing there?' Or they may hear, 'Those Arabs, those Muslims . . .' coming from friends and family. The more they know, the more quickly they feel comfortable within our environment and the better able they are to respond when they find themselves in an uncomfortable situation. That's been a discovery of ours.

"We emphasize that there are no dumb questions, but we stress that they will get different answers because there's no one way in Islam. We do not have a Pope that we look to for a single answer. Answers are really left to individual interpretation. Part of the reason why we are a progressive school is because we're open to different interpretations. So you're gonna hear someone who says music is *haram* and another person say, 'What are you talking about? Music is a part of our culture! Kids should be singing and enjoying music!' You will also find someone who says a *hijab* is required for women. Another person will say, 'No, *hijabs* are not required!' We recommend they ask their questions to two different people. In that way, they can see the spectrum. We try to make them feel as comfortable as we can. This is the ideal. But then there is what actually happens.

"To give you an example, our religious studies teachers are first-generation immigrants. Our Qur'an teacher was born outside of the US. If you look at our Arabic teachers, the same. Islamic studies is the only space where we can hire somebody who was born and raised here, has Islamic knowledge and is better equipped to prepare kids for what's ahead because they themselves have experienced it. The Qur'an and Arabic teachers who came from outside of the country invariably teach the way they were taught. So, there's a little bit of us and them that develops. That's the reality. When you have White American teachers and an immigrant Qur'an teacher, there is tension around 'that's your way, and this is our way.' That's hard to overcome because I think the immigrant teacher doesn't see how different their teaching methods are. That's a very hard thing because they don't understand. It's like this push and pull. The reason why every parent's child is in this school is because of the religious teachers, and yet their teaching methods are not aligned with who we are. If I am hard on them, they feel I'm picking on them when they're the most valuable asset."

"They have a skill set that is needed, yet their methodology is completely counter to what you want," Miriam summarized.

"Yes. I want our religious studies teachers to be the teachers students remember with fondness, but that is not always the case. Sometimes students see the religious studies teachers as uncles and aunties, but their favorite teachers are the ones that actively engage them in their learning."

"In our interviews with teachers from other faith traditions, there was reluctance to talk about their faith experience. They didn't want to accidentally cross the line. Is there a way that you draw the line for them? Do they understand where that line is?" asked Miriam.

"It's complicated. We had an experience with a music teacher who wanted to teach the kids Tchaikovsky during November and December. The music teacher kept saying that *The Nutcracker* wasn't intended to be a Christmas ballet. I replied that culturally everyone knows it as a Christmas ballet. If Tchaikovsky is really the purpose, then teach it in March. She was an evangelical Christian who couldn't bring herself to not honor the season of Christmas. I find that some White teachers come to a point where they want to fix things because they are uncomfortable."

Miriam replied, "So, instead of being mindful of the environment and the purpose of the school, she isn't realizing that the kids get plenty of Christmas outside of the school."

"That's right. Students get bombarded with Christmas. Driving home there are Christmas lights and Christmas trees. Christmas is in every shop. Christmas is all over the television. This school is the one space that can be authentically theirs. So, I hate to sound completely insensitive, but those who feel like they can't be fully Christian within an Islamic school environment shouldn't be working in an Islamic school."

Dr. Ramsey's voice revealed her frustration. "Yes, what's our mission? Of course, you can wear your cross. No one is under the illusion that you're a practicing Muslim. Some of our kids and families will be sensitive and kind enough to give her a Christmas present before the break. But don't expect the

White, Christian colonial perspective to dominate this space. My question is, 'Why does she feel the need to display her Christianity here?' When she's at home, her Christianity is fully on display. It is fully on display with her family and in society. I want her to evaluate that and then come talk to me." Dr. Ramsey laughed, but she was clearly irked.

"That's a great example of drawing the line. Christianity is privileged in public schools and public spaces. Teachers put up Christmas decorations even though not all the students in their classroom are Christian. It's an imposition of their Christian privilege," added Miriam.

"This may be my own issue, but there isn't a Muslim who hasn't had to navigate their own identity on the regular. It's hard for me to open a space for someone who already has privilege. It's really hard. That comes back to when I do the preliminary screening and ask, 'How do you feel about teaching in an Islamic school?' Either the applicant didn't know or wasn't completely honest. We will let this teacher come into our space as a foreigner, learn, and think everything is amazing. Then, all of a sudden, this teacher will want to put out their Christianity. This is completely counter to everything that we're trying to do at this school. We want to give our kids a sense of whatever White privilege feels like outside to those who enjoy White privilege."

Dr. Ramsey took a drink of coffee. Her mood shifted. "I think our teachers, on the whole, embrace the notion of community, and they are also a community among each other. They are also protective of the kids because they've seen them over the long haul. This becomes a discovery when a new teacher comes into the school. The new teacher will complain about a kid, and then all of a sudden, the other teachers don't like that. It's perceived as if this new teacher is picking on one of their relatives. I like this protectiveness. I like that they understand that we're a community and that we're protectors of one another.

"Our teachers want to aspire to something greater than themselves. They want to have an influence and impact on the future. They want to do good. These are admirable things. Those teachers with complete humility are probably the best teachers out there. There are other teachers who just love being in control. Those teachers have a selfish slant to their work. Those are the ones that are hard to work with. It is hard for them to see their selfishness. They call the classroom 'my classroom.' The students are 'my students.' So, when you have a teacher who really does the work with humility, it is 'the students' classroom.' We have many of those types of teachers.

"But right now, we are playing catch-up with our teachers. Before Covid, we had everyone on the same page with Positive Discipline and Leader in Me, but now only half of the teachers are on the same page because the other half are new to the school. My goal is to have a stable, consistent faculty and staff like when we were one campus so we can all get the same professional development where teachers are using the same language and have a common purpose. I hope to achieve that by year three. Yes, it's like starting all over again after Covid."

"Do the teachers from both campuses have a chance to come together?"

"Sure, for celebrations and faculty workdays. These events allow staff to connect. It's hard to have professional development that is applicable to the whole school since it's preschool through eighth grade. We have religious studies, physical education, and specialty teachers. So if we're looking at the English Language Arts program, that might be for Kindergarten through grade five. That means religious studies are out, specialties are out. For me, my focus is Positive Discipline, the Leader in Me, and the grounding of who we are, and only then can we do some creative things. I would say our specialty teachers are the least engaged with professional development. For example, we have one art teacher. What do you do to get an art teacher to think differently?"

"How do you move teachers on if they are not a good fit for the school?" asked Miriam.

"I had a situation where I had to let a teacher go last year. This teacher was liked by some of the families. I knew that she wasn't the right fit for the school. Sometimes, as an educator watching another educator, you know that what you are observing is not right. A teacher could give every student an 'A' grade. Parents will think, 'She's a brilliant teacher because my daughter is getting A's!' But, in reality, that teacher may not be holding kids accountable. They're not really teaching. To relieve themselves of the headache, they are just giving away grades. So, as a leader, I knew this was going to be an unpopular decision, but it was the right decision for the kids. I couldn't sleep. I knew I needed to bring up my courage to potentially hurt her and negatively impact her livelihood. I never want to hurt anybody. I thought about it for a long time, probably a week straight, of not sleeping at night. Finally, I came to this place where I recognized that my role is my role, and my humanity is my humanity. They do not need to be in conflict. In other words, I can still say to somebody, 'This isn't working,' and at the same time, wish them well and want what is best for them.

"Religiously, we believe that *rizq* (sense of giving or apportionment) comes from God; it's not from me. If it's meant for this person to be a millionaire, it's meant for them. If it is meant for this person to be a teacher, they will be a teacher in some other environment. I really want what's best for that person, and I hope this comes through. Of course, I also honor the fact that they're going to be mad at me. In the past, I've experienced some people going out and telling everyone that I was terrible and mean. The way I handled it was horrible, and they wished that I would have let them go in a different way. I don't have the ability to counter that, nor do I need to. It's their story. If they want to paint it that way, if that makes them feel better, it's okay. It's not me against that person. They are going to be mad. There was one time that someone actually came back and thanked me for letting them go because, at the time, they didn't recognize how unhappy they were. My faith tells me I'm in a position to help push a person in the direction they are meant to go because God has set this direction."

Miriam took a minute to collect her thoughts. "I know we'll be out of time soon. May I ask a few questions about the curriculum?

"Sure."

"How has your curriculum changed over the last five years?"

"A few things have changed. Covid created an opportunity for us to enhance the ways we were using technology. Moving forward there are some innovative things that we're exploring, such as measuring students' executive functioning skills and seeing if there's a curriculum that can support the development of these skills. In the co-curricular space, our field trips are back. During Covid, those fell by the wayside. We have some after-school programs again through renting out the facility, such as a new robotics club, leadership clubs, and different sports."

"I know current events are integrated into the Islamic studies and social studies classes. When Ilhan Omar and Rashida Tlaib rose to prominence in the political arena, how was this integrated into the curriculum?" asked Miriam.

"With the school also being a community center, we had organizations rent out the space to host both Rashida Tlaib and Ilhan Omar. They came for two different fundraisers. To be clear, it wasn't me that invited them. Politically, we have to have some separation from the political organizations that rent out our space. But our kids came and met them."

"That must have been a real treat!"

"Yes, and this week we had Ibtihaj Muhammad visit. She is the first Muslim female *hijabi* Olympic medalist and author of *The Kindest Red* and *The Proudest Blue*. She read her books to our kids."

"I saw that on Instagram! She's a fencer," said Miriam.

"Being a known Islamic school and with the facilities we have, these things naturally happen without me having to make them happen."

"You mentioned that the enrollment of students increased exponentially over the last five years. What demographic shifts have you seen, if any?"

"We've seen more families move into Springwater from other states. Post-Covid, we've seen more kids that are behind. We've had to be more flexible with our acceptance policy to accommodate families that might have one or two kids who are falling academically behind. We had families stay with us because we were offering in-person schooling. Even those who were with us but were remote didn't fare as well as those who showed up in person. Teachers are seeing students with a spectrum of needs. They will have a kid who's a year ahead and another kid who's a year behind in the same classroom. That wasn't the reality pre-Covid. We've had to hire instructional assistants to help support students. I'll also say that we've seen more anxiety in parents and kids. I don't know if this is a post-Covid or a millennial generational thing, but they generally worry about everything."

"Do you think the children are more connected? Do they all have phones in middle school?"

"Well, they're not allowed, but they all have them," said Dr. Ramsey with a chuckle.

I'm wondering if social media contributes to this anxiety or is it a sign of the times?" reflected Miriam out loud.

"I think it's all of it. Let me go back to your original question about how we value the interests and humanity of our students. We are part of a sports league that runs in three trimesters. The first trimester is flag football for the boys and volleyball for the girls. The next trimester is basketball with a girls' team and a boys' team. The third trimester is soccer with boys' and girls' teams. For the younger ones, boys and girls play on the same soccer team. The only ones that feel a little off are volleyball and flag football. Our coach found a small group of schools that were willing to do an extra session for four weeks. Girls can play flag football, and boys can play volleyball. That is an example of a conscious effort to try and provide an opportunity for everyone equally.

"What about gender equality in the school curriculum?" asked Miriam.

Dr. Ramsey appeared amused by the question. "I think the best way to talk about this is through our sex ed program. Both boys and girls participate in sex ed. This learning begins in the fifth grade with the human development class, and we include the parents. In fact, today is our father and son pizza night, which we call 'Boys Night Out' because not all of our kids have fathers in their lives. We have to be sensitive to language. We do parent-child activities because we want the kids to have a puberty partner to open the door for communication within the family on a very uncomfortable topic. For instance, in the mother-daughter tea, we want to demystify puberty so that the mom and the daughter can giggle about periods and pads, wearing bras and hair down there, and all that stuff. The dads and the boys can have that same connection. It's to remind the moms and the dads of how they felt when they were going through puberty themselves, so they can have compassion for their kids. It's also to open the doors of communication so kids know that this person not only has experienced everything they're about to experience but also cares deeply about them and will help them through anything. Sex ed is much more clinical. It's biology. It's about asexual and sexual reproduction. So, they learn this in class.

"In seventh grade, we add a piece about Islamic etiquette around sexuality and what's expected. We also do that with mother-daughter tea and father-son pizza. This includes what women need to do after they finish their period. We talk about exemption from prayer and fasting when young women are menstruating. We talk about how sexuality is a positive part of human life. We talk to boys about relationships and love, but this equal approach is not typical. Some alumni shared that their parents wanted them to continue at a private Muslim high school when they left North Star. Our female alum shared that the boys would kick the girls off the basketball court. The girls were shocked. They never heard, 'Girls don't play sports' or 'Girls can't play basketball.' So when they faced this for the first time, it was a surprise. It's not something they experienced here.

"In terms of gender equality at North Star, the only complicated issue is prayer. You know the fact that boys are in the front and the girls are behind. For me personally, I'm very comfortable being in the back because of the way that we bend. I wouldn't feel comfortable with a guy behind me while doing that part of the prayer. I think for our teen girls, who are social justice oriented, they see this as an issue of fairness. They think, 'That's their problem. They shouldn't be looking.' They are right about that. I reached out to some scholars to understand why we can't pray side-by-side because there is room for us to do that here. We do it during Ramadan and even in Hajj, where women and men are literally standing side-by-side. Every scholar I spoke to said that there's absolutely nothing that would prohibit side-by-side prayer, as long as there's enough space as if there's an individual in between. They also said that there's no mosque that they know of that's doing it. For me, we're already progressive enough and innovative enough. Even though there's no prohibition, taking a stand like that as a school, which is not as a mosque, will set us up for unnecessary scrutiny. I'm waiting for a mosque to do it. Once they do it, we can. I am certain that twenty years from now, most of the mosques will be doing side-by-side prayer. So, I'm waiting. It's gonna take another generation."

"Do you know that the center used to be like that in its early years?" asked Miriam. "I was there. We would have the lecture. Then the community members would fold up the chairs in the lecture hall, which also served as the prayer space. Women would stand on one side and men on the other, with an invisible aisle in the middle. When the center moved to a larger building, it all changed. Isn't that something?"

"Yes, it really is something," said Dr. Ramsey. "Last year, we had a cluster of eighth-grade girls who started a rebellion that was prompted by one boy telling them, 'Get in the back!' It triggered a sense of injustice. So, they protested prayer. I told them they could pray by themselves."

"That was an interesting way to stop the rebellion. How do you typically go about problem-solving?"

"Our approach is like a mirror. One kid holds up a mirror to the other and says, 'You did this to me, and it hurt my feelings.' It gives the other kid an opportunity to reflect. He says, 'You hurt me first,' or 'I'm sorry,' or 'I didn't mean it.' It is impossible for me to know the intention or what happened the week before. No problem can be solved by an outside person. It has to be solved between the two kids.

"Now, our parents get mad because they only see one side. 'This kid keeps kicking my kid. You do nothing about it!' It's what they imagine. Our rules are fluid. A kindergartener who kicks another kindergartener is very different from an eighth grader who kicks a fourth grader. Every circumstance looks different, so your judgment, and what you do, is based on the circumstance. There are times when a kid's awareness that they've hurt somebody is enough. I don't need to punish them on top of that, especially if they were sincere and the hurt child forgave him or her. There are times when it's the third time we've talked about this issue, and another step needs to be taken. A student may be suspended to serve as a reminder not to do it again. It's not to make it hurt, it's to make it stick. So the next time you have the impulse, you remember. Conflict resolution is best when it takes place between the two individuals involved. In our faith, the person who is hurt or injured has a right on the person who injured them. So they're the ones we check in with, asking, 'Is that enough? Do you believe him when he says sorry? Do you need more than that? What do you want from them?' It gives them a chance to say, 'I just don't want them to do it again.'"

"So, this philosophy of problem-solving, is it understood amongst the teachers? Do they take that same approach when encountering these issues in the classroom?" asked Miriam.

"I think teachers are so inundated with schedules that they don't have the ability or the space to do what's needed at the moment. They will send the kid to us, which is fine. We resolve it and then send them back. Sometimes a teacher will send a student to me because they're naughty. So, the injured person is the teacher, and sometimes that doesn't come across. I might think that the child was sent to me because of a situation with another kid, but in actuality, they were being incorrigible in class. Sometimes teachers get it; sometimes they don't. In some cases, teachers just want the kid out of the class. They do not have the language to tell me they are fed up. They don't say, 'Hey, can you keep this kid for the rest of the day?' Then it feels like a failure on their part, which is what we talked about earlier. But some days, teachers are just done."

"I totally get that," said Miriam. "As you reflect on the last five years, what are you most proud of?"

"The students. The alumni. Who our students are and what they will become. Also, the community that's been built as a result of the school. Personally, seeing the capital campaign fulfilled and the establishment of this building to serve the community is a great feeling to see our dreams actualize in the way we intended."

9

North Star Academy

A Model for Freedom

Students at North Star Academy were aware that their Muslimness was the target of intensifying hate speech, harassment, and violence perpetrated by American media, far-right politicians, and White supremacists. They were not sheltered from the negative stereotypes, conspiracy theories, and false claims that portrayed Muslims as untrustworthy, violent, misogynistic, and dangerous. They listened to Trump's harmful anti-Muslim rhetoric. They heard reports of the government surveilling Muslim communities through informants and social media monitoring. Instead of insulating students from the realities of the dynamic sociopolitical context, educators at North Star Academy created opportunities to fortify their students through a critical and progressive approach to their faith—a faith that commands through the Holy Qur'an that Muslims bear witness for truth and justice. We liken the beliefs and behaviors at North Star Academy to a progressive Islam that professes a revolutionary proposition:

> Every human life . . . Muslim and non-Muslim, rich or poor, "Northern" or "Southern," has exactly the same intrinsic worth. The essential value of life is God-given and is in no way connected to culture, geography, or privilege. A progressive Muslim is one who is committed to the strangely controversial idea that the worth of a human being is measured by a person's character, not the oil under their soil, and not their flag. A progressive Muslim agenda is concerned with the ramifications of the premise that all members of humanity have the same intrinsic worth because . . . each of us has the breath of God breathed into our being. (Safi, 2003a, p. 3)

Current events and controversial topics were critical components of teaching and learning. Through curricular activities, students connected their lived experiences to individuals enduring similar hardships. They studied Muslim persecution in Myanmar, China, India, and Europe. They learned about the marginalization of immigrants, refugees, women, BIPOC, and those of non-Judeo-Christian faith traditions. Students learned the importance of historical context and its impact on current social norms and mores (El Fadl, 2003). They also practiced perspective-taking and active listening to develop empathy. The collective knowledge and skills gained at North Star Academy enabled students to embrace their identity as proud American Muslims and see themselves as worthy advocates for a more socially just and equitable America.

Through our analysis of the data, we identified the enactment of six freedoms to be at the heart of teaching and learning at North Star Academy (Figure 1). The six freedoms allowed students to make decisions and choices, speak their minds, and share their values and beliefs through cultural, material, and intellectual exchanges (Kassam, 2003). Freedom was not synonymous with anarchy or having free rein. Instead, freedom was exercised with full consideration of one's rights and the human rights of others. Teachers and leaders at North Star Academy were

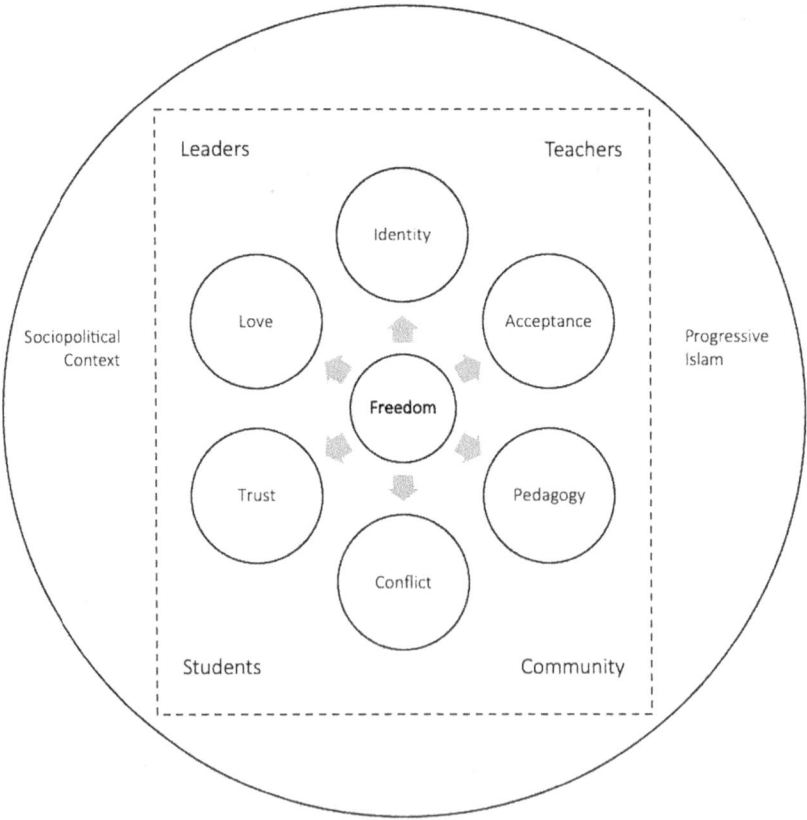

Figure 1 A model for freedom in progressive Islamic schooling.

cognizant of the increasing fragility of freedom and its use as a rhetorical device to justify systemic discrimination, government surveillance, corporate control of media, economic inequality, and disparities in access to education and health care (Kendi, 2019). Accordingly, they sought to develop students who could use their freedom to not fear speaking truth to power (Said, 1994). This approach mirrored the Golden Age of Islamic civilization, where contestation, conflict, and debate inspired innovation, with humility to acknowledge and respectfully disagree (Moosa, 2003). This approach was understood to be entirely in accord with progressive Islam.

The application of the six freedoms liberated North Star teachers to employ questioning, critical thinking, dialogue, and perspective-taking in their lessons. Students learned to analyze sociopolitical hierarchies and the reproduction and perpetuation of societal hegemonies. Students examined the cultural-conservative push to restrict individual freedoms, such as the infringement on women's reproductive rights, falsifying the Black history narrative in America, and protecting police through qualified immunity when accused of using excessive or disproportionate force on Black and Brown bodies. The dynamic and controversial sociopolitical context was not viewed as an unsafe or dangerous threat to learning or being; rather, it was seen as a catalyst for learning that encouraged resistance at the first sign of oppression. However, it was not freedom applied writ large that taught students to see themselves as American Muslims. Rather, it was six specific freedoms (identity, acceptance, pedagogy, conflict, trust, and love) that developed students' American Muslim identities and their critical consciousness. This was an intentional and ongoing process reliant upon Dr. Ramsey's ability to sustain an active and engaged school community that understood freedom as a core component of faith.

The Six Freedoms

Implementing the six freedoms was a continuous process. Dr. Ramsey shared with us the challenges of upholding progressive Islamic values in a sociocultural context that frequently pushed against these principles. However, it was her ability to retain a talented and like-minded leadership team that allowed the school to meet—and arguably exceed—its mission to develop confident and courageous American Muslims. In the section that follows, we elucidate how and in what ways each freedom shaped North Star Academy's progressive learning environment and the influence this had on students' academic and spiritual development.

(1) Through freedom of identity, students became confident and courageous American Muslims who upheld their ethical and moral principles.

>North Star Academy's staff and student population were diverse. Most teachers identified with other faith traditions, and student demographics ranged from those who recently arrived in the United States to third and fourth-generation Americans. Dr. Ramsey's family were long-standing members of the Islamic Center of San Rico. She was raised in the community, participated in its youth group, and was a founding member of the school. Her roots ran deep, and she firmly believed in the Islamic Center's founding mission to propagate "American Muslim identity," a progressive Islamic ideology that teaches American Muslims to see themselves as both American and Muslim without contradiction (Brooks, 2019; Ezzani & Brooks, 2019). This ideology was reflected in the school's pledge of allegiance, which reinforced the school's focus on developing in students an American Muslim identity within a progressive Islamic framework. The framework is grounded in Qur'an and hadith, and supports a progressive worldview that stands firm in opposing a constricting of human dignity and freedom. Therefore, families who disagreed with the school's mission during the enrollment process were counseled to choose nearby Islamic schools that were more conservative in approach. North Star Academy's vision of developing an American Muslim identity permeated school policies and day-to-day practices, and ownership of this vision by families and educators was an essential component of community cohesion.
>
>Freedom of identity was most evident through our conversations with North Star alums, who learned what it meant to be a progressive American Muslim and uphold and advocate for human rights, no matter individual differences (Qur'an, 49:13). North Star's curriculum of resistance provided opportunities for students to grapple with morality and ethical behavior related to contentious topics. Students learned that advocating for women's rights, racial justice, immigrant and refugee rights, and LGBTQIA+ rights were wholly aligned with Islam, as reflected in the God-given human rights to life, dignity, equality, choice, and expression (Qur'an, 17:70).

Classroom discussions focused on moral and ethical principles connected to the fundamental concept of *tawheed* (oneness of God). Omid Safi (2003) defined progressive Muslims as those "relentlessly striving toward a universal notion of justice in which no single community's prosperity, righteousness, and dignity comes at the expense of another" (p. 3). Progressive Islam obliges Muslims to engage in social activism as caretakers of God's creation. This "way of being Muslim" is expressed through the Quranic injunction: "Ye who believe! Stand out firmly for justice, as witnesses to Allah, even as against yourselves, your parents, or your kin, and whether it be (against) rich or poor" (Duderija, 2018, p. 3; Qur'an, 4:135). At North Star Academy, moral learning was reinforced through the Qur'an and *hadith* (the sayings and actions of Prophet Muhammad) and served as benchmarks by which students critiqued hegemonic discourses perpetuated through media representations, political speech and actions, and cultural norms and attitudes that justified power relations in society. This liberatory approach to teaching and learning (Apple, 2019; Friere, 1968; Giroux, 2020; hooks, 1994; McLaren, 2021) obliged North Star teachers to push students to recognize how to behave in ethical ways. The head of school modeled moral conviction by questioning and challenging policies and practices detrimental to a caring and inclusive society (Barakat, 2023; Ezzani, 2014; Furman & Shields, 2005). Buttressing this learning was the day-to-day interactions students had with teachers and one another. This exposed students to different perspectives and life experiences, which broadened their knowledge, challenged their assumptions, and helped them to develop critical thinking skills (Qur'an, 21:67, 39:42). Through this learning, students began to see themselves as agentic American Muslims with a deep understanding of the social, economic, and political forces shaping their lives and the lives of others (Khoury & Mahfouz, 2023).

Students were given myriad opportunities to practice challenging dominant narratives and felt safe to take risks. However, students' ability to practice was contingent upon the confidence and skills of their teachers. Some teachers avoided challenging issues, others expressed a lack of knowledge, and some had concerns about potential backlash from parents as reasons for their silence or avoidance of complex discourse. These instructional and curricular choices created tension between school leaders, who embraced liberatory pedagogy, and the teachers who evaded difficult discussions.

As the head of school, Dr. Ramsey modeled how to facilitate difficult dialogue for other leaders and teachers. When she learned about an inappropriate comment made by a male student on the topic of sexual abuse, she pushed into the classroom to speak about the Me-Too movement and rape as a human rights violation. She made it clear to the teacher and students that the classroom was a space for difficult conversations. She challenged the teacher and students to develop a deeper understanding of male power and privilege in society and what it means to participate in a cultural shift to dismantle victim blaming. As a socially just leader, Dr. Ramsey encouraged teachers' reflective practice and infused anti-oppressive practices in the school (Brooks & Ezzani, 2023b; Ezzani, 2021; Galloway et al., 2019; Khalifa et al., 2019). This learning was vital to developing critical consciousness, as teachers and students learned how they shape (and are shaped by) social structures and systems. Surprising to us, the reluctance of some teachers to engage in difficult discussions did not undermine the development of students' progressive American Muslim identities, as the school's lived practices superseded teacher reticence. This was evident in the dispositions of those who attended the school for five years or longer, primarily the fifth through eighth-grade students and the alumni.

After leaving North Star Academy, students demonstrated their ability to freely express their American Muslim identity. They attended various schools that ranged from large public high schools to prestigious private schools and other Islamic K–12 schools. In all contexts, alumni saw themselves as distinct from other students in these settings. In the public school setting, they courageously identified as Muslim. They were astonished to find "hidden Muslims" afraid to identify or join the Muslim Student Association. Those attending large public high schools with their peers from North Star Academy described themselves as self-reliant and were not compelled to hang out with them as a way to shelter themselves. When challenged with experiences such as partying and drinking, they exhibited a solid moral compass and advocated for themselves and others. Self-assurance also manifested in their interactions with school leaders and teachers, such as requesting to pray during the school day or expressing their need to dress modestly when engaged in theater, dance, and soccer activities.

Alumni faced challenges of marginalized identities in both public and private school settings. They recognized that the history taught outside of North Star Academy legitimized and privileged Eurocentricity at the expense of neglecting Black and Brown histories. When minoritized peoples and their histories were included, teachers taught and sanctioned erroneous information (Brooks et al., 2020b). Some North Star Academy alumni were assertive, while others were nervous about challenging and correcting their teachers' misstatements about Islam, the Middle East, and Muslims. However, this apprehension did not stop students from respectfully speaking to their teachers to correct misconceptions and inaccuracies. In some cases, their efforts were rejected entirely. In other cases, alums changed attitudes and/or knowledge about Muslim identity and Islam. Some alum demonstrated leadership by advocating for progressive issues, such as keeping *Persepolis* as a core text despite conservative Muslim pressure to remove the book from a public school library. On the whole, the alumni shared with us their concerns that the broader American public had little knowledge of Islam. To their dismay, their textbooks perpetuated misconceptions about their faith tradition. For that reason, they welcomed silly (and potentially offensive) questions. They answered all questions in an effort to correct harmful stereotypes. They leaned on their faith to minimize stress and anxiety and wished their less assured Muslim peers could do the same.

Freedom of identity offered students the agency to be confident American Muslims. They learned this through a curriculum of resistance that increased their awareness and understanding of their own biases and systemic societal issues (Ezzani & Brooks, 2019). They developed the skills to challenge the status quo and advocate for themselves and others. They solved problems and were able to analyze complex issues and identify underlying causes. North Star students showed empathy and understanding of others (Qur'an, 21:107), which led to a deeper understanding of themselves and different cultures, beliefs, and experiences. Freedom of identity was fundamental to students' development of what it means to be a critically conscious American Muslim.

(2) Through freedom of acceptance, students learned the importance of cultivating positive relationships with individuals, regardless of their differences.

Exclusivist and intolerant attitudes and behaviors toward people of different backgrounds, beliefs, and worldviews were viewed as counter to the school's values. Parents chose to enroll their children because of its diversity of staff and students. Parents spoke of how accepted their children felt at North Star Academy. The students supported these sentiments and spoke of their differences in food preferences, prayer rituals, dress, dogs as pets, and interfaith marriage. Rather than reinforcing a right or wrong answer to these contested concepts, leaders and teachers instructed that there was no one "right" way to be Muslim and that students should follow their families' preferences.

Students experienced acceptance and gained self-confidence from interacting with teachers of different backgrounds and faith traditions, recognizing that they cared deeply about their academic development and socio-emotional well-being. In some cases, teachers of other faiths engaged with Islamic texts, such as the Christian kindergarten teacher who read *surahs* from the Qur'an to students. Freedom of acceptance fostered a school culture that respected diverse ways of being. This acceptance did not equate to agreeing with others' beliefs or values. Rather, through freedom of acceptance, students learned greater understanding and empathy (Qur'an, 5:48). One parent described the school as providing "true acceptance" because everyone belonged, no matter their difference.

Although freedom of acceptance was integral to North Star Academy, Dr. Ramsey knew teachers and parents could fall short in their day-to-day interactions. She was mindful that anti-Muslim and anti-Islamic prejudice adversely affects young Muslims in the identity formation process in a society hostile to them (Aalberg et al., 2016; Brooks et al., 2021; Sirin & Fine, 2008). Consequently, she and other leaders in the school viewed the shortcomings of teachers and parents as an opportunity for teachable moments, professional learning, workshops, and discussions. Freedom of acceptance allowed Dr. Ramsey opportunities to promote trusting relationships, inclusive interactions, and belongingness for teachers, students, and families. She wanted students to take pride in their identities as American Muslims while, at the same time, valuing human diversity. However, this was not always enacted by teachers and parents, as our findings indicated instances of race evasiveness, internalized racism, and the need to normalize Christian values.

During focus group discussions with teachers, there were examples of ambiguity, vagueness, and even fright about navigating challenging situations about race, which we viewed as race evasiveness. Some North Star teachers who were White avoided uncomfortable conversations about race. We viewed this evasion as a shortcoming that prevented meaningful dialogue, understanding, and learning (Gay, 2018). For example, Ms. Carpenter's comment, "It's almost like with Martin Luther King, Jr.'s skin color doesn't matter. We are all people," reflected her avoidance of discussing race, which seemed to cause her discomfort. Such responses were problematic, and a common tactic used by teachers to disengage from conversations when they had limited awareness about race and racism (Bonilla-Silva, 2003; Bouley & Reinking, 2021; Diem et al., 2016; Ezzani & Brooks, 2015). Such responses signified the erasure of student identity and hampered teachers from addressing race. However, when teachers raised these challenges with their school leaders, school leaders moved into action, modeling and providing classroom opportunities for learning. For example, the lower school director, Ms. Fatemi, read *The Color of Us*, a book on skin color, when a child interpreted another peer's comment about her skin color to mean "she's ugly."

Internalized racism was evident through parent and student responses, reflecting American society's negative messaging and stereotypes about Islam and Muslims (Suleiman, 2017). One mother used the term "ghettoized" to describe neighboring conservative Islamic schools (David et al., 2019; Lipsky, 1987). The use of this term denoted these Islamic schools as inferior due to their insular cultural norms and ways of being. The people within these Islamic school communities were relegated to a "ghettoized" group identity, creating a hierarchy between North Star Academy and other Islamic schools (Kendi, 2019). During the parent focus group discussion, other parents listening to this language gave tacit approval through their loud silence and by nodding their heads.

Internalized racism was often subconscious. Parents in the focus group discussion described their students' negative self-images (Suleiman, 2017). A mother shared that her daughter, Qadira, wanted to change her name to fit in with her mostly White soccer teammates. Rather than encourage the mother's choice of birth name, another mother recommended "White" names that Qadira could use, such as Emily and Emma. One mother shared her eight-year-old son's hesitancy to reveal that they are Muslim when the housekeeper began to talk about Christmas. In response, one mother understood this to mean that "he needs to hide part of his identity sometimes." In both cases, students' "ingestion of problematic notions" revealed internalized oppression and feelings of powerlessness to discrimination and hate (Suleiman, 2017, p. 1). Students and parents were well aware of the social and cultural dominance of anti-Muslim racism (Brooks et al., 2021), an understanding that permeated their day-to-day lives. The youngest students were the most susceptible to internalized racism (Clark & Clark, 1966).

There were also instances of Christian hegemony, whereby Christian norms and practices were treated as the default or customary way of life. Christian holidays entered the schoolhouse, with students at the elementary school level wanting to sing Christmas songs and discuss who had Christmas trees in their homes. Students shared if they participated in Easter egg hunts or went trick-or-treating on Halloween. Some teachers used dialogue to unpack the meaning and help students check their ideas regarding their level of engagement with different Christian holidays. Other Christian teachers expressed trepidation as to how much they should or should not support these discussions out of fear of "getting into trouble." These teachers did not seek clarification from school leaders.

Christian hegemony also surfaced in more subliminal ways. For example, Ms. Flores said, "Even though I'm Catholic, we believe the same things, such as doing the right thing . . . even though it's not the same religion." This concealment undermined Islam's importance and significance, positioning it as invisible (Blumenfeld, 2006). As Christianity is socially embedded in American society, Christian teachers were shaped by cultural hegemonies of Christian privilege and power (Yukich & Edgell, 2020). Enacting freedom of acceptance in a context of pervasive xenophobia, Islamophobia, White supremacy, and Christian privilege in the United States revealed the "historical power differences that remain between white [sic] people and people of color" (Diem et al., 2022, p. 7).

Accepting and valuing self and others was an ongoing challenge and journey for the school community, more so in the lower elementary grades. Shortcomings on the issues of race, faith, and privilege were met with learning opportunities such as workshops for parents and professional learning for teachers. The students were Dr. Ramsey's primary concern, and she wanted them to be discerning even in their current school environment. She and other leaders entered classrooms to model pedagogical strategies for teachers and students in an ongoing effort to work toward freedom of acceptance.

(3) Through freedom of pedagogy, school leaders promoted a reciprocal approach to teaching and learning that fostered the development of students' critical consciousness.

Most Islamic schools inculcate one interpretation of Islam, which is often based on the Islamic school's sociohistorical context, the demographic make-up of the community, geographic location, funding sources, or the preferences of leaders (Breen, 2018; Brooks et al., 2020a; Driessen & Merry, 2006; Merry, 2018; Zine, 2008). As schools of thought are tied to religious authority and interpretation of scripture, how religious knowledge is taught can in/advertently promote and/or uphold the faith of some students while diminishing, devaluing, or denigrating the beliefs of students not aligned with the majority faith tradition in a particular school (Brooks & Brooks, 2019). At North Star Academy, progressive Islam prevented one particular school of thought from dominating its ethos due to its focus on human rights, pluralism, and social justice (Khuwaja & Ezzani, 2022; Safi, 2003b). This freedom of pedagogy encouraged students to identify and challenge injustices so that they could work toward creating a more equitable and just society (Qur'an, 2:62, 213, 256).

The standard of academic excellence was high at North Star Academy. Freedom of pedagogy gave teachers the autonomy to teach the California state standards in ways that were culturally responsive, student-centered, and grounded in the values of justice, equality, freedom, and human rights. Teachers designed bespoke learning that was meaningful, inquiry-based, innovative, and interactive. Integrated into this learning were current and controversial events that provided students with opportunities to develop their skills and capabilities in identifying, critiquing, dialoguing, and challenging societal oppressions and inequalities (Ezzani & Brooks, 2019; Freire, 1972; Jamal, 2023). As enumerated in a number of Hadith, learning about justice was wholly aligned with the Islamic faith and the lived examples of Prophet Muhammad (Suleiman, 2020). Dr. Ramsey referred to the content as a curriculum of resistance—imparted through pedagogical strategies that furthered the development of students' critical consciousness.

To provide a few examples, young students participated in the *Global Read Aloud* project, where they discussed the book *Refugee*, by Alan Gratz, with a classroom from Nebraska. Students learned about gun laws, gun safety, and gun sense. They discussed Trump's hatred toward

Muslims and were beginning to understand racial, ethnic, cultural, and religious differences. Upper school students learned about the Holocaust and current-day anti-Semitism. Teachers used critical dialogue to unpack the ongoing oppression and subjugation of Uyghur Muslims in China and refugees on the US-Mexican border. Students also examined Trump's exclusionary policies, such as the Muslim Ban and the conservative backlash against the Black Lives Matter Movement. They discussed terrorism, police brutality, and protest movements. Learning was tied to Islamic values and stressed the importance of Muslims adopting a morally upright character, which advocates for justice in ways that honor the social interdependence of humans within society. These discussions generated conflict and debate, which was expected and addressed.

Freedom of pedagogy at times resulted in teachers restricting student learning. In a focus group discussion with first through third-grade teachers, a teacher described a writing lesson that "didn't go over well." Ms. Davis' annual "Letter to the U.S. President" lesson became a "Letter to Kids Bop" (a company that produces children's music). Changing the lesson was intentional. Ms. Davis was surprised and caught off guard when a student shared her feelings about President Trump: "You know he hates Muslims." Although she responded to the child with, "I kind of agree with you," Ms. Davis reflected that she did not want to upset her six-year-old students and chose to change the lesson's direction. Throughout the year, Ms. Davis frequently squelched her students' anti-Trumpism in her classroom and redirected them back to their learning activity. Ms. McLean, a third-grade teacher, shared that she told students that everyone is entitled to their opinion and that it is okay to disagree. However, she stressed that respect needs to be shown to the president because he is the country's commander-in-chief. Some teachers did not view the classroom as a space for reciprocal teaching and learning.

Ms. McLean's unwillingness to entertain a student's worldview hampered freedom of pedagogy. However, teachers with cultural humility understood the limitations of their knowledge and viewed the classroom as a place to learn from their students. There was an essential connection between teachers' beliefs, their actions in the classroom, and what their students learned (Gay & Howard, 2000; Ladson-Billings, 1995; Villegas, 2007). For instance, Ms. Davis believed she needed to shield her students from the harsh realities of anti-Muslim hate. She turned her gaze, conveying to the students the unimportance of fairness and justice in society toward Muslims. Ms. McLean promoted patriotism and ran the risk of celebrating a past and a present that condones White supremacy and undermines justice. Most importantly, these beliefs and actions were counter to freedom of pedagogy and limited students' opportunities to develop their critical consciousness.

Dr. Ramsey trusted teachers to make the right decisions about curriculum and instruction but was also acutely aware that freedom of pedagogy was a risk. Teachers with the skills to lead students through discussions on challenging topics allowed students to question and interrogate power dynamics and how they operate in American society and the wider world. North Star Academy's less confident teachers frequently chose the path of least resistance, redirecting students to safer learning. At worse, White teachers tried to fix things that did not align with their religious or sociopolitical worldview (Villegas, 2007). Dr. Ramsey understood the complexity of measuring teachers' dispositions in the hiring process and, at times, discovered that some teachers had difficulty actualizing freedom of pedagogy in a way that honored and valued their Muslim students' experiences. Other teachers were malleable, and when she became aware of their learning gaps, she took the opportunity to push into classrooms and model critical discourse for teachers and students. Freedom of pedagogy was a continuous process of learning and development.

(4) Through freedom for conflict, the school community created valuable opportunities to address challenges through accountability, open dialogue, empathy, and forgiveness.

Students at North Star Academy were not sheltered or protected from conflict. Instead, school leaders recognized that conflict was a central teaching of Prophet Muhammad and a necessary part of community life and human relationships. Prophet Muhammad was known for his skill in resolving conflicts peacefully and justly (Qu'ran, 21:78-79). Muslims today are encouraged to forgive those who have wronged them as a means of finding peace and reconciliation (Qur'an, 42:37). At North Star Academy, freedom for conflict provided students, teachers, school leaders, parents, and the wider school community with myriad opportunities to develop and practice their faith through *akhlaq* (moral character and disposition), *ihsan* (goodness or excellence), *sabr* (patience), *shukr* (gratitude), *istiqama* (consistency), and *tawakkul* (reliance on God) (Abdalla, 2001; Cader, 2017). It allowed freedom for conflict to occur (with individuals free to express their differing opinions and engage in debate and dialogue) and positioned North Star Academy as a courageous community of learners.

Dr. Ramsey expected the other school leaders and teachers to directly address conflict, whether it was brought into the schoolhouse through current events, parental concerns, or student discord. Conflict encouraged critical thinking and required school community members to evaluate their perspectives and consider alternative viewpoints. However, some teachers avoided conflict, ignored problems, and chose silence rather than confronting challenging issues. Freedom for conflict was complex to navigate. Yet, our data analysis revealed it to be an essential component of education at North Star Academy.

North Star Academy's approach to conflict focused on emotional regulation and respectful nonpunitive approaches to behavior management. Grounded in the philosophy of Positive Discipline, school leaders and teachers emphasized mutual respect, clear communication, logical consequences, and problem-solving. The youngest students learned to express their feelings and identify solutions through The Zones of Regulation and the Wheel of Choice programs. For older elementary students, the Leader in Me program offered opportunities to develop their leadership skills, increase their self-confidence, and practice respect, responsibility, and kindness. The school-wide Value of the Month program established behavior expectations and a shared language to create a safer, more respectful, and inclusive school.

School leaders and teachers did not solve problems for students but led them through a constructive problem-solving process. To illustrate this, Dr. Ramsey provided a typical example of a student taking another child's ball. Rather than a teacher solving the problem for the students and taking the ball away, teachers were expected to lead the students through a dialogue about the problem and push them beyond the requisite "I'm sorry" to "I'm sorry because . . ." and "What can I do to make it better?" This approach developed empathy and understanding while also encouraging students to understand and empathize with a peer's perspective of the situation.

Freedom for conflict also extended into the wider community. A prospective family was concerned that girls past puberty were not wearing *hijabs* at North Star Academy. Dr. Ramsey informed the father that the *hijab* was not required for girls at the school. She suggested a nearby school to this family that would be a better fit for what they envisioned for their child. In another incident, a mother complained that her child imitated the bad habits of a classmate. In response, Dr. Ramsey replied to the mother, "The other child is gifting you the knowledge that your daughter is a follower. What are you going to do to fortify your kid so that she doesn't get easily sucked in?" In another case, a father, angry over his son's injury, told Dr. Fatemi how she should resolve the conflict. She listened and acknowledged his concern but advised the father to focus on his relationship with his child rather than correct her and upset other parents. Although these responses might be confronting to families, Dr. Ramsey insisted on straightforward communication and seeing disagreements as opportunities for learning.

    Dr. Ramsey had an open-door policy. She made herself available to the entire North Star community and felt assured that this was widely known. She preferred to handle issues of conflict on an individual and case-by-case basis, using a Socratic style of questioning with students. However, parents proved more challenging. Dr. Ramsey said she often has difficult conversations with parents who want immediate answers or solutions. She told parents that conflict provided learning opportunities and cited this as a reason to refuse their requests. In the same vein, Dr. Ramsey frequently reminded teachers that decisions on *halal*, what is im/permissible, were in the hands of the parents. Due to the progressive Islamic ideology, teachers were not to correct family decisions on food preference, prayer, dress, or holiday celebrations. This injunction was in keeping with the school's ideology.

    Freedom for conflict shaped teacher experience. In our first through third-grade teacher focus group, Ms. Davis shared that WhatsApp was a place for parents to plan events for their children outside of school, but it also had become a place for parents to complain. Gossiping, bullying, and passive-aggressive behaviors from parents targeted at specific teachers caused conflict. Freedom for conflict, when left unchecked, placed all of the power into the hands of the parents. Some teachers felt powerless. They were insecure about sharing their concerns with Dr. Fatemi or Dr. Ramsey. Teachers viewed this as a "test" of their abilities and felt they had no recourse to address this ongoing conflict. Some parents, who befriended teachers, reached out to assure teachers that parents' gossip was inappropriate. This brought into question how school leaders could bridge the gap between parents and teachers by providing specific support to help teachers negotiate tensions.

Freedom for conflict created a culture that shaped how the school community interacted with one another. When conflicts were addressed directly, tensions were reduced, collaborations improved, and trust grew in the school. When conflicts were not addressed, negativity, stress, anxiety, and poor communication increased. Some teachers avoided conflict with parents to maintain peace and politeness (Dillon & Nixon, 2019), and this further exacerbated divisions. This impacted the well-being of some teachers, who found it challenging to confront conflict or leverage leadership support. In this case, the inability to effectively manage conflict undermined trust within the school community.

(5) Through freedom to trust, the school community emphasized the importance of building relationships through openness, integrity, and personal regard.

In Islam, leadership is understood as a sacred trust (*amana*). In other words, a leader should lead others with sincerity and devote the necessary time and energy to justly fulfill the obligations of the position. Leaders are expected to guide their followers toward goodness and righteousness for the betterment of individuals, communities, and society (Brooks & Mutohar, 2018). They are accountable to Allah, and to those whom they serve, for the decisions they make—as inattentiveness can result in undue harm to others. Leaders model trust by serving and interacting with others with compassion, fairness, honesty, and integrity (Brooks & Ezzani, 2023a). In keeping with Islamic teachings, Dr. Ramsey viewed her leadership role at North Star Academy as a sacred trust and a heavy responsibility.

Dr. Ramsey co-constructed (Louis, 2007) trust over time through bonding and bridging social capital (Patulny & Lind Haase Svendsen, 2007; Putnam, 2000). Networks of long-standing relationships provided access to resources and opportunities that generated interpersonal trust within the school community (Patulny, 2004). Dr. Ramsey's longevity as the Head of School not only reflected her competence and capabilities but also served as the glue for community cohesion. The School Board chair Mr. Hassan characterized North Star Academy's school leaders as "a team," albeit with Dr. Ramsey as the lead educator and the steward of the school's mission and vision. We concurred with this statement. In our interviews and observations, Dr. Ramsey often returned to the school's mission, vision, and her Islamic faith as her raison d'être.

Dr. Ramsey's central focus was on the student's socio-emotional development and their academic learning. Co-constructing a space of inclusion and acceptance granted students the freedom to trust, share feelings, and find solutions to problems. Khadija, an eighth grader, shared, "Dr. Ramsey doesn't want to betray your trust and stays in contact often." Daniel, a sixth-grade student, shared, "I can cry at this school because they're always nice about it." Ahmed added, "At this school, everyone is connected, and we can tell everyone our feelings." This was irrespective of conflict, noting, "If you have a problem with someone, you can always find a way to solve it." From the students' point of view, freedom to trust required little effort and was easily given.

Freedom to trust extended to teacher-student relationships. The consistently positive attention students received from teachers created a sense of belonging, established reliability, raised their confidence, and encouraged students to see themselves as valued members of their community. Teachers helped students practice vulnerability through dialogue, a critical component of building collective trust (Forsyth et al., 2011). Jana noted, "Sometimes people get into fights . . . the teacher will come over and ask what happened, but she doesn't solve it. She would ask the two people in the fight to solve it." Importantly, students trusted their teachers from different faith traditions to act with integrity and reliability. These interactions taught students to not only respect other belief systems but also build relationships on nonjudgment and mutual understanding (Sahih Al-Bukhari, 1:54:2707; Qu'ran, 49:13, 29:46). Affirming interpersonal encounters enhanced positive affect and nurtured freedom to trust throughout the school (Tschannen-Moran, 2014). As we learned from the alumni, this learning was indispensable to navigating their life beyond North Star Academy.

Yet, trust at North Star Academy was also fragile. Freedom to trust required nurturing interactions that enhanced community cohesion (Forsyth et al., 2011). Parents took an active role in their children's education through volunteer activities and attendance at events and other school-related activities. Yet, some teachers were intimidated by difficult, demanding, and entitled parents. As a result, some teachers struggled to have difficult conversations with some parents. They did not seek support from Dr. Ramsey. In other words, they did not come to her to rehearse what they would say or seek advice on how to approach a particular parent or issue. Dr. Ramsey reflected on the teacher's reluctance to reach out to her for help, direction, or support. She attributed this to teacher autonomy. However, data analysis revealed that some teachers experienced North Star Academy as having low relational trust (Bryk & Schneider, 2002). Some with this perception left within the first three years of employment.

Dr. Ramsey sought to hire teachers with integrity and passion. She wanted to see prospective teachers "tear up" in the interview and show their strong sense of purpose and deep commitment to the teaching profession. She compared teaching to being a member of a clergy, as both are responsible for guiding and mentoring others, having deep moral and ethical responsibilities, and possessing strong interpersonal and communication skills (Carter, 2009). Yet, Dr. Ramsey struggled to freely trust some teachers of the Christian faith. Christian teachers could go too far in having students complete Christmas-themed lessons. For example, an evangelical teacher insisted on teaching Tchaikovsky's *The Nutcracker* in December, making the claim that it was not based on a Christmas story. Dr. Ramsey had to ask the teacher to move the lesson to the month of March.

Thus, freedom to trust was not as freely given or received by the adults in the school. Trust between the adults grew and diminished based on sociocultural pressures and the day-to-day interactions experienced within the school community (Hoy & Tschannen-Moran, 1999). In the final analysis, freedom to trust was most evident in students' willingness to be vulnerable. Vulnerability provided an avenue for students to connect with their peers on a deeper level. This freedom to trust was remarkable to observe, and we noted that this might be the precursor to freedom to love.

(6) Through freedom to love, the school community fostered supportive relationships grounded in respect, compassion, and care.

In the Islamic tradition, the concept of love holds a significant place and encompasses various dimensions and expressions. Allah is referred to as the all-loving (Qur'an, 7:157), the all-compassionate (Qur'an, 1:1), the most generous (Qur'an, 28:77), the gentle (Qur'an, 22:63), and the all-merciful (Qur'an, 11:90). Muslims are encouraged to develop a deep and sincere love for Allah (God) and His final messenger, Prophet Muhammad. Prophet Muhammad's exemplary character and his championing of social justice and compassion, particularly in relation to the marginalized and vulnerable members of society, inspire Muslims to work toward a just and compassionate society. We observed these various dimensions and expressions of love at North Star Academy and saw how transformational a role love played in shaping the school community.

Similar to Freire's (1985) concept of "armed love" as the sine qua non of teaching, Dr. Ramsey held a deep love for North Star Academy's students and the wider school community. This was a "fierce and unequivocal" love-in-action, whereby Dr. Ramsey advocated on behalf of North Star students and believed wholeheartedly in their abilities to achieve at their highest levels (Daniels, 2012; Rivera-McCutchen, 2019, p. 237). Dr. Ramsey's love-in-action created a positive and nurturing school environment, evident in the teachers, parents, and students' many expressions of care, selflessness, acceptance, understanding, and forgiveness of others.

This freedom to love was evident in the student wall decorations that included messages of care and compassion for others: "Don't be racist," "Black Lives Matter," "Believe," and "Love." A classroom poster displayed messages of generosity and justice: "Love Wins," "People and Planet Are Valued over Profit," and "Immigrants & Refugees Are Welcome." In our conversations with students, current social justice issues were linked to Islam's perspective on humanity: the equality of all human beings before *Allah*; the sanctity and inviolability of human life and human dignity; brotherhood and solidarity; and the social responsibility to care for the poor, the vulnerable, and the oppressed. Students learned that human beings are equal in their basic human dignity and have inherent worth, regardless of race, ethnicity, social status, or gender—this love for humanity was foundational to the school's progressive ideology. Students had the freedom to love others (and themselves) for who they were, no matter their difference.

Freedom to love extended to the wider school community. Over the years, families at North Star Academy developed a network of relationships that offered support, understanding, and empathy. Parents had opportunities to connect with others, form friendships, and develop meaningful relationships around a shared purpose. In some interviews, parents expressed their love for the school through strong emotions. Freedom to love strengthened relational bonds, with many calling the school a "first" or "second" home. This harmonious integration fostered a school community brought together by shared values and reinforced through similar ways of thinking and problem-solving. To provide an example, Dr. Ramsey removed competition. She viewed a "competitive environment exactly the opposite of building a community." She questioned, "How do you wish for your brother when you want to beat him?" Freedom to love at North Star required taking into consideration the feelings of others and how decisions would affect the wider community. In this case, competition and winning were wholly counter to loving others and maintaining an integrated, supportive, and loving community.

Dr. Ramsey modeled freedom to love through: active listening; making time for students, teachers, and parents; showing affection through hugs, high-fives, and words of appreciation; and supporting teachers' and students' goals and aspirations. She expected teachers to love their profession and, by extension, their students, acknowledging the boundary that educators cannot love their students more than parents. She spoke of her willingness to retire, given they can find a school head "soaked in that special sauce" to lead the school. In other words, freedom to love requires a trusted caretaker to carry the school into the future.

Toward a Hopeful Future

We concluded the study in 2023, a time of increasing political polarization and consumed by contentious political discourses on gun control, immigration, health care, the aims of education, climate change, gender/sexual identity, and reproductive rights. Misinformation has amplified tensions, leading to heated debates in all sectors of society. Mass shootings in schools and police violence on Black and Brown bodies are commonplace, with the Southern Poverty Law Center documenting over 700 hate groups in the United States, with Muslims being the target of many of these groups. Consequently, Muslims continue to experience hate crimes, profiling, employment discrimination, and anti-Muslim racism. As a response, Muslim-led advocacy groups have joined others to work toward advancing understanding at a time when individual rights and democratic norms are compromised and conflated with anti-Americanism. Despite what is happening today, hope prevails at North Star Academy. The school has doubled its enrollment over the last five years. This necessitated the hiring of additional teachers and administrators at both the lower and upper school campuses. The school's endowment has likewise grown, allowing families of modest income to enroll their children with the support of tuition waivers.

As we conclude this study, we must emphasize that North Star Academy is not typical of other schools in the United States. It did not restrict freedom to "America, mom, and apple pie"—concepts often used to symbolize quintessential American values and ideals often relegated to lessons in civics, government, and US history. Rather, North Star Academy situated freedom broadly, as a universal ideal within Islam, and a core component of students' American Muslim identities. Freedom at North Star Academy allowed students to explore their full potential, become active participants in their own education, and develop the capabilities necessary to navigate evolving, dynamic, and contested sociopolitical contexts through a progressive Islamic framework. Dr. Ramsey's astute and discerning leadership was essential to sustaining a culture of freedom at North Star Academy. Using her words, freedom was the "special sauce" that empowered every student to see themselves as valued American Muslims with unlimited potential and a strong sense of purpose.

Methodological Appendix

This qualitative methodological appendix provides additional details about our research design, data collection, and data analysis methods used in conducting this case study.

As the purpose of this study was to better understand the role of freedom in an American Islamic school, we aimed to generate rich, contextualized insights to contribute to the existing body of knowledge in the field of educational leadership. To this end, we purposefully selected North Star Academy because it is one of the few Islamic schools that outwardly identify as progressive and whose mission is to develop in students an American Muslim identity. The school opened its doors in 2001, a day before the 9/11 attacks on the World Trade Center and the Pentagon. The tragic events of 9/11 drew the community together and strengthened the mission of the school: to offer outstanding academics in a progressive Islamic environment and develop in each child an American Muslim identity so that they are well-prepared to succeed, lead, and serve.

Dr. Ramsey was the founding principal of North Star entering her fifteenth year of leadership at the start of the study. She espoused Islam to be a faith of social justice and believed schooling should develop students' critical consciousness. North Star Academy's mother organization was the Islamic Center of San Rico, a large Islamic community focused on propagating American Muslim identity, civic engagement, and open-mindedness alongside a strong commitment to sustaining an inclusive and welcoming community. We spoke with the head of school, Dr. Ramsey, and the Islamic Center of San Rico's Chair of the Board of Directors, Daod Bianchi, to convey our intent and to seek permission to study the school and its community. They both agreed to participate and were excited to gain feedback and learn from the community.

All of the study's participants were from the North Star Academy community and the Islamic Center of San Rico. The head of school informed the school about the study and scheduled interviews with school leaders, teachers, parents, community members, and students. We interviewed fifty-six participants in total, engaging them through multiple interviews that ranged from sixty to 90 minutes in length. Interviews and focus group discussions were semi-structured, audiotaped with permission, and transcribed by a professional third-party service. We sought to learn about American Muslim identity, diversity and inclusion, curriculum and instruction, relationships, school policies and practices, values, progressive Islam, social justice, and anti-racism. We achieved a comprehensive understanding of the school by triangulating information from various sources. For example, school and classroom walk-throughs and observations were conducted on the lower and upper school campuses. Anecdotal notes were collected that captured events and interactions between members of the school community. We took photos of students' academic work, posters, artwork, and displays. The entirety of data collection was performed by both researchers simultaneously, which allowed for immediate debriefing and exchange of ideas. Researcher bias was mitigated through peer debriefing (Williams & Todd, 2016) and through member checking (Clandinin & Connelly, 2000). After conducting interviews and observations, peer debriefing helped to correct instances of over or underemphasis, provide clarity to ambiguous descriptions of observations, and identify potential errors in the data.

Data analysis was guided by a six-phase approach to coding and theme development. These phases included familiarization with the data through multiple readings, coding, searching for themes, reviewing themes, and defining and naming themes (Braun & Clarke, 2006; Clarke et al., 2015). We spent extensive time pondering, interrogating, discussing, and conceptualizing how the school community engaged with the concept of freedom. We also used an iterative process of questioning and analytic note-taking during our initial readings of the data. Through weekly discussions, we developed a codebook with mutually agreed-upon definitions. We utilized simultaneous and pattern coding that included structural, descriptive, and conceptual coding schemes based on the language used in the research, interview, and focus group questions (Clarke et al., 2015; Saldaña, 2011). We questioned and clarified our understanding of codes for exclusion or inclusion. We utilized this recursive process to reconcile our contradictions and merge codes into categories, which were winnowed and sifted into the final six themes (Miles & Huberman, 1994; Patton, 2015). We triangulated findings within and across interview and focus group data, observations, anecdotal notes, and documents to confront subjectivities and minimize investigator bias. All feedback confirmed our interpretations and findings. As a qualitative case study, the findings are not intended to be generalized to a larger population; however, the situations discussed hold the potential for transferability.

This study is limited in that it tells the story of one Islamic community and as such, does not represent the wide-ranging diversity found within the American Muslim community. We were also limited by both time and funding. However, the openness of participants to share their thoughts, feelings, and experiences provided richness and depth to the data collected which countered these limitations. We encourage future research on freedom in Islamic schools in other regions of the United States and in countries around the world. This is an overlooked concept that is increasingly at risk in schools, most notably in societies experiencing sociopolitical movements seeking to undermine freedom and democracy. Social justice and freedom are foundational teachings in Islam, and these concepts should be centered in Islamic schooling research.

Glossary

abaya a loose-fitting, full-length robe worn by some Muslim women
akhlaq moral character and disposition
Allah God
amana a sacred trust
Assalamu alaykum greetings of peace
ayah verse in the Qur'an
ayat verses in the Qur'an (plural)
dabka Palestinian folk dance
dawah inviting people to embrace Islam
Eid Muslim religious holiday
fitnah behavior that causes a state of trouble or chaos
hadith saying/teaching of Prophet Muhammad
Hafiz a title of respect given to a person who memorized the Qur'an
halal permissible food
haram forbidden or unlawful
hijab head covering worn by Muslim females
huwa grammatical word in Arabic for third-person singular male
ihsan goodness or excellence
ilm knowledge
istiqama consistency
jihad spiritual struggle
jum'ah Friday midday prayer
masajid masjid (plural)
masjid an Arabic word for a place of prayer, also called mosque
mihrab arches that are niches in the wall of a mosque that indicate the direction of Mecca
minaret a slender tower connected to mosques used to project the call to prayer
najis ritually unclean
Qur'an The holy text of Muslims
rizq provision or sustenance, a sense of "giving" or "apportionment" from God
sabr patience
Shaykh a scholar
Shi'a one of the two main branches of Islam
shukr gratitude
shura a collective and consultative form of decision-making
sunnah traditions and practices of Prophet Muhammad

Sunni one of the two main branches of Islam
surah a chapter in the Qur'an
tajweed rules governing how to pronounce the words of the Qur'an during recitation
ta'lim teachings of the Qur'an and hadith
tawakkul reliance on God
tawheed oneness of God, the creator and sustainer of the universe
thobe ankle-length robe with long sleeves
ummah global Muslim community
Wa-alaykum assalam and peace be upon you
wudu cleaning ritual before prayer
zabiha meat slaughtered in a permissible way
zulm injustice

Note

Introduction

1 In everyday conversation, it's common for people to use the demonym "America" to refer to anything related to the United States of America. This usage is derived from the country's formal name, which incorporates the term "America." However, this practice might lack precision and can exhibit a viewpoint that places emphasis on the United States while potentially disregarding other countries and regions that constitute the larger landmass of the Americas. In the writing of this book, we employ the terms "United States" and "America" as they were used by the individuals we interviewed, reflecting prevalent colloquial language, which may reveal bias.

References

Aalberg, T., Esser, F., Reinemann, C., Stromback, J., & De Vreese, C. (Eds.). (2016). *Populist political communication in Europe*. Routledge.

Abdalla, A. (2001). Principles of Islamic interpersonal conflict intervention: A search within Islam and western literature. *Journal of Law and Religion*, *15*, 151–184.

Abdullah, Z. (2013). American Muslims in the contemporary world: 1965 to the present. In J. Hammer & O. Safi (Eds.), *The Cambridge companion to American Islam* (pp. 65–82). Cambridge University Press.

Abu El-Haj, T. R. (2006). Race, politics, and Arab American youth: Shifting frameworks for conceptualizing educational equity. *Educational Policy*, *20*(1), 13–34.

Acquisti, A., & Fong, C. M. (2012). An experiment in hiring discrimination via online social networks. *Management Science*, *66*(3), 1005–1024.

Aizpurua, A., Singer, A. J., Butler, L. F., Collier, N. L., & Gertz, M. G. (2017). 15 years later: Post 9/11 support for increased security and criminalizing Muslims. *Journal of Ethnicity in Criminal Justice*, *15*(4), 372–393. http://dx.doi.org/10.1080/15377938.2017.1385556

Ajrouch, K. J., & Jamal, A. (2007). Assimilating to a white identity: The case of Arab Americans. *The International Migration Review*, *41*(4), 860–879.

Apple, M. W. (2019). *Ideology and curriculum* (4th ed.). Routledge.

Apple, M. W., & Buras, K. L. (Eds.). (2006). *The subaltern speak: Curriculum, power, and educational struggles*. Routledge.

Araujo, A. L. (2020). *Slavery in the age of memory: Engaging the past*. Bloomsbury Publishing.

Barakat, M. (2023). Qasim Amin: Champion of women's liberation. In M. C. Brooks & M. D. Ezzani (Eds.), *Great Muslim leaders: Lessons for education* (pp. 23–34). Information Age Publishing.

Bayoumi, M. (2001). East of the sun (west of the moon): Islam, the Ahmadis, and African America. *Souls*, *3*(3), 39–49.

Bell, C. (2014). *Terrified: How anti-Muslim fringe organizations became mainstream*. Princeton University Press.

Bleich, E., Nisar, H., & Abdelhamid, R. (2015b). The effect of terrorist events on media portrayals of Islam and Muslims: Evidence from New York Times headlines, 1985–2013. *Ethnic and Racial Studies Review*, *39*(7), 1109–1127.

Blumenfeld, W. J. (2006). Christian privilege and the promotion of "secular" and not-so "secular" mainline Christianity in public schooling and in the larger society. *Equity & Excellence in Education*, *39*(3), 195–210.

Bonet, S. W. (2011). Educating Muslim American youth in a post-9/11 era: A critical review of policy and practice. *The High School Journal, 95*(1), 46–55.

Bonilla-Silva, E. (2003). "New racism," color-blind racism, and the future of whiteness in America. In A. W. Doane & E. Bonilla-Silva (Eds.), *White out: The continuing significance of race* (pp. 271–284). Routledge.

Bouley, T. M., & Reinking, A. K. (2021). *Implicit bias: An educator's guide to the language of microaggressions.* Rowman & Littlefield.

Boustan, L. P. (2017). *Competition in the promised land: Migrants in northern cities and labor markets.* Princeton University Press.

Bowen, P. D. (2011). The search for "Islam": African-American Islamic groups in NYC, 1904–1954. *The Muslim World, 102*(2), 264–283.

Braun, V., & Clarke, V. (2006). Using thematic analysis in psychology. *Qualitative Research in Psychology, 3*(2), 77–101. http://dx.doi.org/10.1191/1478088706qp063ia

Breen, D. (2018). *Muslim schools, communities and critical race theory: Faith schooling in an Islamophobic Britain?* Palgrave Macmillan.

Brooks, M. C. (2019). *Education and Muslim identity during a time of tension: Inside an American Islamic school.* Routledge.

Brooks, M. C., & Brooks, J. S. (2019). Culturally (ir)relevant school leadership Ethno-religious conflict and school administration in the Philippines. *International Journal of Leadership in Education, 22*(1), 6–29.

Brooks, M. C., & Ezzani, M. D. (2023a). *Great Muslim leaders: Lessons for education.* Information Age Publishing.

Brooks, M. C., & Ezzani, M. D. (2023b). Zainab Salbi: Leadership begins within. In M. C. Brooks & M. D. Ezzani's (Eds.), *Great Muslim leaders: Lessons for education* (pp. 223–229). Information Age Publishing.

Brooks, M. C., Brooks, J. S., Mutohar, A., & Taufiq, I. (2020a). Principals as socio-religious curators: Progressive and conservative approaches in Islamic schools. *Journal of Educational Administration, 58*(6), 677–695.

Brooks, M. C., Cutler, K. D., Sanjakdar, F., & Liou, D. D. (2020b) Teaching jihad: Developing religious literacy through graphic novels. *Religions, 11*(11), 1–16.

Brooks, M. C., Ezzani, M. D., Sai, Y., & Sanjakdar, F. (2021). Racialization of Muslim students in Australia, Ireland, and the United States: Cross-cultural perspectives. *Race, Ethnicity, and Education.* https://doi.org/10.1080/13613324.2021.1997977

Brooks, M. C., & Mutohar, A. (2018). Islamic school leadership: A conceptual framework. *Journal of Educational Administration and History, 50*(2), 54–68.

Bryk, A., & Schneider, B. (2002). *Trust in schools: A core resource for improvement.* Russell Sage Foundation.

Burney, S. (2012). Orientalism: The making of the other. *Counterpoints, 417*, 23–39.

Cader, A. A. (2017). Islamic principles of conflict management: A model for human resource management. *International Journal of Cross Cultural Management, 17*(3), 345–363.

Cainkar, L. A. (2011). *Homeland insecurity: The Arab American experience after 9/11*. Russell Sage Foundation.
Cantor, P. A. (2012). *The invisible hand in popular culture: Liberty vs. authority in American film and TV*. University Press of Kentucky.
Carter, C. (2009). Priest, prostitute, plumber? The construction of teachers as saints. *English Education*, *42*(1), 61–90.
Chabon, M. (2020). *Fight of the century: Writers reflect on 100 years of landmark ACLU cases*. Avid Reader Press.
Chande, A. (2008). Islam in the African American community: Negotiating between Black nationalism and historical Islam. *Islamic Studies*, *47*(2), 221–241.
Clandinin, D. J., & Connelly, F. M. (2000). *Narrative inquiry: Experience and story in qualitative research*. Jossey-Bass.
Clark, K. B., & Clark, M. P. (1966). Emotional factors in racial identification and preference in Negro children. In M. M. Grossack (Ed.), *Mental health and segregation* (pp. 53–63). Springer. http://dx.doi.org/10.1007/978-3-662-37819-9_7.
Clarke, V., Braun, V., & Hayfield, N. (2015). Thematic analysis. In J. A. Smith (Ed.), *Qualitative psychology: A practical guide to research methods* (pp. 222–248). Sage.
Council on American-Islamic Relations (2019). Hijacked by hate: American philanthropy and the Islamophobia network.
Covey, S. R. (1989). *The 7 habits of highly successful people*. Fireside.
Curiel, J. (2015). *Islam in America*. I.B. Tauris.
Curtis, E. E. (2005). African-American Islamization reconsidered: Black history narratives and Muslim identity. *Journal of the American Academy of Religion*, *73*(3), 659–684.
Curtis, E. E. (2009). *Muslims in America: A short history*. Oxford University Press.
Curtis, E. E. (2013). The Black Muslim scare of the twentieth century. In C. W. Ernst (Ed.), *Islamophobia in America* (pp. 75–106). Palgrave Macmillan.
Daniels, E. A. (2013). *Fighting, loving, teaching: An exploration of hope, armed love and critical urban pedagogies*. Sense Publishers.
David, E. J. R., Schroeder, T. M., & Fernandez, J. (2019). Internalized racism: A systematic review of the psychological literature on racism's most insidious consequence. *Journal of Social Issues*, *75*(4), 1057–1086.
Deflam, M. (Ed.). (2008). *Surveillance and governance: Crime control and beyond*. Emerald Publishing Group.
Diallo, I. (2012). Qur'anic and *Ajami* literacies in pre-colonial West Africa. *Current Issues in Language Planning*, *13*(2), 91–104.
Diem, S., Welton, A. D., Frankenberg, E., & Jellison Holme, J. (2016). Racial diversity in the suburbs: How race-neutral responses to demographic change perpetuate inequity in suburban school districts. *Race Ethnicity and Education*, *19*(4), 731–762.
Diem, S., Welton, A. D., & Brooks, J.S. (2022). Antiracism education activism: A theoretical framework for understanding and promoting racial equity. *AERA Open*, *8*. https://doi.org/10.1177/23328584221126518

Dillon, R., & Nixon, M. (2019). *Powerful parent partnerships: Rethinking family engagement for student success*. Routledge.

Dionne, E. J., & Diiulio, J. J. (Eds.). (2000). *What's God got to do with the American Experiment?* Brookings Institution Press.

Diouf, S. A. (1998). *Servants of Allah: African Muslims enslaved in the Americas*. New York University Press.

Diouf, S. A. (2021, February 10). Muslims in America: A forgotten history. *Aljazeera*. https://www.aljazeera.com/features/2021/2/10/muslims-in-america-always-there

Dooley, P. L. (2017). *Freedom of speech: Reflections in art and popular culture*. ABC-CLIO.

Douglass, F. (2009/1846). *Narrative of the life of Frederick Douglass*. Oxford University Press.

Douglass, F. (1852). What to the slave is the fourth of July? https://www.blackpast.org/african-american-history/speeches-african-american-history/1852-frederick-douglass-what-slave-fourth-july/

Douglass, S. L. (2009). Teaching about religion, Islam, and the world in public and private school curricula. In Y. Y. Haddad, F. Senzai, & J. I. Smith (Eds.), *Educating the Muslims of America* (pp. 85–108). Oxford University Press.

Driessen, G., & Merry, M. S. (2006). Islamic schools in the Netherlands: Expansion or marginalization? *Interchange, 37*, 201–223.

DuBois, W. E. B. (2015). *The suppression of the African slave trade to the United States of America 1638–1870*. CreateSpace Independent Publishing Platform.

Duderija, A. (2018). Progressive Islam: Reawakening authenticity. *Tikkun, 33*(1). https://www.muse.jhu.edu/article/692998

Einboden, J. (2020). *Jefferson's Muslim fugitives: The lost story of enslaved Africans, their Arabic letters, and an American president*. Oxford University Press.

El Fadl, K. (2003). Islam and the challenge of democratic commitment. *Fordham International Law Journal, 27*(1), 4–71.

Eltis, D. (2018). *Slave voyages: The trans-atlantic slave trade database*. https://www.slavevoyages.org/about/about#faq/8/en/

Esposito, J. L. (2011). *What everyone needs to know about Islam*. Oxford University Press.

Etzioni, A. (2005). *How patriotic is the patriot act: Freedom versus security in the age of terrorism*. Routledge.

Evanzz, K. (2017). The FBI and the Nation of Islam. In S. A. Johnson & S. Weitzman (Eds.), *The FBI and religion: Faith and national security before and after 9/11*. University of California Press.

Ezzani, M. (2014). Ethical leadership: A Texas school district's efforts toward cultural proficiency. *Values and Ethics in Educational Administration, 11*(1), n1.

Ezzani, M. D., & Brooks, M. C. (2015). (Mis)Understanding Islam in a suburban Texas school district. *Religion & Education, 42*(3), 237–254.

Ezzani, M., & Brooks, M. (2019). Culturally relevant leadership: Advancing critical consciousness in American Muslim students. *Educational Administration Quarterly, 55*(5), 781–811.

Ezzani, M. (2021). A principal's approach to leadership for social justice: Advancing reflective and anti-oppressive practices. *Journal of School Leadership*, *31*(3), 227–247.

Forsyth, P. B., Adams, C. M., & Hoy, W. K. (2011). *Collective trust: Why schools can't improve without it*. Teachers College Press.

Freire, P. (1968). *Pedagogy of the oppressed*. Continuum.

Freire, P. (1972). Education: Domestication or liberation? *Prospects*, *2*(2), 173–181.

Freire, P. (1985). *The politics of education: Culture, power, and liberation*. Greenwood Publishing Group.

Friedman, M., & Friedman, R. D. (1982). *Capitalism and freedom*. University of Chicago Press.

Furman, G. C., & Shields, C. M. (2005). How can educational leaders promote and support social justice and democratic community in schools? *A new agenda for research in educational leadership* (pp. 119–137). Teachers College Press.

Galloway, M. K., Callin, P., James, S., Vimegnon, H., & McCall, L. (2019). Culturally responsive, antiracist, or anti-oppressive? How language matters for school change efforts. *Equity & Excellence in Education*, *52*(4), 485–501.

Gates, H. L., Jr. (2019). *Stony the road: Reconstruction, white supremacy, and the rise of Jim Crow*. Penguin Press.

Gay, G., & Howard, T. C. (2000). Multicultural teacher education for the 21st century. *The Teacher Educator*, *36*(1), 1–16.

Gay, G. (2018). *Culturally responsive teaching: Theory, research, and practice*. Teachers College Press.

Giroux, H. (2020). *Critical pedagogy*. Springer.

Gomez, M. A. (1994). Muslims in early America. *The Journal of Southern History*, *60*(4), 671–710.

Grant, D. (2015). "Civilizing" the colonial subject: The co-evolution of state and slavery in South Carolina, 1670–1739. *Comparative Studies in Society and History*, *57*(3), 606–636.

Green, T. H. (2019). *The fear of Islam: An introduction to Islamophobia in the West*. Fortress Press.

Greenawalt, K. (2007). *Does God belong in public schools?* Princeton University Press.

Grewal, Z. A., & Coolidge, R. D. (2013). Islamic education in the United States: Debates, practices, and institutions. In J. Hammer & O. Safi (Eds.), *The Cambridge companion to American Islam* (pp. 246–265). Cambridge University Press.

Griffiths, M. (1998). *Educational research for social justice: Getting off the fence*. Open University Press.

Guhin, J. (2018). Colorblind Islam: The racial hinges of immigrant Muslims in the United States. *Social Inclusion*, *6*(2), 87–97.

Hall, S. (2001). The spectacle of the "other." In M. Wetherell, S. Taylor, & S. Yates (Eds.), *Discourse theory and practice* (pp. 324–344). Sage.

Halverson, J. R. (2016). West African Islam in colonial and antebellum South Carolina. *Journal of Muslim Minority Affairs*, *36*(3), 413–426.

Hammer, J., & Safi, O. (Eds.). (2013). *The Cambridge companion to American Islam*. Cambridge University Press.

Hannah-Jones, N. (2021). *The 1619 project: A new American origin story*. Random House.

Hayes, K. J. (2002). How Thomas Jefferson read the Qur'an. *Early American Literature*, 39(2), 247–261.

Heinrich, J. (2013). The devil is in the details: In America, can you really say "God" in school? *Educational Review*, 67(1), 64–78.

Herman, S. N. (2011). *Taking liberties: The war on terror and the erosion of American democracy*. Oxford University Press.

Hing, B. O. (2018). *American Presidents, deportations, and human rights violations: From Carter to Trump*. Cambridge University Press.

hooks, b. (1994). *Teaching to transgress: Education as the practice of freedom*. Routledge.

Howell, S. (2013). Laying the groundwork for American Muslim histories, 1865-1965. In J. Hammer & O. Safi (Eds.), *The Cambridge companion to American Islam* (pp. 45–64). Cambridge University Press.

Hoy, W. K., & Tschannen-Moran, M. (1999). Five faces of trust: An empirical confirmation in urban elementary schools. *Journal of School Leadership*, 9(3), 184–208.

Jackson, S. A. (2005). *Islam and the Blackamerican: Looking toward the third resurrection*. Oxford University Press.

Jamal, Z. N. (2023). Aga Khan IV: "Education is an intensely moral enterprise." In M. C. Brooks & M. D. Ezzani (Eds.), *Great Muslim leaders: Lessons for education* (pp. 91–108). Information Age Publishing.

Jefferson, T. (1824). From Thomas Jefferson to Lydia Howard Huntley Sigourney, 18 July 1824. *Founders Online*, National Archives, https://founders.archives.gov/documents/Jefferson/98-01-02-4419

Jefferson, T., & Washington, H. A. (2019/1853). *The writings of Thomas Jefferson: Autobiography, with appendix. Correspondence*. Creative Media Partners.

Jeffries, J. L. (2004). Juneteenth, Black Texans and the case for reparations. *Negro Educational Review*, 55(2), 107–115.

Johnson, S. A. (2017). The FBI and the Moorish Science Temple of America. In S. A. Johnson & S. Weitzman (Eds.), *The FBI and religion: Faith and national security before and after 9/11* (pp. 55–66). University of California Press.

Kamali, S. (2017). Informants, provocateurs, and entrapment: Examining the histories of the FBI's PATCON and the NYPD's Muslim surveillance program. *Surveillance & Policy*, 15(1), 68–78.

Karim, K. H. (2006). American media's coverage of Muslims: The historical roots of contemporary portrayals. In E. Poole & J. E. Esposito (Eds.), *Muslims and the news media* (pp. 116–127). I.B. Tauris.

Kassam, T. R. (2003). On being a scholar of Islam: Risks and responsibilities. *Progressive Muslims: On justice, gender and pluralism* (pp. 128–144). One World.

Kendi, I. X. (2019). *How to be an anti-racist*. Penguin.

Keyworth, K. (2015, May 18). Fast facts about full-time Islamic schools in the United States. Islamic Schools League of America. https://theisla.org/wp-content/uploads/resources/Fast%20Facts%20about%20Full%20Time%20Islamic%20Schools%202015.pdf

Khalifa, M. A., Khalil, D., Marsh, T. E., & Halloran, C. (2019). Toward an indigenous, decolonizing school leadership: A literature review. *Educational Administration Quarterly, 55*(4), 571–614.

Khoury, N., & Mahfouz, J. (2023). Amina Wadud: Critical self-reflection in Islam toward radical transformation. In M. C. Brooks & M. D. Ezzani (Eds.), *Great Muslim leaders: Lessons for education* (pp. 171–182). Information Age Publishing.

Khuwaja, S., & Ezzani, M. D. (2022). Notions of pluralism in religion education: Islam as a case study. In J. S. Brooks, A. H. Normore, M. C. Brooks, & N. Sum (Eds.), *Globalization and education: Teaching, learning and leading in the world schoolhouse* (pp. 241–261). Information Age Publishing.

Kuypers, L. (2011). *The zones of regulation: A curriculum designed to foster self-regulation and emotional control.* Think Social Publishing, Inc.

Ladson-Billings, G. (1995). Toward a theory of culturally relevant pedagogy. *American Educational Research Journal, 32*(3), 465–491. https://doi-org.ezproxy.ecu.edu.au/10.2307/1163320

Lipsky, S. (1987). *Internalized racism.* Rational Island Publishers.

Louis, K. S. (2007). Trust and improvement in schools. *Journal of Educational Change, 8*, 1–24.

Maghbouleh, N. (2017). *The limits of whiteness.* Stanford University Press.

McLaren, P. (2021). *Critical pedagogy manifesto: Teachers of the world unite.* DIO Press Incorporated.

Mearsheimer, J. J. (2021). Liberalism and nationalism in contemporary America. *PS: Political Science & Politics, 54*(1), 1–8.

Meer, N. (2007). Muslim Schools in Britain: Challenging mobilisations or logical developments? *Asia Pacific Journal of Education, 27*(1), 55–71.

Merry, M. S. (2018). Indoctrination, Islamic schools, and the broader scope of harm. *Theory and Research in Education, 16*(2), 162–178.

Miles, M. B., & Huberman, A. M. (1994). *Qualitative data analysis: An expanded sourcebook.* Sage.

Moosa, E. (2003). The debts and burdens of critical Islam. *Progressive Muslims: On justice, gender and pluralism, 4*, 111–27.

Nguyen, T., & Danticat, E. (2005). *We are all suspects now: Untold stories from immigrant communities after 9/11.* Beacon Press.

Patel, F., & Levison-Waldman, R. (2017). The Islamophobic administration. Brennan Center for Justice. https://www.brennancenter.org/our-work/research-reports/islamophobic-administration

Patton, M. Q. (2015). *Qualitative research and evaluation methods: Integrating theory and practice* (4th ed.). Sage.

Patulny, R. (2004). *Social capital norms, networks, and practices: A critical evaluation*. Social Policy Research Centre.

Patulny, R. V., & Lind Haase Svendsen, G. (2007). Exploring the social capital grid: Bonding, bridging, qualitative, quantitative. *International Journal of Sociology and Social Policy, 27*(1/2), 32–51.

Pavlick, J. (2019). Reproducing patriotism: An exploration of "freedom" in US history textbooks. *Discourse & Society, 30*(5), 482–502.

Plunkett, S. H., & Kimble, J. J. (2018). *Enduring ideals: Rockwell, Roosevelt & the four freedoms*. Abbeville Press.

Poole, M. (2015). The feasibility of educating trainee science teachers in issues of science and religion. *Cultural Studies of Science Education, 11*(2), 273–281.

Powell, K. A. (2018). Framing Islam/creating fear: An analysis of U.S. media coverage of terrorism from 2011–2016. *Religions, 9*(9). http://dx.doi.org/10.3390/rel9090257

Putnam, R. D. (2000). *Bowling alone: The collapse and revival of American community*. Simon and Schuster.

Ragosta, J. A. (2013). *Religious freedom: Jefferson's legacy, America's creed*. University of Virginia Press.

Railton, B. (2021). *Of thee I sing the contested history of American patriotism*. Roman & Littlefield.

Rashid, H., & Muhammad, Z. (1992). The Sister Clara Muhammad Schools: Pioneers in the development of Islamic education in America. *The Journal of Negro Education, 61*(2), 178–185.

Reeves, R. (2015). *Infamy: The shocking story of the Japanese American internment in World War II*. Henry Holt and Company.

Reichman, H. (2019). *The future of academic freedom*. John Hopkins University Press.

Reynolds, D. (2010). *America: Empire of liberty*. Penguin Press.

Rivera-McCutchen, R. L. (2019). Armed loved in school leadership: Resisting inequality and injustice in schooling. *Leadership and Policy in Schools, 18*(2), 237–247.

Romanowski, W. D. (2012). *How American Protestants fought for freedom at the movies*. Oxford University Press.

Roth, K. (2005). Getting away with torture. *Global Governance, 11*(3), 389–406.

Saada, N. L. (2017). Schooling, othering, and the cultivation of Muslim students' religious and civic identities. *Journal of Religious Education, 64*(3), 179–195.

Safi, O. (2003a). *Progressive Muslims: On justice, gender, and pluralism*. OneWorld.

Safi, O. (2003b). What is progressive Islam? *ISIM Newsletter, 13*(1), 48–49.

Sahih Al Bukhari 1: Chapter 54, Hadith 2707.

Said, E. W. (1978). *Orientalism*. Pantheon Books.

Said, E. W. (1994). *Culture and imperialism*. Vintage.

Said, E. W. (1996). *Covering Islam: How the media and the experts determine how we see the rest of the world*. Vintage Publishing.

Saldaña, J. (2011). *Fundamentals of qualitative research*. Oxford University Press.

Saunt, C. (2020). *Unworthy republic: The dispossession of Native Americans and the road to Indian territory*. W. W. Norton & Company.

Selod, S., & Embrick, D. G. (2013). Racialization and Muslims: Situating the Muslim experience in race scholarship. *Race & Ethnicity, 7*(8), 644–655.

Shalaby, I. M. (1967). *The role of the school in cultural renewal and identity development in the Nation of Islam in America* (Order No. 6711958) [Doctoral dissertation, University of Arizona]. ProQuest Dissertations and Theses Global.

Sirin, S. R., & Fine, M. (2008). *Muslim American youth: Understanding hyphenated identities through multiple methods*. New York University Press.

Smithsonian (2019). *African Muslims in early America: Religion, literacy, and liberty*. National Museum of African American History & Culture. https://nmaahc.si.edu/explore/stories/african-muslims-early-america

Snowden, E. (2019). *Permanent record*. Macmillan.

Spellberg, D. A. (2013). *Thomas Jefferson's Qur'an: Islam and the founders*. Alfred A. Knopf.

Suleiman, O. (2017). Internalized Islamophobia: Exploring the faith and identity crisis of American Muslim youth. *Islamophobia Studies Journal, 4*(1), 1–12.

Suleiman, O. (2020). 40 Hadith on social justice. https://yaqeeninstitute.org/series/40-hadiths-on-social-justice

Suleiman, Y. (2004). *A war of words: Language and conflict in the Middle East* (Vol. 19). Cambridge University Press.

Sutliff, P. (2016). *Civilization jihad and the myth of moderate Islam*. Tate Publishing & Enterprises.

Tschannen-Moran, M. (2014). *Trust matters: Leadership for successful schools*. John Wiley & Sons.

Van Es, M. A. (2016). The Dutch organisations and Islam. In *Stereotypes and Self-Representations of Women with a Muslim Background. Citizenship, Gender and Diversity* (pp. 119–157). Palgrave Macmillan.

Villegas, A. M. (2007). Dispositions in teacher education: A look at social justice. *Journal of Teacher Education, 58* (5), 370–380.

Wallenstein, P. (2004). *Blue laws and black codes: Conflict, courts, and change in twentieth-century Virginia*. University of Virginia Press.

Warner, B. (2020). *Measuring Mohammed*. CSPI.

Weisenfeld, J. (2016). *New world a-coming: Black religion and racial identity during the Great Migration*. NYU Press.

Wiencek, H. (2012). The dark side of Thomas Jefferson: A new portrait of the founding father challenges the long-held perception of Thomas Jefferson as a benevolent slaveholder. *Smithsonian Magazine*. https://www.smithsonianmag.com/history/the-dark-side-of-thomas-jefferson-35976004/

Williams, J. K., & Todd, R. H. (2016). Debriefing the interpretive researcher: Spider sniffing with a critical friend. *Qualitative Report, 21*(12), 2161–2175.

Williams, O. (2010). Slavery in Albany, New York, 1624–1827. *Afro-Americans in New York Life and History, 34*(2), 154–168.

Wingfield, M. (2006). Arab Americans: Into the multicultural mainstream. *Equity & Excellence in Education, 39*(3), 253–266.

Winters, C. (1978). Afro-American Muslims: From slavery to freedom. *Islamic Studies, 17*(4), 187–205.

Wolcott, H. F. (2002). *Sneaky kid and its aftermath: Ethics and intimacy in fieldwork*. Altamira Press.

Wong, L. S., & Mishra, P. (2021). Reforming our school systems around a humanizing curriculum: Schooling during and after COVID-19. *ECNU Review of Education, 4*(4), 890–898. https://doi.org/10.1177/2096531120980750

Wuthnow, R. (2011). *America and the challenges of religious diversity*. Princeton University Press.

Yukich, G., & Edgell, P. (2020). Introduction: Recognizing raced religion. In *Religion is raced* (pp. 1–16). New York University Press.

Zeus, L. (2018). Dis-orienting western knowledge: Coloniality, curriculum, and crisis. *Cambridge Anthropology, 36*(2), 7–20.

Zine, J. (2004). Anti-Islamophobia education as transformative pedagogy: Reflections from the educational front lines. *American Journal of Islamic Social Sciences, 21*(3), 110–119.

Zine, J. (2008). *Canadian Islamic schools. Unveiling the politics of faith, gender, knowledge and identity*. University of Toronto Press.

Index

advocate 11, 158, 166, 174
   the center 26
   for others 43, 73, 161, 173
   the school 15, 156
   for self 19, 22, 36, 40-2, 160
Africa 3-9, 60
agency 71, 161
Ahmadiyya 5-6, 9
American Muslim identity 24
   development of 22, 64
   expression of 160
   in mission 18, 135, 140, 158
angels 45, 60, 64-5
anxiety 39, 66, 151
Arabic 35
   in curriculum 10, 63, 88-9, 118-19
   language 3-4, 92, 116, 139
   teachers 146
art 10, 34, 36, 63, 89, 116
   teacher 149
Asia 10, 60, 87

Bible 4, 45
Biden, President Joseph 133
Bilal 3, 86
Black Lives Matter 116-17, 133, 166, 173
bullying 61, 137, 169

California state curriculum 63, 80
   standards 165
care 123, 152, 173
   for others 78, 94
   by school head 119, 127
   by teachers 36, 40, 162
   as a value 67, 74, 115
Catholic 45
   parents 58, 107
   school 135
   teachers 50, 70, 164
character
   building 67, 70
   exemplary 130, 155, 172
   as a trait 39, 41, 79, 166-7
China, *see* Uyghurs
Christian 20, 61
   faith tradition 156
   hegemony 4, 8, 164
   teachers 53, 67, 128-9, 147-8, 162, 172
Christmas 20, 61, 91, 111, 163
   in curriculum 50, 54, 147-8, 164, 172
critical consciousness, *see* curriculum of resistance
curriculum 10, 68, 109, 142, 167, *see also Zones of Regulation*
   change 150
   discriminatory 7-9
   humanizing 4, 63 (*see also Leader in Me*)
   social justice 136
   values 67
curriculum of resistance 22, 64-5, 70-1 79, 158, 161, 165

dance 35-6, 160
democracy 25, 130, 133, 179
dogs 96, 162

Easter 50, 91, 164
Eid 28, 76, 92
Ellison, US Representative Keith 5, 101
empathy
   develop 156
   practice 49, 83-4
   show 161-2, 167-8, 173
equality
   for all human beings 120, 173
   in curriculum 64, 165
   defined 61
   gender 28, 30, 63, 151-2
   in Qur'an 25, 71, 158
eurocentric 8, 46, 161

expectations
    of behavior   38, 65–6, 130, 168
    high   15, 37, 57
extreme right politics   2, 136

fairness, *see* justice
Farewell Sermon (Khutbat al-Wada)   49
Farrakhan, Minister Louis   9
FranklinCovey, *see* Leader in Me

gay   23, 27, 121–2
gender   11, 55
    in curriculum   151–2
    equality   28, 30, 63, 173
    justice   70–1
    segregation   35
Gratz, Alan, *see* Refugee
Guatemalan   78, 94

hadith   10, 45–6, 70, 158
    anti-racism   49
    in curriculum   72–4, 159
    justice   165
halal   10, 25, 31, 58, 169
Halloween   50–1, 94, 111, 164
haram   25, 95, 146
hijab
    disagreement about   146, 168–9
    identity   21, 58, 103, 112
    ignorance about   43
    The Kindest Red and *The Proudest Blue*   150
    personal decision   16, 36, 114
homelessness   26–7, 76, 121
homosexuality, *see* gay
human dignity   25, 158, 173
human rights   11, 47, 63, 94, 116, 133, 156, 160, 165
    in Qur'an   158

inclusion   11, 55, 129, 171
injustice
    challenging   26, 76, 78, 138
    in the classroom   22, 80–1, 153
    in curriculum   64–5, 79, 85, 120–1, 165
integrity   37, 101, 170–2
interfaith   14, 61, 136
    activities   91–2
    marriage   63, 162

ISIS   27, 95
Islamic studies
    in curriculum   10, 41, 51, 63–5, 85, 137
    Director   22–4
    related to current events   75–6, 78–9, 95, 120, 150
    teachers   146
Islamophobia   16, 133, 164

Jews   60–1, 77, 120
jihad   2, 42
justice   11
    Black Lives Matter   133
    in curriculum   63–4, 73, 80, 85, 116, 121, 136
    economic   77
    gender   70
    in hadiths   73
    in Qur'an   25, 159
    racial   158
    restorative   76, 86
    social   14, 23, 26–7, 76, 89, 138, 152, 165, 173
    undermining   166–7
    universal notion of   120, 130, 138, 155, 159
    in US Pledge of Allegiance   32
    as a value   67

Kaepernick, Colin   78
King, Jr., Dr. Martin Luther   51, 86, 163

law enforcement   2, 26–7
Leader in Me   15, 68–70, 138, 148–9, 168
LGBTQ+, *see* gay
Lighthouse Certification, *see* Leader in Me

Malcolm X   77, 116–17
media
    American   155
    corporate control   157
    literacy   79
    and misinformation   6, 92
    representation of Muslims   16, 27, 44, 95, 159
mercy   23, 119, 121, 138
    in Hadith   74
    in the Qur'an   25
Mexicans   60, 94, 120

misinformation   8, 57, 92, 133, 174
mission   18, 22, 109, 124, 130, 139, 147
  progressive   157–8
  safeguard   63, 135, 140, 170–1
morals   38
Muhammad, Ibtihaj: author of *The Kindest Red* and *The Proudest Blue*, see hijab
multiculturalism   21–2
music   66
  Christmas   50, 147
  in curriculum   9–10, 34, 63, 166
  individual interpretation of   146
  musicals   36
Muslim Student Association   23, 41, 43, 47–8, 54, 160

Nation of Islam   6, 8–9

Omar, US Representative Ilhan   101, 150
oppression
  challenging   4–5
  in curriculum   20, 65, 157, 165–6
  in Qur'an   26, 64
  societal   83, 100, 163

Parent Association   52–4, 57–9, 89, 108, 112
  socialization   114, 124–31
patriarchy   71, 75
peace   60–1
  in Qur'an   25, 83, 167
  reconciliation   51, 116, 120, 170
pedagogy, *see* curriculum of resistance
Persepolis   43, 161
pets   96, 162
plays in theater   34, 160
pluralism   25, 63, 165
police   27, 105, 120
  brutality   166
  violence   78, 133, 138, 157, 174
positive discipline   85–6, 108, 138, 148–9, 168
poverty   76–7
privilege   4, 19, 64–5, 71, 155
  Christianity   148, 164
  male   75, 160
  White   9, 138, 161

progressive Islam
  ideology   18, 63, 155, 157–8, 169
  interpretations of   71, 159
Prophet Muhammad   10, 25–6, 44–6, 49, 64, 73, 83, 86, 137, 159, 165, 167, 172
protest   78, 133, 153, 166

Qur'an   3–5, 10, 45, 53, 88–9, 96, 118, 128, 146–7
  critical thinking   64
  empathy   161–2
  equality   28, 165
  forgiveness   83
  freedom   158
  gender   71
  human dignity   27
  human rights   95, 158
  justice   155
  mercy   25
  peace   167
  references to God   73, 159, 172
  social justice   26
  values   25
  wrongdoing   60

race   7, 9, 11, 137, 164, 173
  evasiveness   162–3
racism
  anti-Black   5, 9, 138, 178
  anti-Muslim   3, 10, 133, 174
  The Color of Us   87, 163
  internalized   162–4
  Intragroup   83
Ramadan   46, 76, 92, 135, 152
refugee   133
  crisis in Syria   77
  in curriculum   117, 156, 158, 173
  Refugee   64, 109, 165
  on US and Mexican border   166

Saudi Arabia   60, 133
school board   43, 55–6, 89, 140, 170
school culture   83–4, 104, 127, 162, 168
security   1–2, 105–6
self-confidence   36, 47, 162
September 11, 2001   2, 7, 14, 16
slavery   2–4
soccer   34, 116, 134, 163
  girls playing   54, 136, 151, 160

social justice, *see* justice
social media   2, 56, 105–6, 121, 136, 139, 151, 155
   Facebook   56, 98, 105–6, 121
   Instagram   56, 106, 150
   Snapchat   56
   WhatsApp   87, 97–8, 169
socio-emotional   84–5, 162, 171
Socratic method   90
South Africa   52, 129
stereotypes   47, 49, 52, 155, 161, 163
strategic planning   134–5
stress
   managing   66
   students and   34, 39, 161
   teachers and   170
synagogues   60–1

tawheed   9, 159
terrorist   15, 21, 42, 44, 77–8, 95
Tlaib, US Representative Rashida   101, 150
transgender   27, 121
Trump, President Donald J.
   anti-Muslim racism   10, 54, 155
   bigotry   10
   in curriculum   78–80
   election of   129, 133, 137
   exclusionary policies   60–1, 166
   hate speech   10, 155

ummah   7, 10, 83
The University of Islam   8–9
Uyghurs   133, 166

value of the month   67, 69, 168
violence   6, 27
   against Black and Brown people   137–8, 174
   gun   78, 116
   against Muslims   3, 133, 155
   physical   4–5
   sexual   75
vision   4, 63, 105, 113, 124, 135, 158, 170–1
voice   137–8
   parental   98
   student   90
   teacher   140
volleyball   56, 136, 151

Wheel of Choice   85, 168
wudu   59–60, 96

youth group   21, 23, 35, 158

zabiha   10, 59–60, 65, 94, 121
Zionist   91
Zones of Regulation   65–7, 84–5, 168

www.ingramcontent.com/pod-product-compliance
Lightning Source LLC
Chambersburg PA
CBHW052113300426
44116CB00010B/1644